THE STUART PAPERS
AT WINDSOR

THE STUART PAPERS
AT WINDSOR

BEING SELECTIONS FROM HITHERTO
UNPRINTED ROYAL ARCHIVES, WITH
INTRODUCTION AND NOTES, BY

ALISTAIR & HENRIETTA TAYLER

PUBLISHED BY THE GRACIOUS PERMISSION OF
HIS MAJESTY THE KING

NEW YORK
E. P. DUTTON AND COMPANY INC.

First Edition . . . *1939*

Made and Printed in Great Britain by Butler & Tanner Ltd., Frome and London

Printing Statement:

Due to the very old age and scarcity of this book, many of the pages may be hard to read due to the blurring of the original text, possible missing pages, missing text and other issues beyond our control.

Because this is such an important and rare work, we believe it is best to reproduce this book regardless of its original condition.

Thank you for your understanding.

James Francis Edward Stuart in 1745

From a picture (artist unknown) at Alloa House

[*Frontispiece*]

Contents

List of Illustrations

vii

Preface

THIS book is the outcome of a project formed as long ago as the autumn of 1934 when my late brother, who had already done so much for Jacobite history, and I, having obtained permission to study the Stuart papers at Windsor, were filled with the desire to give some of these later ones to the Public, and the gracious consent of his late Majesty King George V having been obtained, we began to make a selection (among the thousands of unpublished letters) of those which seemed to us of intrinsic interest, and capable of being woven into a personal history. The task of selecting, transcribing and annotating these was necessarily a very long and absorbing one and has taken over three years.[1] Owing to the sudden death of my brother in November 1937, I am left to complete it alone, without the benefit of his very careful eye and acute sense of humour and fitness. It is, however, still a joint work, and as such I venture to offer it to an indulgent historical public, feeling that, whatever its defects, it certainly throws new light on one aspect at least of the eighteenth century.

HENRIETTA TAYLER,
Fellow of the Royal Historical Society.

DUFF HOUSE,
    ARUNDEL, 1938.

[1] The present selection is only a portion of those which have been prepared.

Introduction

THIS Collection, which is one of the most remarkable in the world, because of its marvellous completeness as to personal as well as political details of the life of a Court, has, it appears, been strangely neglected. For over 120 years the vast mass of letters and papers, now collected into 541 volumes, has been in the possession of the Crown of Great Britain and available for consultation by any accredited student or writer. But among the hundreds of historians, of memoir writers and of novelists who have dealt with the eighteenth century and particularly with the Jacobite Risings and the protagonists in them, those who have made really practical use of this collection could be counted on the fingers of both hands.[1] A list of those who seem, as far as the present writers can ascertain, to have drawn *any* real material, however small, directly from them, will be found on page 37. The number who might have done so, and would thereby have avoided many of the errors into which they have fallen, is *legion*.

It is true that only within the last few years has the systematic cataloguing of these papers been undertaken by the staff of His Majesty's Archives and prior to that any information required had to be sought for like the proverbial needle in a bundle of hay, by steadily reading through hundreds of letters and memorials, three-quarters of which might not bear

---

[1] Browne, Lord Stanhope, Lang, Haile, Fitzroy-Bell, Dickson, Thornton and Petrie.

on the matter in question. The present writers can, however, bear witness to the fact that this was an enthralling pursuit, and revealed most unexpected "streaks of life"; they will, moreover, always feel grateful for the fact that they were the last serious historians (if they may venture to arrogate to themselves this title) who were privileged to "sail the uncharted sea" of the "Stuart papers," making on the way the most thrilling discoveries. The earliest historian, as apart from the biographers of Prince Charles Edward and his father, who has hitherto made really extensive use of these documents, and printed many, is James Browne, Esq., LL.D., Advocate, in his Monumental *History of the Highlands*, and he actually printed verbatim 279 of the thousands of letters available. The word *verbatim* is perhaps not strictly accurate, for Dr. Browne, though, according to his title-page, he had published a monograph in French, seems to have been incompetent to cope with that tongue in manuscript, and over and over again prints peculiar words which are not French, or which do not make any sense, *and are not in the originals*. He was, it seems, unable either to read the manuscript or to supply the missing French word from the context or from his knowledge of the language. He also ascribes some of the letters unsigned (or signed with initials) to the wrong people. His subject being the entire history of Scotland,[1] he had not, of course, been able to make such an intensive study of the Jacobite period nor to become so personally acquainted with the actors in the Jacobite drama and their handwritings as is the duty of the exclusively Jacobite historian.

It is, however, safe to say that it matters less, since this hundred-year-old history of Scotland is not now read by

[1] Which is apparently what *he* understood by "the Highlands"!

2

anyone ; it was always rather for the specialist than the general reader, with its four volumes (sometimes bound as *eight*), its very small print and its absence of Index. The 279 letters, also, are placed in the volumes in a somewhat confusing manner and seem to have been selected very much at haphazard.

At the end of Vol. II in which the history of the Highlands has been brought down to "the Spring of the year 1745" there is an Appendix of thirty-three letters and papers, of which the first nine are taken from other printed books. From No. 10 onwards they are from the Stuart papers and exclusively concern the Rising of 1745. The first letter is wrongly dated, as can be seen from the original, the remaining twenty-four are of the years 1743 to 1745 and contain a few errors of transcribing. No. 22 is very long and really consists of extracts from thirty-two letters, concerning Sempill and his intrigues.[1]

Vol. III completes the history of Prince Charles Edward to his death in 1788, and ends the actual work. It is followed by an Appendix of eighty-seven letters of dates from June 16th, 1745, to May 9th, 1747 ; the errors in these are many.

Vol. IV continues the Appendix of Vol. III and has 201 letters down to 1759 and two without dates ; many of these also are full of errors. The rest of Vol. IV is occupied with Appendices on the various Highland Regiments and on particular clans, as to which no information was forthcoming from the Stuart papers.

Dr. Browne in his Preface, while enumerating the letters he has transcribed and published, and the wonderful new

[1] Francis, the Jacobite Lord Sempill as distinct from Hugh, his cousin, the holder of the title in Great Britain.

light they are to throw on the history of the Forty-Five, explains that he was unable to continue his examination of the papers down to the death of the Cardinal York, because Buckingham House was being prepared for the reception of King William IV and his Consort and the papers formerly kept there were being removed to Windsor, whither it was apparently impossible for him to follow them !

In Lord Mahon's (afterwards Lord Stanhope's) history, letters are printed bearing upon the special points he wished to illustrate. They were, of course, reprinted in the volume Lord Mahon called the "45." No errors have been detected in these.[1]

Besides these historians, several biographers have made a fairly extensive use of the Stuart papers, but more as a source of information than of actual quotation.

Andrew Lang, in the Life of Prince Charles Edward, which he wrote for the Goupil series, makes ample acknowledgment to Queen Victoria for the opportunity of drawing material from Windsor. It is, however, somewhat unsatisfactory that he rarely indicates the date of the particular letter from which he, somewhat loosely, quotes. In his later works, *Pickle the Spy*, and *The Companions of Pickle*, he weaves his story almost entirely from the Windsor material, but again usually by indirect quotation, or quoting from memory.

In Lang's later work, written in collaboration with Miss Alice Shield, *The King Over the Water*, which was the long-called-for first biography of Prince Charles's father, full use is made of the letters down to the death of King James, and Miss Shield, who was responsible (as stated in the Preface) for "almost all the writing," has been exact in giving the

---

[1] Save that the name of the Prince's vessel is given as the *Du Bellier*.

dates, if not the text, of the letters, material from which she was using.

In her Life of Cardinal York she also made good use of the Windsor material.

The other Life of James Francis Stuart, published in the same year (1907) with that of Shield and Lang, by Martin Haile (Marie Hallé) and entitled *The Old Chevalier*, is much more carefully documented, as is the same writer's equally attractive Life of the King's Mother, Marie of Modena, for which the Stuart papers at Windsor, with those at Chaillot, formed the principal documentary sources.

Among other biographers, the painstaking Miss Agnes Strickland consulted the papers for her lives of the latest Stuart Queen and Princess, and very charming letters exist from her stating that she felt herself to be thus "a humble instrument in the hands of God for stemming the fatal tide of Republicanism," and offered her work to Queen Victoria in this spirit.

The Contessa Campana di Cavelli drew a few details and printed some letters direct from the papers for her *Derniers Stuarts*, but the Marchesa Vitelleschi in her *Court in Exile*, and Ewald in his Life of Prince Charles Edward only quoted from those already printed by other writers.

The Marquis de Ruvigny, of course, compiled his Jacobite Peerage from study of the Warrant-books, among these papers, but seems not to have read the letters or he would not have fallen into so many errors as regards family history, dates of deaths, etc.

Dr. Dickson, in his *Jacobite Attempt of 1719*, prints a number of letters directly bearing on that period, chiefly from the Duke of Ormonde and Cardinal Alberoni.

F. Williams, the author of the *Life of Atterbury*, would appear to have seen some letters and so would Callaghan, author of *The History of the Irish Brigade*. Among quite modern writers, Major Skeet consulted them for details relating to Charlotte of Albany, and Major Eardley-Simpson took the precaution of looking up at Windsor one or two facts important for his specialized work on *Derby and the Forty-Five*, otherwise drawn from local sources ; Sir Charles Petrie also made a comprehensive study of these papers. Most other writers on Jacobite themes, if they quote the letters at all, do so only at second hand from those printed by Browne and Mahon. Even the eminent Jacobite historian Dr. Blaikie did this, and *quoted Browne's errors*. He himself never went to Windsor, but gives, in his admirable Itinerary of Prince Charles Edward, *one* hitherto unpublished letter sent to him by Mr. afterwards Sir Richard Holmes, the then Librarian.

The present writers are acutely conscious of their good fortune in being the first to be privileged to publish a selection from all those letters, subsequent to the date of the seven volumes issued by the Historical MSS. Commission, which came to an end with the close of the year 1718. An endeavour has been made to survey the field for the next forty-one years, that is until the Jacobite cause received its *coup de grâce* in the defeat and virtual annihilation of the French fleet by Hawke at the Battle of Quiberon Bay, November 22nd, 1759 (see page 249). This defeat destroyed all hope of a Stuart restoration by help from France ; moreover, the sentimental desire of a part of the British Nation for a return of the old reigning house was practically extinguished in the following year by the accession to the throne of the young British-born Prince who became the popular King George III.

It was extremely difficult for the present writers to decide how to treat so vast a field. The official publications of the Historical MSS. Commission, of course, printed the documents chronologically as they are now sorted and bound, and printed practically *all* of them ; but since the present work sets out to be a selection of the more interesting letters, throwing light upon various more or less well-known personalities of the first half of the eighteenth century, it has seemed better to give the letters of the Royal family chronologically as far as possible, interspersing them with those of others, introduced in each case with a brief account of the correspondent—all alike being Jacobites who either resided at or wrote to others in the Jacobite Court at Rome, and whose letters were preserved there.

The history of how these documents came to Windsor at all is something of a Romance in itself.

The "Stuart papers" now so carefully bound in 541 volumes and safely lodged in the Round Tower, have passed through the most amazing vicissitudes, and would seem to have had a charmed life. They consist of a certain number of documents that must have been carried by the Old Chevalier with him to Avignon in 1716 and to Rome in 1718 or more likely sent to him at the latter place from Paris, when it was made clear that the Papal City was to be his permanent abode. As most of the early ones have been printed in the first volume issued by the Historical MSS. Commission, they do not particularly concern us here. There is one holograph letter of Charles II and a great number of those of Queen Mary of Modena when she was on the throne of England, i.e. between 1685 and 1688, a good many to her from her uncle and her brother, the Cardinal Cesare d'Este and the Duke of Modena and others, and a few from King James II himself, with many warrants and certificates issued from St. Germain en Laye, after the Exiled Court was settled there, and a number of letters from the Duke of Berwick to his father.

From the year 1701, after the death of James II, there are letters and warrants of James III. From 1713 onwards great numbers from Berwick to his half-brother and after August 1714 these are still more numerous (about 200 in all, of which the great majority have been printed). There are others from and to Bolingbroke about the proposed expedition to Scotland of 1715, and after September in that year the letters of Mar, Huntly and other Scottish Jacobites, with fairly full details of the disastrous Rising of that year. From 1716 begins the vast correspondence which the *de jure* King James III was to carry on for fifty years, both with his own unfortunate subjects, first from Avignon, then from Pesaro and Urbino and finally from Rome (which was his home from 1718 to his death in 1766) and with foreign potentates and others, and after December 31st, 1718, *all these are unpublished*.

The monarch without a throne was himself a most voluminous writer of letters, and almost every one he wrote was painstakingly copied and preserved, usually by James Edgar of Keithock in Angus, that most faithful of private secretaries, who remained by his master's side till his own death in 1764 and was succeeded by Andrew Lumisden.

Letters to the King and to his various secretaries and letters between Jacobites, were innumerable and nearly all were preserved, while the volume of the "Stuart papers" is further swelled by a mass of petitions, claims to and receipts for pensions, and a great many wholly uninteresting bills, stable and kitchen accounts and even menus !

This mass of papers, accumulating year by year, lay in the Palazzo Muti in Rome, until the death of King James in 1766, when it passed into the possession of Charles Edward and at his death, twenty-two years later, some of the collection (it is not quite clear how much, but that part which had gone to Florence) became the property of his natural daughter, Charlotte, Duchess of Albany, who had tended him in his last months and herself died in the following year. Whatever was not taken to Florence and thus retained by her, passed into the possession of her uncle, Henry, Cardinal York, who lived for nineteen years longer. Both portions of the Collection eventually reached England, but in very different circumstances, now to be narrated.

It is interesting to note that in neither case had the ostensible owner of the papers any real right either to the possession of them or to sell them (see below, and p. 23).

On the death of the Duchess of Albany, it was stated that she had left, by will, all her property, including those of her father's papers then in her possession, to her confessor, Abbé James Waters (Procurator-General of the English Benedictines in Rome since 1777), who at once removed the papers which, from the death of Prince Charles had remained in his library in Florence, first to the Cancelleria in Rome and later to Waters's own house in that City.[1] A few years after this, Waters became very friendly with Sir John Coxe Hippisley, the unofficial link between the Papal Government of Rome and that of Britain, and Hippisley relates that he had frequently had opportunity to see some of these papers, in the years 1794 and 1795 and knew them to be very interesting

[1] Actually she had instructed Waters to destroy what was of no value and hand the rest to her uncle.

and valuable, but it was not until 1804 that he first had the idea that the papers should by rights come to England, and thereupon started tentative negotiations for this purpose on his own account, backed by the authority of Charles James Fox, who wrote as follows :

Charles James Fox to Sir John Coxe Hippisley
ST. ANNE'S HILL.
3 *Oct.* 1804.

"The Prince of Wales would be very glad to purchase the Stuart papers at any reasonable terms, such as the annuity you hint at or any other mode of satisfying the Person you mention. But perhaps one ought to know with more certainty than we now do, that the papers are not merely transcripts of or from a narrative (not the original letters) which was in the Scotch College at Paris and which is now in Scotland. If you think they can be purchased reasonably, H.R.H. would wish that they should be consigned to Mr. H. Elliot, Lord Minto's brother, who is I understand at Naples, and who will bring them over or send them by some safe conveyance.[1] If the papers are not mere duplicates, they must at any rate be extremely valuable, though not particularly so to *me* unless unless [*sic*][2] they relate to the period between 1672 and 1690 or thereabouts.

I am dear Sir,
Yours ever,
C. J. Fox."

After having perhaps seen the above letter, or anyhow been

[1] Elliot was not, however, concerned in the actual rescue of the papers.
[2] Perhaps written when Fox was drunk. He had earlier in the year 1804 been definitely excluded by the personal wish of the King from Pitt's Coalition Ministry and all his Whig friends had refused to serve without him, the party then attaching itself firmly to the Prince of Wales, in whose name he now writes.

told of its contents, the Abbé Waters wrote to Sir John Hippisley: "I value my honour and reputation, therefore can or will give you *no* other proofs of the authenticity and originality of the papers, but what you may gather from the observations and remarks I have made on some in the descriptive list sent." He sent at the same time a very full list of most of the papers and says he knows the handwriting of "the Old and Young Chevaliers" very well, but cannot vouch for all the others.[1] The transaction was therefore carried out.

The usually received story is that it was entirely owing to Sir John Coxe Hippisley's friendship with Abbé Waters that the English Government *discovered* and had the opportunity of acquiring the "Stuart papers" in his hands, but letters at Windsor reveal that Mr. Jackson, envoy to the King of Sardinia, had also heard of their existence and had been, by the instruction of Pitt, also conducting diplomatic enquiries into the possibility of purchasing them; by the orders of his Principal he, however, now withdrew from the pursuit (1804).

But besides this, an article in the *Scottish National Review* of April 1921, by Mr. Walter Seton of the London University, which quotes a letter in his own possession of the year 1793, shows that these papers had been known to the English Court eleven years earlier. The letter, though unsigned, is in the well-known handwriting of Sir William Hamilton, ambassador to the Court of Naples.[2] Hamilton was known to have

[1] This letter as well as an earlier one from Waters now only exist in a copy in Hippisley's handwriting; the latter explains that Waters's original letters were much injured in the process of disinfection, which accounts no doubt for the fragmentary condition in which many *more interesting* papers are now found.

[2] Curiously described by Mr. Seton as a great sailor, presumably because of the connection of Lady Hamilton with Nelson!

been in Rome in 1792 and 1793 and a reference in his letter to the Cardinal of York as nearing 70 (which age the latter would reach in the spring of 1795), helps to fix the date. Hamilton was also on terms of intimacy with the Abbé Waters and was allowed to see and handle the collection of papers, presumably not only the portion which had come from Florence but something more like the whole collection, since he describes it as filling two presses of 7 feet high, 5 or 6 feet broad and 18 inches deep ! He had many conversations with Waters on the subject, closely examined some of the manuscripts and saw of what great value they would be to the Royal Family of Great Britain. The member of the family whom he interested in them was Augustus Frederick, Duke of Sussex, sixth son of George III, who on a visit to Rome in 1792 had called on the aged Cardinal, giving him his title of Royal Highness and treating him with great respect ; it was also he who arranged in the following year for an augmentation of the old man's much-needed pension, and later for its extension for one year after the Cardinal's death, to pay off his old servants.

Sussex was president of the Society of Arts and of the Royal Society and much more really interested in the documents, pictures, miniatures and jewels than his brother, the future Prince Regent, into whose possession they ultimately came.

Hamilton thought he had extracted a promise from Waters that the papers should not be disposed of to anyone without warning himself and Sussex. He was aware that those still in the possession of the Cardinal could not be moved till after his death, and Waters apparently said (in 1793) that the same restriction applied to those in his own possession. Hamilton in this letter remarks on the Cardinal's great age and Waters's poor health and opines that the Royal Family may not have long to wait. However, as already seen, Hippisley received the papers (which had been in the Duchess of Albany's possession) for the Prince of Wales, without waiting for the death of the Cardinal. Abbé Waters was not at all rapacious in the matter of price and said the reward he would prefer would be a modest annuity settled on him for life. (The exact sum is not mentioned anywhere in the Hippisley correspondence which has come down to us, but is elsewhere stated to have been £200 a year.)[1] This arrangement was made, but the valetudinarian priest died soon after receiving the first quarterly instalment, so the British Government may be said to have made a good bargain.

Before his death, Waters personally conveyed the precious papers in his own possession to the care of the British Consul at Civita Vecchia, Mr. Richard Bartram, whose receipt for them still exists—"Received from the Rev. Mr. James Waters of Rome, a case marked R.B. contents unknown, with orders to hold the same at the disposal of Admiral Collingwood, or Sir John Coxe Hippisley of London. Civita Vecchia, 15 March 1806." (The date of this receipt is a little puzzling—as the papers were certainly at Civita Vecchia in 1805 and Waters was dead by 1806. It was probably a copy made afterwards and dated when made.) Certainly on September 6th, 1805, no less a person than Henry Dundas, Lord Melville (once "the uncrowned King of Scotland" and now first Lord of the Admiralty until his disgrace in this year), wrote from Weymouth to Hippisley (who was at Southsea) that the latter

---

[1] Many letters formerly at Mells Park, Somerset, have unfortunately now been lost.

was to settle with Lord Nelson, then fitting out for the Mediterranean, to go to Civita Vecchia and fetch the precious documents, that "the Prince of Wales was very anxious about the papers and hopes Lord Nelson will keep them on board his own ship till he finds a safe conveyance to England." Nelson's death at Trafalgar, of course, prevented him from carrying out this commission, which devolved on Collingwood, but the French had occupied the port, and in spite of repeated attempts by sending gunboats throughout 1806 and 1807, the British Admiral was unable to effect a peaceful landing and was at last told to desist, as he only drew suspicion on the English residents in Civita Vecchia. The unfortunate Bartram had been arrested and taken to the Castle of St. Angelo in Rome—all his property was confiscated and he himself narrowly escaped being shot on suspicion of having in his possession things belonging to the English (*as indeed he had*). He had skilfully concealed the incriminating box of papers, which four years later was recovered by Dr. Paul Macpherson, Principal of the Scots College in Rome. Bartram refused any compensation for all his sufferings, of which he wrote a long account on July 31st, 1817.

For four years, then, the papers lay "perdu" in the safe hiding-place arranged by Mr. Bartram, but neither the Prince of Wales nor Sir John Hippisley had forgotten about them. In the year 1810 the engraver Nathaniel Marchant, who knew Rome well, and must have been a personal friend of Hippisley, suggested that an acquaintance of his, Angiolo Bonelli, an Italian merchant living in London, and about to make a journey to Italy, would be a good man to entrust with the commission of bringing the box of papers to England.

A further complication arose from the fact that Cardinal

York, who had died in July 1807, had instructed his executor, Monseigneur Ange Cesarini, Bishop of Milievi, to send to the Prince of Wales some valuable mementoes of him. Cesarini had selected for this purpose the Cross of St. Andrew worn by Prince Charles Edward, and a ruby ring, marked with a cross, which had belonged to King Charles I and had traditionally been used at the Coronation of all the Stuart Kings of Scotland.[1] Also (some accounts say) an emerald. Cesarini wrote to the Prince of Wales on August 30th, 1807, and Sir John Hippisley was told of this valuable bequest, when he at once arranged that it should be taken care of by his brother-in-law, Count Cicciaporci, who commanded the Vatican Guard, and the latter had the jewels removed to his house in Florence. They formed a somewhat inconvenient deposit, since by Tuscan law it was death for any Italian to have in his possession anything belonging to an Englishman, but there they apparently remained till 1810. Bonelli's first attempt to fetch them, by Sir John Hippisley's order, failed, as Cicciaporci, who did not know Bonelli, stoutly denied having any such thing in his possession. However, the small box of jewels seems at last to have joined the cases of papers at Leghorn, and all were eventually shipped to England. How this was managed must be told by Bonelli himself.

Letter of Angiolo Bonelli to Sir John Coxe Hippisley
GOLDEN SQUARE, 23 *April* 1813.

"SIR,

Agreeably to your request, I now commit to paper the outlines of my situation under the circumstances of the commission which I was honoured with on account of H.R.H. the Prince Regent, by your authority.

[1] Now among the Scottish regalia in Edinburgh Castle.

15

On the 5 Sept. 1810 I left London for the Continent, with permission from the British Government to proceed to Italy, when I was entrusted by you, Sir, with the important commission to recover the several cases lying at Civita Vecchia and to use my best endeavours to forward them by the surest means to England.

I obtained also a Swedish passport and went to Leipsic ; there I met a M. Arenberg, a Venetian merchant who, after shewing me various precious stones and antiques, produced a large sapphire surrounded with 16 brilliants of about 6 grains each, assuring me that it had belonged to the Stuart's crown, and that *Cardinal de York* had worn it on his Mitre. Having ascertained this to be a fact, from the evidence he gave me, and knowing that Cardinal York had sold at Venice during the Conclave many of his valuable articles, I wished to purchase it, but M. Arenberg declined parting with it, observing he was resolved to carry it to England himself and there present it for sale to his Royal Highness. At length however I succeeded, after a hard struggle, in obtaining it for 679 Louis d'ors in Bills upon England, upon which, at that time, there was a loss of 33 per cent by the Exchange (amounting, with the Interest of the money for 2 years, to above £1000). I then pursued my way to Weisberg, where I procured a German passport and thence I went to Vienna and Venice, where being accused of coming from this country, I was forthwith put under arrest and a strict search of my effects followed at the Albergo ; but before the Officers came to my person for examination, the Secretary of Police, Mr. Minio, on the promise of paying him a thousand sequins (*about £600*) took possession of my portfolio, containing the commission of his Royal Highness and your own letters, which papers, if discovered by the Agents of the Police, would have been sufficient to deprive me of my liberty for ever, if not of life, and the seizure of the cases would of course have been ultimately inevitable. After the search was over the Officers drew up a *procès verbal* and sent it to Milan and Paris, and an answer was returned, to send me to Rome, there to remain under the vigilance of the police. I having paid down the thousand sequins, the Portfolio was restored to me by Mr. Minio and I was passed on to Rome, where I was so closely watched that I found no other way to accomplish the wish of you, Sir, than by sending persons to Civita Vecchia to endeavour to remove the Cases, but they all returned without being able to do anything. At length I requested the Rev. Mr. Macpherson, President of the Scots College, to go to Civita Vecchia with unlimited powers to pay whatever sum might be requisite so that the said Cases might be saved. On Mr. Macpherson's arrival, he found they were stopped by mortgages on them, which were to be paid down before the person in whose hands they were, would permit their removal.[1] After great trouble and personal risk, the activity and interest of Mr. Macpherson at length surmounted every obstacle and he succeeded in shipping off the cases for Leghorn, where the house to which they were consigned placed the cases with other things under several books and papers of little consequence to conceal them from the vigilance of the custom house officers at Leghorn, whence with very great difficulty, they were embarked on board a Tunisian vessel bound to Tunis and thence forwarded to Malta and finally to London. All the expenses in employing several persons besides Mr. Macpherson, their journeys from Rome to Civita Vecchia, presents, freights, etc. till their arrival in London amount to about £460 sterling. I, being apprized that the cases had been punctually forwarded to their destination, then endeavoured to get off for Germany and proceed to England, but was again detained under arrest and my Passport taken from me on the suspicion of my having sent papers to England of great importance. Nor was I per-

---

[1] They had in fact been lying in store for four years and some fees were no doubt due.

mitted, before the lapse of 6 months more, to go on to Paris and this as a special favor, leaving behind me as security my wife and children who had been included in my English passport, also much property. At Paris I was under the condition of shewing myself every week at the Police, thus rendering my escape almost next to impossible. I contrived however to get on to *Bruges* by the assistance of my friends and at length at the peril of my life succeeded in getting off and was taken up and carried into the Fleet at Deal and I must appeal to you, Sir, for this latter part, as you have heard it yourself from the Admiral.

I have now, Sir, to observe that this paper is intended solely for your private information for should it eventually reach France it might endanger both my family and the several other persons alluded to. I am ready to make oath of the truth of the contents. You have heard also from the worthy Mr. Macpherson in person before he left England the circumstances as far as related to him, as well as the hardships which befell myself, of which he was an eye-witness and indeed was near sharing with me the embarrassments. My wish, Sir, was to give content to the Prince Regent and to yourself, who honoured me with this important commission. I had hoped from what you first mentioned that there would have been no difficulty in my obtaining the Grace which you solicited for me, of letters of Denization which I had indeed solicited before I left England, but by some secret enemies failed to procure. I should be sorry that you should appear to protect a character unworthy of yr favour, but I am sure no person can accuse me with any justice of any dishonourable action. I wish to look to England as my country and to find in it that comfort and protection which is denied to me in my own.

I have the honour to be, etc.

ANGIOLO BONELLI."

One detail omitted by the writer of this letter, and vouched for by the Admiral concerned, was that when picked up by a British vessel and carried into Deal, the intrepid Bonelli, after all his former hardships, was actually endeavouring to make his way to the shores of England in a *home-made boat*, and that this boat had been built in his garret lodging in Bruges, and presumably been launched on the Canal and so made its way to the open sea. Angiolo Bonelli seems to have been a man of infinite resource ; posterity can only regret that the Home Secretary, Lord Sidmouth, should have made so many difficulties and finally refused to grant him the one reward he asked, i.e. to become a naturalized Englishman, which he thoroughly deserved.

Lord Sidmouth, formerly Henry Addington (and by that name Prime Minister for two years—1801–03), was a timorous, narrow-minded man. Of him it was said "As London is to Paddington so is Pitt to Addington." He distrusted all foreigners and though Angiolo Bonelli had been known and respected for long as a merchant in Leghorn, in partnership with the Consul, John Udny, and since for many years in partnership with Isaac Pitterin, Golden Square, though his application was backed by Lord Hardwicke, Lord Kinnaird and other prominent persons [1] and though Sir John Coxe Hippisley offered to guarantee him in any way required, he never, apparently, received his "Letters of denization." It is to be hoped that at least his wife and family were allowed to rejoin him in England.

He, like Bartram, refused to accept any pecuniary reward for his arduous services. Only the money he had actually

[1] Three marquises, Douglas, Lansdowne and Stafford, with Lords Darnley and Radstock, were also his friends and wrote on his behalf.

disbursed for bribing the various officials was eventually paid him. These payees included the remarkable police secretary in Venice (then under Italian rule), who, before a suspected person was searched, obligingly took possession of the only incriminating object that might have been found, and subsequently restored it to its owner. A carefully detailed account of all expenses was given to Sir John Hippisley, was paid and receipted. Paul Macpherson on seeing this, maintained that the sums put down as paid to or for him were too large, but no steps were taken about it. The total amounted to £1,060,[1] exclusive of what Bonelli had paid for the Cardinal's jewel and no record of his having been repaid this amount exists, though one letter notes that the Prince Regent was unable to return the jewel, as he had given it to the Princess Charlotte !

A further episode in the history of this jewel is given in Greville's memoirs, under June 24th, 1821 :

> The King dined at Devonshire House last Thursday sen'night. Lady Conyngham had on her head a sapphire which belonged to the Stuarts and was given by Cardinal York to the King.[2] He gave it to the Princess Charlotte and when she died he desired to have it back, Leopold being informed that it was a crown jewel. This crown jewel sparkled in the head-dress of the Marchioness at the ball.

The laws of Tuscany, at that time, *still* made it death to have or conceal anything that belonged to the English, so

	£	s.	d.
[1] To the Secretary of Police in Venice	600	0	0
To different persons at Civita Vecchia. . . .	358	10	0
Freight Leghorn to Tunis	42	0	0
Tunis to Malta and London	59	10	0
	£1060	0	0

[2] This statement was erroneous.

20

the three cases of papers [1] which remained for a time in Cicciaporci's house were an active source of danger. He tried to induce the Rev. Paul Macpherson to take them with him to England as personal luggage, but this was refused as the packages were too bulky, and they were at length sent by sea, as related in Bonelli's letter, duly addressed "by the hand of an English woman," Hippisley's sister and Cicciaporci's wife, one consigned to the Prince Regent and two to Hippisley himself. Cardinal Consalvi [2] wrote anxiously in March 1813 to know if they had arrived and hoped they would at least afford the Prince Regent "some amusement."

The final adventure of these remarkable papers with the nine lives was that the Tunisian vessel having reached a British port with "a foul bill of health," had to have all her cargo disinfected, and the three cases were opened and thoroughly "rummaged" by the Sanitary Officers at Standgate Creek in the Thames ; which accounts for a good deal of disorder among the papers, and the fragmentary condition of many.

They were, however, now actually in England, where they were finally handed over by Bonelli to Sir John Hippisley on June 19th, 1813, and duly delivered at Carlton House. They had to wait four years for the arrival of the second contingent.

The fact that the two consignments of "Stuart papers," now at Windsor, were, quite properly, amalgamated by the Commissioners when sorting them in chronological order, has tended to obscure the fact of the difference of their secondary *provenence*, though both, of course, originally formed part

[1] Apparently repacked from the original case, marked R.B.!
[2] He was Secretary of State to Pius VII and in 1814 went to London as envoy to arrange the peace.

of the Archives of King James III & VIII at the Palazzo Muti in Rome.[1]

The first lot to arrive in England in 1813, after the romantic adventures already related, came as seen from the hands of Prince Charles Edward's daughter, Charlotte, through her executor, the Abbé Waters, who had not, as already stated, the faintest right to sell them, since her own instructions in her Will (*which still exists*) directed him to burn what was not important and hand the rest over to her uncle, the Cardinal. The second lot of papers which reached England in 1817, came from the repositories of the Cardinal himself, having also passed through some curious vicissitudes, and the *Deus ex machina* in this case was not an ecclesiastic, but a Scottish adventurer, Dr. Robert Watson, who had already had a most strange career. Born in Elgin and, according to the most reliable accounts, in the year of Culloden (1746), he had, in the course of his long life, been an M.D., a "colonel" in Washington's army and a revolutionary agitator in England, at which time he became Secretary to the notorious Lord George Gordon and afterwards wrote his life. He is said to have been the original of Gashford of *Barnaby Rudge*, in which book the Gordon riots are so thrillingly described.

Besides being a friend of Washington, Robert Watson was also well known to Napoleon, who made him Principal of the new non-ecclesiastical Scots College in Paris, and he held that office for six years, 1802–8. It was at this period that he became known as "Chevalier." In 1816 he stated that he had been for twenty-five years preparing a history of the Stuarts and had come to Rome in 1809 (where he set up as

---

[1] Annotations on the back of some of them in the handwriting of Abbé Waters, prove particular ones to have been among those in his hands. But he had long had access to the whole collection.

a teacher of English), because he knew that some of the papers from the Old Scots College in Paris had been deposited there, as well as many others of later date which had accumulated and that he was there on purpose to institute a search for them.

The documents belonging to the Cardinal York had in fact been quite lost to sight, since the date of his death, which occurred July 13th, 1807. They had been bequeathed in entirety to his executor, Cardinal Cesarini, and *some* of them Cesarini gave or bequeathed to a niece, who sold them to Lord Oxford ; these were bought in Rome by the Baroness Braye in 1842 and are now in the British Museum.[1] The bulk of this immense collection already described, however, remained in the hands of Cardinal Cesarini, who seemingly did not value it at all, being ignorant of the two languages, French and English, in which most of the documents were written. At Cesarini's death they passed into the possession of his executor, Monsignor Tarsoni, auditor to the Pope (an office grandly magnified by the splendour-loving Dr. Watson into the equivalent of Lord Chancellor). Tarsoni took even less interest in the "Stuart papers" than had his predecessor, and in the year 1816, nine years after the Cardinal's death, their whereabouts was discovered with some difficulty by the persistent Watson. They were found to be in a garret in the Palazzo Monserati in Rome, exposed to wind and rain and the ravages of rats and mice, nominally in the care of the Abbate Lupi. The following paper in the French Foreign Office well describes their condition.

---

[1] They have not been printed, though sometimes consulted. They are not of historical interest, being largely concerned with the ecclesiastical and diocesan affairs of the Cardinal.

Février 1817.

A la mort du Prétendant la plus part des papiers qui'étaient en sa possession furent envoyés au Cardinal d'Yorck qui prit alors le titre de Charles IX (*really Henry IX* !) (Il en ont resté cependant quelques uns entre les mains de la fille naturelle du prétendant, la dernière Duchesse d'Albany, qui furent depuis rendus au prince régent par M. Waters, moine anglais, ami intime de la princesse.)

Ce dépôt de documents de famille fut soigneusement gardé à Rome jusqu'à l'époque de la mort du cardinal d'Yorck, apres laquelle le Duc Cesarini, son executeur testamentaire, les fit transporter et placer dans le palais Monsferrati. A la mort du duc Cesarini, les mêmes papiers restèrent à la dis-position de Monsignor Tarsoni, executeur testamentaire du duc. Ce dernier dépositare, ignorant, comme le premier, les langues dans lequelles les documents sont écrites et attachant peu de prix à leur contenu, les laisse comme object inutile dans le lieu où on les avait fait placer ; ils devinrent la pâture des rats et des insectes, et demeurèrent exposés aux vents et à la pluie qui entraient de tous côtés, attendu que les fenêtres du grenier étaient, depuis longtemps, sans carreaux.

Cette collection aurait été perdue pour la posterité sans la découverte qui en a été faite par M. Watson le 16 décembre 1816 et les soins qu'il a eu de les retirer du galetas où ils étaient enfouis, pour les faire transporter dans sa maison. Parmis les papiers rendus par M. Waters au prince régent, il n'y avait d'important, ainsi que l'assure M. Macpherson, principal du college écossais à Rome, que le testament politique du roi Jacques, adressé à son fils, tandis que les papiers acquis par M. Watson et qui n'ont été connus que par le Cardinal d'Yorck, forment une collection immense de documents de ce temslà.

Ils consistent en 250,000 pièces originales ou copies de differens genres d'écrit.

Il y a environ 10,000 lettres autographes de la famille Stuart

adressées à differens souverains de l'Europe et aux partisans
Jacobites de la Grande Bretagne. Le document de la date la
plus reculée est un régistre commencé à Whitehall en 1623—
il contient plusieurs centaines de lettres, toutes de la main
propre de la reine Marie Stuart. (*Mary of Modena, wife of
James II.*)

Il y a aussi les lettres écrites aux Stuarts par Pierre le Grand,
Charles XII, les rois et reines de France et d'Espagne et d'autres
princes regnans à cette époque.

Les correspondances secrètes de plusieurs papes, cardinaux
et autres princes italiens paraissent être du plus grand intéret.
Les notes, depêches des Ambassadeurs et autres Agens accre-
dités par les Stuarts, auprès des differents cours de l'Europe,
forment la plus grande partie de cette collection. Les Lettres
de Fénelon, aussi bien que celles de l'évêque de Rochester,
du docteur Swift, des Lords Bolingbroke et Marshall sont
tres curieuses sous le rapport litéraire.

Il existe aussi d'autres papiers très importants au sujet des
rebellions de 1715 et de 1745 et differens autres projets qui
tendaient au rétablissement des Stuarts sur le trône de l'Angleterre. En un mot, il n'y a pas de guerres, de traitées de paix,
de conspirations politiques, dans un laps de temps d'un siècle,
auxquels les Stuarts et leurs fidèles adherens n'aient participés
directement ou indirectement ; il se sont adressés à toutes les
autorités de leur temps, depuis le Czar de Moscovie, jusqu'aux
pirates de Madagascar.

Ces papiers, renfermés dans cinq caisses, ont été saisis à
Rome le 12 Janvier dernier (1817) au domicile de M. Watson,
et portés aux palais du Gouverneur ou ils sont actuellement
déposés.[1]

(The final sentence carries the story a little further than
has been reached in our account.)

---

[1] *Documents historiques* from the "Archives des affaires étrangères, Quai
d'Orsay. *Fonds Stuart*."

Watson approached Lupi—(it is said he also bribed Tarsoni) and after a prolonged negotiation in which the value of the collection as waste paper was the only thing discussed, Watson became the owner at the price of 170 piastres, about £23 (others say for 300 crowns), and losing no time, had the whole collection transferred *that same night* to his own lodgings.[1] There is no doubt that he was well aware that he had secured a prize. His intention was to convey the papers to England or Scotland, offer some to the Prince Regent and write family histories based upon many of the others. He contemplated publishing in America and it is probable (from the character of the man) that political and social blackmail may have entered into his calculations. In any case, he felt he had now a provision for life. Then his Scots caution forsook him ; he was unable to keep his successful coup to himself and boasted to his fellow countrymen (and women !) in Rome of what he had done ; especially to the Duchess of Devonshire, who then invited him to a soirée and begged to see specimens of these wonderful documents. Watson brought a packet with him and as these lay on the Duchess's table they were examined by Cardinal Hercule Consalvi, who had been in England and knew many of the families mentioned. He laid the letters down again without a word. Next morning, however, Dr. Watson was surprised by a visit from the Italian Police, sent by the orders of the Cardinal to seal up the papers and the room in which they were contained, as being valuable property which could not be removed from the Papal States without express permission.

[1] It was said it filled two wagons !—but the size of the wagons was not given. When removed to England they filled five large chests ; Watson's lodgings were in the Strada dei Tre Cannelli, 149, quite near the Palazzo Muti whence the papers had originally come.

Watson protested and blustered and, on examination, was exceedingly rude to the Cardinal who told him that any Roman who had used similar language would have found himself a prisoner of the Inquisition ! Lupi, who had sold what did not belong to him, was put in prison for a year and Watson had eventually to submit to the inevitable, though he still maintained that the papers were *his*, since he had paid for them and refused to be reimbursed the modest sum he had expended, claiming that if they were to be handed over to the British Government, as he learnt was the intention of His Holiness, he, who had discovered them, ought to have the honour of doing this, and to receive a reward for it. The British Government did indeed assign £500 to be paid to the discoverer of the papers, but Cardinal Consalvi decreed that Watson had forfeited all right to this by his violent and insulting behaviour, and did not hand it over.

Long afterwards, in England, Watson made ridiculous claims for immense sums, but he seems on the whole to have been treated better than he deserved and to have netted in all over £3,000 from the Commissioners appointed to deal with the papers. This he refers to as an "alimentary subsistence" and further said he "hoped to get enough from them (the papers) to pass the remainder of his days in comfort, in Scotland !"

Some accounts say that being unable in the first instance to raise the very modest sum which he paid to Lupi for the collection, he had entered into negotiations with the future Lord Brougham then in Rome from whom he tried to borrow the money, but Brougham insisting that in that case the papers would be his, the arrangement fell through.

Brougham (who was editor of the *Edinburgh Review*) had certainly realized the political if not literary value of so many records of plots, etc., in which the ancestors of his colleagues or opponents in Parliament had been involved. Watson represented to Lord Castlereagh that as early as January 19th, 1817, he had announced to Mr. Dennis, the English Consul at Civita Vecchia, that he was in possession of these papers, and that he meant to present them to the Prince Regent. He certainly expected that many of them would have been published, and that he would have received "the emoluments from the publication." They had, however, reached England without further adventure, and not sent by him,[1] and are announced as having been *"received"* by October 2nd, 1817, and again in a Foreign Office Minute of January 12th, 1818, as being at Carlton House, where they were placed with the other Stuart papers, obtained from Waters.

Shortly after this, in May 1819, a Commission to deal with the whole was appointed consisting of : J. W. Croker (the editor of Johnson, pilloried by Macaulay) ; Sir James Mackintosh, the historian ; Charles Watkins William Wynne (descendant of one of the undecided English Jacobites) ; William Richard Hamilton, Under Secretary of State for Foreign Affairs ; Richard Pollen ; and Dr. Stanier Clark, the King's Librarian, with James Pullen as Secretary.

Before, however, going on to relate what the Commission did with the "Stuart papers," the after career of Robert Watson must be briefly sketched. Chevalier Watson, as he still called himself, continued to profess ardent Republican principles and it is said to have been concerned in the *Cato*

---

[1] They had been repacked in nine boxes, handed over to Consul-General Parke at Civita Vecchia and despatched from thence in an English brig, the *Satellite*, on June 21st, 1817, reaching the Thames on August 20th.

St. Conspiracy, that absurd plot, hatched in a little street off the Edgware Road in February 1820, with a design to murder the entire Cabinet at a dinner-party and carry away their heads in sacks ! Someone turned King's evidence and the ringleaders were tried and executed. Watson was imprisoned for a time, but nothing could be proved against him, and he was released. The manuscript Diary of H. J. Ellis in the British Museum, Add. MSS. 36653, contains a curious passage, referring to Watson.

Feb. 6, 1820.

I dined at Highgate with Mr. Lackington where I met the Chevalier Watson, the owner of the papers which he calls the Archives of the Stuart family—obtained by him from the Chancellor of Rome the Executor to the Cardinal of York. Mr. Watson it appears gave seventy piastres for them,—I suppose about sixteen pounds. He states they made two waggon loads. He nam'd near eighty letters from Bishop Atterbury among them. A great many also from Sir Robert Walpole . . .

Mr. Watson is a Scotchman—A Highlander he calls himself. He said he had been Chairman formerly to the Executive Committee of the London corresponding Society and had been outlawed. He afterwards received a pension from the French Directory and was appointed Director of the Scots College. He spoke of himself as having been at one time Preceptor to the son of Admiral Greig ; had been imprisoned at another at Fontainebleau, after having had an interview with Bonaparte. That he ingratiated himself so far with an agricultural Society there, by writing 2 or 3 papers for them, as to become a honorary associate to them and through the means of some of the principal persons ultimately obtained his enlargement upon condition of not going beyond the limits of the French Empire . . .

I think I can have no doubt that Mr. Watson has been a spy . . .

I have promised to call and see his curiosities.

Watson was then an old man, over 70, but he lived for eighteen years longer and in 1825 wrote a remarkable letter to a friend in Scotland, dated from Paris, and asking for the loan of money that he might not lose a wonderful collection of treasures, comprising as he said, the Constantinople Bible, the Missal of Mary Queen of Scots, the chronicles of St. Denis, the baton of Marshal Ney, the carriage of the Emperor Napoleon taken at Waterloo, etc. What happened to any of these is not known, save the last item which was certainly later to be seen at Madame Tussaud's.

The ultimate act in the life of this extraordinary old Scot was his committing suicide at the Blue Anchor Inn in Thames Street on Monday, November 19th, 1838, by strangling himself with his own neck-cloth in which he had inserted the poker. Suicide of such a determined character at the advanced age of 92 seems almost unique. Besides his discovery of the "Stuart papers" in Rome, he claimed that he knew of two other depositories of valuable documents of the same nature. One emanating from the Scots College in Paris, probably those now at Blair's College, Aberdeen,[1] and another in Rome, which may have been those purchased by Lady Braye.

His portrait from the National Portrait Gallery in Edinburgh is reproduced opposite.

His veracity was certainly a very doubtful quantity. On one occasion he stated that he had been allowed by "the Abbate Lupi" *in 1812* to see and take copies of some of the

[1] Which have not yet been printed, though Monseigneur Buti many years ago made a rough catalogue of them.

"Stuart papers"—which hardly agrees with the story that Lupi looked on the whole collection as so much waste paper and as waste paper valued it at 200 piastres. (Watson offered 150 and the 170 was a compromise.)

Watson further stated in his own defence that he had already, before the papers were seized, made offer of them to the Prince Regent, but no one believed him. He added also that he had had, during his brief ownership of them, advantageous offers from foreign ambassadors and English M.P's to sell them the collection, and mentioned that his expenses in all had been 600 piastres, in which he boldly included his own expenses of living and various bribes. He seems not, in fact, to have known very much of the actual contents of the collection which he owned for a month, being in this unlike the Abbé Waters, whose catalogue raisonné is of deep interest and was of great use to the Commissioners when they began their task two years after the arrival of the second contingent of "Stuart papers" in England.

It is obvious that, even when re-united, these two collections did not represent the whole of the archives of the Palazzo Muti. Among the missing would be those brought to England as samples by Sir John Hippisley, given to the Prince of Wales and subsequently lost, those which fell victims to the ravages of weather and vermin in the Palazzo Monserati, those which it is more than likely Watson managed to abstract,[1] besides those given to Consul Dennis and others to the Rev. Edward Bury, as detailed in Hippisley's letters, and those sold by Cesarini's niece.

The collection of miniatures was dispersed and it is not known whether any found their way to England or not.

[1] He also gave a few to Brougham.

Two large pictures belonging to the Cardinal were bought by Sir John Hippisley, but not, it seems, brought to England owing to difficulties of transport. One was a portrait of Pope Benedict XIV, (Lambertini d. 1758) by the well-known Pompeo Battoni, the other a full-length of King James by Cavaliere Benedetto Luti, and was at one time thought to be the picture bought long after in Rome and now in the possession of the Earl of Mar and Kellie at Alloa House,[1] but *if* the date on the picture is right Luti was then dead. In Crofton Croker's notes, quoted by Ellis as above (Add MSS. 36653), occurs also (under 28 Nov. 1826), the following passage :

> James's letters to his son are filled with parental fondness. It is impossible not to esteem the writer. Comparatively speaking, few English men attached to the Stuart cause. The principal adherents to this unfortunate family were Scotch and Irish, and there appear many instances of the most devoted attachment to the "right cause" as it is termed, in which friends, family, fortune and country were sacrificed without the prospect of any return.

Croker quotes one letter of King James's beginning "I have much business to transact, moreover I am much troubled with Mulligrubs." This is now missing !

Croker seems to think that the King's letters were all collected long after from the recipients, and remarks on the magnitude of the task, not realizing that most of them are either drafts or copies by Edgar, in his hand.

He says "there was a letter from the Duke of Norfolk to the Pretender, endorsed in the Pretender's own writing, 1720, in which the Duke declares his attachment to the Pretender's cause." This also is no longer to be found.

As stated on page 28, the Commission appointed to deal with the "Stuart papers" began its labours in May 1819, and

[1] Reproduced as frontispiece.

the first thing to do was to remove the collection from Carlton House to St. James's Palace where a special room was set apart for it.

The next was for the Commissioners to attempt to take stock of the whole of the material, and in this they were greatly helped by the very full list supplied by the Abbé Waters and copied by Sir John Hippisley. This appears to have been largely a list of *all* the "Stuart papers," since some of those appearing in it were certainly among those obtained by Dr. Watson ; Waters of course as chaplain had had many years of undisturbed possession to study the whole collection, both those which had come from Florence and those which were still the property of the Cardinal. Among those which he handed over to Sir John Hippisley he enumerates as of special interest the four volumes of the *Life of James II*, afterwards published by Dr. Stanier Clark (Waters notes that he himself had *copied out* the whole of this), the Instructions of King James to his son and the will of the former ; the five volumes of Entry books and Warrants ; the History of the Royal House of Stuart in Italian ; the accounts of Prince Charles's expedition to Scotland, by eye-witnesses [1] (access to which had been refused to the historians, Home and Chambers, and secretly granted to Sir James Mackintosh, who made *some* use of them), and a very large number of letters specially detailed—the whole catalogue running to many pages.

The Commissioners were unanimously of opinion that this collection, though less in bulk than the second consignment obtained four years later, was decidedly more "curious and interesting."

[1] These are probably the accounts by O'Sullivan and Sir John Macdonald, and a third not yet published, as it contains nothing strikingly new.

The second consignment of Stuart papers consisted entirely of letters, being the correspondence amassed in the Palazzo Muti during the years between 1718 and 1788, together with what may be termed "domestic papers." (The later corre-spondence of the Cardinal himself (all *after* that date) forms another collection, of which some is now in the British Museum and some still in the hands of Lord Braye.)

Having ascertained what they had to deal with, the Commis-sion proceeded, chiefly by means of their invaluable secretary, to arrange both sets of papers together in chronological order, and by the 22nd of August, *1821*, were able to issue a report that this had, as far as possible, been done. Besides the 400 bundles into which they were originally made up, there were always a certain number undated, which now fill some of the ten most exciting boxes of the collection.

The result of this first report was that the Commissioners were ordered to compile a full and explanatory Catalogue, which, however, has *never yet been done* ; but the report issued on February 12th, *1822*, definitely recommends the publishing of several volumes of selected papers, which the Commissioners are sure would be "well received by the public." They specially advised that the names of all those who had received grants of nobility, etc., from King James II in exile, and from his son and grandson after him, with other particulars from the Warrant and Entry books should be published. This was, to some extent, eventually done by the Marquis de Ruvigny in his *Jacobite Peerage*, which, however, as already pointed out, is inaccurate in many particulars.

They further proposed that a certain number of volumes of selected papers should be published in quarto form, which they decided any publisher would do for £1000 each, and, since they could not themselves undertake the editing, that some literary hack (it could not have been anyone more qualified), should be paid the sum of £250 per volume to do this. It was considered that the sale of such volumes would pay for their production, but the project never materialized.

The Commissioners at this stage became aware that the Collection was far from being complete, as was indeed obvious, for the reasons given on page 31 and others which would account for the disappearance of a certain number and why some papers definitely alluded to by Waters, Scott, etc., are not now to be found.[1]

In conclusion the Commissioners suggested that the proper home of the Collection was the British Museum !

In January 1823, the Commission invited Mr. Canning, the Foreign Secretary, to "take the King's pleasure on what they had submitted to him," but apparently received no answer, nor did they to another application in 1826, but in the last year of the reign of George IV, June 30th, 1829, Lord Aberdeen, the Foreign Secretary, announced that the King had decided that the Commission should be wound up, and that the papers now lying in a room in St. James's Palace should be handed over to the care of Sir Walter Scott, and his son-in-law, John Gibson Lockhart, who with Dr. Good might themselves arrange for the publication of some of them.

In a dignified letter the Commissioners requested Lord Aberdeen himself to take charge of the key of the room that it might be handed over to Sir Walter Scott when he should arrive from Scotland. They also placed it on record that no one but themselves had had any access to the papers save Scott

---

[1] Long after, Dr. Croker found and purchased fifty odd papers, which he added to the collection.

himself on one occasion and on one other Dr. Sumner, Bishop of Winchester. Scott himself, as might be expected from the state of his health and his own affairs, did nothing, but Lockhart and a subordinate named John Hall, did some further arranging for about six months. Some time after the death of the King the papers were removed from St. James's Palace first to Buckingham Palace, next to the Castle Hotel, Windsor, and then to Cumberland Lodge, where Lord Mahon worked on them ; seven years later they finally came to rest in the Round Tower at Windsor Castle where Mr. Glover and Mr. Holmes arranged them more or less in the condition in which we now find them.

In 1847 Dr. Glover (the Librarian) published a volume entitled *The Stuart Papers—Correspondence*—further described on the Title Page as "letters of Francis Atterbury, Bishop of Rochester, to the Chevalier de St. George, and some of the Adherents of the House of Stuart."

It contains a few letters from other persons down to the year 1725. Only one volume was ever published, though apparently others were projected. The book is now rare and when found is usually uncut. The dedication of Dr. Glover's work, or rather of his first volume, was as follows :

TO HER MOST GRACIOUS MAJESTY THE QUEEN
THIS WORK ELUCIDATING AN IMPORTANT PERIOD OF ENGLISH HISTORY AND PRESENTING FACTS BY WHICH THE BENEFITS ARISING FROM THE ESTABLISHMENT OF THE PROTESTANT HOUSE OF HANOVER ON THE THRONE OF THESE REALMS CAN BE PROPERLY ESTIMATED, IS DUTIFULLY INSCRIBED BY HER MAJESTY'S FAITHFUL AND DEVOTED SUBJECT AND MOST HUMBLE SERVANT AND LIBRARIAN
JOHN HULBERT GLOVER, LIBRARY, WINDSOR CASTLE.
January 1, 1847.

List of those who have used the Stuart papers at all

1. Browne, *History of the Highlands.*
2. Lord Mahon, *History.*
3. Strickland, *Lives of the Queens and Princesses.*
4. Percy Thornton, *Stuart Dynasty* (all printed afterwards by the Historical MSS. Commission).
5. F. Williams, *Life of Atterbury* (the letters here used were probably taken from Dr. Glover's volume).
6. O'Callaghan, *History of the Irish Brigade.*
7. Ruvigny, *Jacobite Peerage.*
8. Campana de Cavelli, *Les Derniers Stuarts.*
9. Andrew Lang, *Life of Prince Charles Edward, Pickle,* etc.
10. Lang and Shield, *King over the Water, Life of Cardinal York,* etc.
11. Martin Haile, *The Old Chevalier* and *Mary of Modena.*
12. Hon. Evan Charteris in his Introduction to Lord Elcho's *Affairs of Scotland,* 1744–46, makes allusions to the Stuart papers which he had studied for the period in question and prints one letter from them and one from the Cumberland MS.
13. Sir Charles Petrie, *The Jacobite Movement.*
14. Alex. Mackenzie, *History of the Camerons.*
15. Major Skeet, *Life of Charlotte of Albany.*
16. Thirty-four letters are printed by Mr. Fitzroy Bell in his edition of *Murray of Broughton's Memoirs.* These, of course, are concerned *only* with the '45, and are of dates from 1740 to 1747. Unfamiliarity with the Italian language, results in one or two errors of transcription.
17. Dr. Dickson, *Jacobite Attempt of 1719.* Letters of the Duke of Ormonde and Cardinal Alberoni.
18. Major Eardley Simpson, *Derby and the Forty-five.*
19. Miss Mitchiner, *No Crown for the Queen* (i.e. Louise of Stolberg).

The Letters

AFTER the story of how the Letters reached Windsor come the documents themselves, and with them we are transported to the Rome of the early eighteenth century, distant by many weeks from Britain and at that time the home of hundreds of exiled English, Scots and Irish who had followed the Stuart Sovereign, in most cases from pure devotion to his cause and his person, but in some instances also merely for daily bread.

Many of the Scottish Chiefs who should have been "little Kings" at home (*so* James Stuart had called them when he landed in Scotland in 1715), ruling their clansmen and managing their estates, were now dragging out a wearisome, useless existence, living perhaps in one room in an old palace and forming themselves into groups called Clubs, so that they might dine more cheaply. (Lord Pitsligo [1] well describes this.) Having nothing to do, they unfortunately quarrelled frequently among themselves, and the echoes of these bickerings reached Paris, London and Scotland. All the exiles wrote too much. It was one of their few occupations, but some of their inordinately long epistles provide future generations with quaint details which would otherwise have been lost.

[1] See p. 49.

Letters from the following have been selected and annotated

KING JAMES

QUEEN CLEMENTINA

PRINCE CHARLES

PRINCE HENRY

LORD AND LADY MAR

SIR THOMAS SHERIDAN

JOHN HAY AND HIS WIFE (LORD
AND LADY INVERNESS)

JAMES MURRAY, LORD DUNBAR

JOHN GRAEME

JAMES EDGAR

ANDREW LUMISDEN

LORD DUMBARTON

LORD WINTOUN

AND OTHER PETITIONERS

The Royal Family

The letters of the King, Queen, and Princes are here given in nearly chronological order, as illustrating their family life by hitherto unpublished and very human documents, and interspersed with others from some of their most prominent followers.

The main facts of their lives must be well known to any-one sufficiently interested to read these letters, but the re-capitulation of the dates will make things clearer.

James Francis Edward Stuart was born on June 10th, 1688, the sixth child of the unfortunate King James II and his second wife, Mary of Modena, and the first of these who lived to grow up. His father's abdication and the flight of the family to France took place when the little Prince was six months old, and the rest of his life was passed in exile. On his father's death, on September 6th, 1701, young James succeeded to the nominal Sovereignty of Great Britain and Ireland and was proclaimed as King by Louis XIV. In March 1708 a promising French expedition was fitted out to invade Scotland and put him on his throne, but by a series of unfortunate accidents never even landed in Scotland. Seven years later took place the better-known Rising of 1715, in which the cause was lost by the incompetence of the Earl of Mar, before poor James Stuart reached Scotland, where nevertheless he did spend an uncomfortable six weeks and then beat an ignominious retreat with his lieutenant and a band of devoted but ruined followers, back to France and then to Avignon. In 1717 he was constrained by European politics to move farther from England to Urbino, and began his residence of nearly fifty years in Rome. Vague projects of restoration arose, died down or failed in the next two years. Then came his marriage with Clementina Sobieska, after her imprisonment by the Emperor's orders and thrilling rescue by Wogan and his Musketeers. Owing to James Stuart's absence in Spain, preparing for another Scottish expedition, the wedding did not actually take place till September 1st, 1719, after all the bridegroom's hopes had been shattered at Glenshiel, on the 10th of June of that year.

From December 31st, 1719, onward, the Stuart papers at Windsor are unpublished, save for those selected ones already described. The history of the Royal family of Stuart, now established for good in the Palazzo Muti, Piazza Santi Apostoli, can be illustrated by extracts from letters to and from the various members, while the lives of the other Jacobites, some in Rome, many in Paris and elsewhere, are shown also separately by their own letters written in or sent to Rome.

King James III, *de jure* King of England for nearly sixty-five years (though he never occupied the throne), was a most prolific letter writer ; as the Earl of Mar said of him when in Scotland in the winter campaign of 1715–16, "He has fine parts and despatches all his business himself with the greatest exactness. I never saw anybody write so finely." In his old age his hand became somewhat illegible, but the greater number of the letters at Windsor despatched by the King exist in copies written in the small neat script of James Edgar [1] (his secretary for nearly fifty years) often with annotations or postscripts by the King himself.

[1] See p. 190.

The first letters to be given, among the earliest of those un-published, are from Mar and his wife, and deal with the King's departure for Spain and Mar's own failure to join him there and subsequent actions. Some of the letters of Lady Mar are of date before December 31st, 1718, and are given here as showing the conditions of travel for those who joined the King in Rome.

The Earl of Mar (*Jacobite Duke*)

John, Earl of Mar, born at Alloa House in 1675, took his seat in the Scots Parliament in 1696 and attached himself to the party of the King, i.e. William, throwing over the early Jacobitism of his father. He was made a Privy Councillor and under Queen Anne became one of the Commissioners for carrying out the hated Act of Union. In 1711 he was appointed Secretary of State for Scotland, and had he been continued in this office by King George I, it is safe to say that he, at any rate, would have had no hand in the Jacobite Rising of 1715. But George turned his back on him and Mar went north, to raise the Standard for King James on September 6th, 1715, at Braemar, and thereafter to muddle away all the chances of the party, which never recovered from his long dallying at Perth, culminating in the indecisive battle of Sheriffmuir (November 13th, 1715). Poor King James arrived in Scotland after this, on December 23rd, but when he fled again six weeks later, took Mar with him and the latter followed his master to Avignon, Urbino and then Rome, and was Secretary of State to the exiled monarch for three years when he dismissed himself, left Italy, and entered into various discreditable dealings with the British Government, while continuing to correspond with King James and fellow-Jacobites, almost till his own death in 1732. The opinion of the Master of Sinclair on the Earl of Mar during the campaign in Scotland is well known. "No man can paint him so natural or so crooked as

44

Earl of Mar and Son

From a picture by Sir Godfrey Kneller at Alloa House

[44]

he does himself." [1] Besides this may be set Bishop Atterbury's, given in a letter (at Windsor).

To John Hay

Oct. 1, 1725.

"I thank you for the sight of Lord Mar's Vindication, which is a very extraordinary piece. As far as I am acquainted with the matter of it, I find there is not a sincere line in it, from one end to the other. . . . Lord Erskine [2] is soon going to Scotland and Lady Mar to England, and nothing, I dare say, would keep Lord Mar here (for whom an Act of Parliament might be obtained, as well as for Bolingbroke) but that this is the spot wherein he can do most mischief as things now stand, and best earn his appointments."

In any collection of Jacobite letters it is inevitable to have some from this man, the evil genius of the Rising of 1715 and a most prolific correspondent with his master, his brother-in-law John Hay, James Edgar and many others, during the thirteen years of life that remained to him after he left Rome. Numbers of his letters have already been printed in the volumes of Stuart papers issued by the Historical MSS. Commission, and others by the Scottish Historical Society in 1938.

The two following are sufficiently curious, since they were written when Mar and his master were both in Rome, the day before the former set out for Genoa with the expressed intention of joining the latter who was to start at the same time for Spain. Great mystery enshrouded both departures. It was hoped to conceal them altogether for some days, and when known, that it might be thought James had gone to meet his bride from Germany, and not to Spain to take part in an invasion of Great Britain. The invasion of course did not

[1] " The affairs in Scotland."

[2] Mar's son.

eventuate, because once again a storm scattered alike a Spanish fleet and the hopes of the Roman Catholics. The King reached Spain, where he remained as a visitor, until asked to leave, but Mar was taken prisoner when he entered the territories of the Holy Roman Emperor, and never saw his master again. Not that he spent the rest of his life in prison. He was very soon released from the Castle of Milan and returned to Rome, but he left it again before the King got back, and after another short imprisonment in Geneva, he drifted to Paris in the neighbourhood of which most of the remaining years were spent. These two letters give his private advice to the King in 1719, and were evidently sent by hand to the King's apartments :

The Duke of Mar to the King (original endorsement)
Feb. 4, 1719.

I was unwilling to trouble you before you parted, and had so many things of moment to think of, wt anything in relation to myself, but I thought my doing it in this manner might be of use to you and for your ease in case it should please God to give you a speedier passage to your intended place than me.

I have often taken the liberty to tel yr Majesty that whenever it should please God to restore you to yr Dominions, that I had no desire or project of haveing any eminent hand in business. At that time, what I have so much wisht for all my life will be accomplished and yr Majesty will be in no want of people to serve you in each of yr kingdoms and who are much more capable of it than I, and it will be farr from giving me any grudge to see any you think fitt emploied in the most eminent posts of yr three kingdoms.

As for the seals I have the honour to hold of your Majesty at this time, you may very freely without any apprehension of giving me a mortification dispose of them as soon as you land in England and not only those for that Kingdom, but also for that of Scotland and Ireland. I never aimed at being what is commonly called to Princes a favorite but my ambition is to have the honour, as it will be a pleasur, of being near your person. You have been pleased already to give me a post, wh entitles me to that, and if you think it fitt to add to it any emploiement which would make me to be of your Cabin Council (as it is called), though of ever so little business, that it may not be thought that after serving you abroad, I am quite turned off

Your Majesty has been pleased to lay more honours on me alreddy than I deserve and I can have nothing further to think of or wish for in that way. You will have the goodness, I hope, if my family by its cariage deserves it, to make it easie for them. God grant yr Majesty a good and safe voage and journie and success in your project. May I be so luckie as to arrive in time to attend you on your expedition, but if unfortunately I do not, let me beg your Majesty to leave directions for my following of you, directly, wherever you go. As to other things, the Duke of Ormond is the fittest to advise you. He was the first who publickly embraced your M'ys service who were in any business at your Sister's death,[1] and I heartily wish he may have the honour to finish the glorious work of your restoration, for which your kingdoms would be so much beholden to him and have occasion to love him better, if that can be, than they do. I am with the most profound submission and respect, etc.,

MAR.

The Duke of Mar to the King

February 5, 1719.

"I think it incumbent on me at this time, when your Majesty may be in England before I have the happiness of seeing you again, to lay before you for yr own privat use what occurs to

---

[1] Queen Anne.

47

me by my having been a considerable time in business there which gave me opportunitys of knowing things and persons that your Majesty cannot possibly have, till some time after your arrivall, and offer this to your Majesty wt all submission as the best service I am capable of rendering you at this junctur.

As the Church of England and the party that goes by its name which is now called Torys are the Majority of the people, so they have ever been the supporters of the Crown and your Majesty will find by supporting and countenancing of them that you will have a quiet and happie reine.

Yr royal unckle King Charles found the fatall consequences as the late King yr father and yr Majesty has dearly since, of his neglecting those at his restoration who had been most zealous for him and the royal cause and preferring in too partiall and eminent a way those who had been otherways, in hopes by that to gain them. Some exceptions are to be made in employing fit persons of experience and knowledge of the opposite party, if such are not to be found in the King's own. (*Here speaks the experienced statesman.*)

As to Scotland, I hope I may be so happie as to be with yr Majesty at furthest before the time of yr settling your affairs there, so all I will trouble yr Majesty with at this time is, after the dissolution of the Union you should set about the re-establishment of the Church of England.[1] . . .

I beg your Majesty may pardon this presumption and may soon have occasion for putting these things, or what are *better* in practice."

Mar then departed for Genoa, whence he was to have joined his master in Spain. He left his wife behind him in Rome,

---

[1] Which shows that he did not well understand the temper of his fellow-Scots ; his own church views were that "the Church of England ritual holds the medium between the bare, unbecoming nakedness of the Presbiterian service in Scotland and the gaudy, affected and ostentatious way of the Church of Rome."

only three months after she had joined him from England, passing through perils by land and sea as shown in her own letters. In a letter written on February 7th (the day he started) Mar recommended his wife to the care of Lord Pitsligo who was remaining on in Rome.

"I have been obliged to leave my wife here, after her making a very long journey to me, but that is not the first proof I have had of her affection, and her own good sense will make her bear with my leaving her now, without her knowledge in the same discreet way she did upon a former occasion [1] and she is in a strange place and will have need of somebody to advise with in severall things. Allow me therefore as my friend to recommend her to your care, etc."

Lord Pitsligo's own comment on this was a handsome testimony to Lady Mar's competence to deal with any emergency. He himself was an exile for his exertions in Scotland in 1715, but went home in 1720, not being among those attainted. He "came out" again in 1745, though an old man, and being placed on the list of exceptions to the Act of Indemnity of 1747, he lived the life of a hunted fugitive till his death in 1762 at the age of 84.

Mars poor wife had had, indeed, much trouble in joining her lord at Rome, with her little daughter.

The Duchess of Mar to the Duke of Mar (*Jacobite creation*)

BOULOGNE. *Sept.* 12, 1718.

I'm afraid you've been in pain for me, since the Squire sent you word I went from Dover. I thought to have writ from Calais, and my letter would have come at the same time, but

---

[1] When he took ship for Scotland in a collier on August 2nd, 1715, on his way to raise the Jacobite standard at Braemar.

very strange things have happened to me since. I lay two
nights for a wind at Dover, and the third morning the packet-
boat went off with a side wind that they thought they could
make Calais with, and, my courage being greater than my
wisdom, I went aboard rather than stay for the next. When
we had not been very long at sea, the wind rose very high and
directly contrary and I, that had been three days at sea both
going and coming last year and had never been sick, was so ill
the whole time that I thought I should have died and everybody
was the same and the poor little thing too, so you may imagine
my distress. After tossing four hours, we were blown to a
little place two leagues from this, called Andresselles. We left
the ship and made towards the land in a boat, which was surrounded, when we came near the shore, by a great number of
raggedest frightful people I ever saw in my life and I was more
frightened at being touched by them than at anything else I met
with, for there had been a very bad fever all hereabouts, but
we were forced to be lifted out of the boat upon men's
shoulders that waded through the water and then carried us
into the town, where they told me nobody had been since
three years ago the same accident had happened to a packet-
boat and, when we came there, we had the whole village
gathered about us ready to pull us to pieces. A younger son
of Lord Nottingham's was on board with his governor and
they had a chaise that held two, which they had brought to
travel into Italy with, and my daughter and I and her maid got
into that and with much ado got hither last night. The wind
was very high and cold and the chaise quite open, so that I
really thought I should have died with cold and sickness on the
road. We laid the child between us and covered her up and
she slept the whole way. I'm something better today and
have sent to Calais to Mr. Forbes [1] to bring something to
convey us to Paris. George Hay, a comical person you've
heard me speak of, came from London with me and 'twas very

[1] Charles Forbes of Brux, who had been given her as an escort.

50

Countess of Mar and Daughter

From a picture by Cavaliere Francesco Trevisani at Alloa House

lucky he did so. He's gone this morning for Calais and returns to England as soon as Mr. Forbes comes here. We left him and the other passengers with the baggage at Andresselles and they came in the middle of the night in a cart, which was all this town afforded to fetch them in. The child is perfectly well and mightily pleased with travelling and the only one that was not at all tired and she's too young to think of danger. She diverts me with her notions of everything she sees but is mightily disturbed she has not yet found her papa. The first inn she came to she thought was the end of her journey and asked everybody why her papa did not come.

I hope we shall leave this tomorrow, but, if I had found a coach here, I could have not gone on today, for I've got a violent cold but no other harm.

The Duchess of Mar to the Duke of Mar

CALAIS. *Oct.* 2, 1718.

I arrived here late last night. My first setting out from Boulogne was a little unfortunate. The day after I arrived there, Mr. Forbes and Father Graeme brought me a very good chariot, as they thought, from Calais, which held four, my daughter, the two servants and myself, but we had not gone two leagues before the springs broke and the chariot overturned. By good fortune the little thing was uppermost and nobody was hurt, but I was excessively frightened, imagining the child was killed. We returned to Boulogne and accidently found a very good chaise for two, which I bought and came post hither, Peggy and I with the little one in our laps, and left her maid to come in the Calais coach. The child, instead of a trouble, serves to divert me and everybody else. She has never been tired, sick or out of humour the whole way. I never saw such a child in my life for quietness.

The Duchess of Mar to the Duke of Mar

LYONS. *Oct.* 15, 1718.

I am at last arrived safe here. I can't but say I thought the time very long. The guide you alloted me (*Charles Forbes*) sometimes makes me laugh and sometimes makes me cry. I fancy you chose him for his strength that, in case the voitures failed, he might bring me on his back, which I dare say he would do very willingly. His courage is very great, but his conduct is but small. We've been no less than seven days coming from Paris and with as much fatigue as if we had come in four, so at this rate you may expect me in the spring, not sooner. The weather has been very hot and the poor little child exposed to the sun and dust to that degree, I expected she would have been in a fever, but she is perfectly well, except being violently tanned and a little leaner. I had a single chaise for myself and a double one for the two maids, and the child was sometimes with them and sometimes in my arms, but I can't tell whether I suffered most by the fatigue of holding her or my concern lest she should come to any harm. Indeed my heart aches, when I think of the journey I still have to make, and I don't find the squire I have to conduct me has much knowledge of the way or judgment to find it out and he piques himself too much on his performances to suffer me to advise with anybody else. If we do not meet soon, I'm afraid my patience will be quite out, which was never more tried than in this journey. I've kept my thoughts to myself, but really my heart is very full, and, if I do not meet you at the end of my journey, I shall have much reason to complain of my fortune and, if I do, I shall soon forget all I have suffered to come to you. Lord Nottingham's son and his governor have travelled thus far with us. I was much the better for the assistance of his servant and equipage, but very little for his company. He's mighty like his eldest brother in everything but his conversation, as *he* never holds his tongue, and this never speaks. He's very sickly and going to Montpellier for his health. I wish I may pick up somebody else to accompany me the rest of my journey, for how I shall get over the Alps without the assistance of anybody but your Highland gentleman I can't tell. I turned away the cook I brought from London to Paris, because he was very troublesome on the road, with an intention to get one there, but Mr. Gordon and Mr. Forbes would not let me take any till I came here, because they said it would be cheaper and better. I wish I may find it so. I hope to hear from you at Turin and that will be some comfort, and I am sure I shall want it by the time I get there. I can't find it in my heart to be angry with my guide, when he has done any silly thing, he is in such concern about it, and, if I do come safe, I shall make you laugh with the detail of what has happened.

I was heartily tired of Paris, which you may easily guess by the company I was in there, but could not get away a day sooner and was forced to leave the picture to be finished at last. I was a great favourite of the painter's and I'm persuaded it will not be his fault, if it is not a very good picture. He has taken a great deal of pains and is mightily pleased with it.[1]

The Duchess of Mar to the Duke of Mar

TURIN. *Oct.* 26, 1718.

I am just come here after the most terrible journey that ever poor mortal had. I was too careless of myself and too easily advised and took the voiturini from Lyons, who agreed to bring me here in my own chaises with their horses, so I came with one single chaise and a double one for the two maids, but such roads and such weather I never saw nor had no notion of. By good fortune it neither snowed nor rained, while I crossed

---

[1] This is the portrait by Trevisani of herself and her little daughter, reproduced at p. 50. Frances, Lady Mar, seems to have been a woman of as high a spirit as her sister, Lady Mary Wortley-Montagu, and her little girl to have been a worthy daughter.

Mont Cenis, which was the only fair weather I had except to-day and the day I left Lyons. The night I lay at the foot of the mountain it snowed all night and the people gave me very little hopes of there being any possibility of going over the Alps the next day and gave me so terrible a description of it that I found it better than I expected. There was a great deal of snow, but I was so wrapped up I felt no cold, and, for the danger, I had run so many hazards in my chaise on those terrible hills and precipices of the other side, that I thought passing the Alps nothing at all and had rather do it twice than sit in my chaise as I did up some of those hills by Lanslebourg and other places. I was in great danger of breaking my neck several times. I never got out of my chaise but once on a little hill, that the horse could not get up, but at last I am come safe, but how I shall get on the rest of my journey I can't imagine, for your squire can speak no language at all, nor, I can answer for him, never will. Indeed my patience was never so much tried, though I very often cannot help laughing at the absurd contrivances of M. le Gouverneur, as the people call him in the inns, and the speeches he makes me. I have taken the chairs I came over the Alps in as far as Susa, but he assured me the road was good, though he had never been it, and made me get into the chaise at Naverese (Norallese) at 5 at night and came that terrible road in the dark, but by good luck we broke neither our necks nor the chaises. He was in a chaise himself and we had but one poor man on horseback to look after us all, but now 'tis over, we are very good friends and I hope there'll be no more dangers to go through. The poor little poppet is running about the room, not a bit the worse for her fatigues. I hoped to have found letters from you here, for I know neither where to find you nor what to do. I intend to take post as soon as I can for Bologna, where sure I shall find some directions.

The weather is cleared up. Though they tell me the roads are so good, I shall travel very easily. Mr. Forbes is so very slow that I shall be twice as long as if I was without him and he's excessively saving, which makes us worse served everywhere. If I don't hear from you at Bologna, I shall think you have quite forgot me. Your daughter's patience is quite out and she asks every minute for her papa. She has been very merry all the way, but I believe the people thought me mad for bringing her.[1]

She had at length joined her lord at Rome, four months before the date of the King's setting out for Spain, and Mar's own departure and imprisonment. While King James was absent in Italy, the little Princess Clementina arrived from Innsbrück where she had been imprisoned and whence she had been rescued by Charles Wogan and his three Musketeers, Gaydon, Misset and O'Toole. She was received in Bologna by James Murray, afterwards Lord Dunbar (see p. 71) whom the King had deputed to arrange matters for him, and to represent him at a proxy marriage which took place on May 10th and "Queen Clementina" then proceeded to Rome where she resided in a convent assigned to her by the Pope, and great heartburnings arose among the Jacobite Lords and Ladies there because they thought James Murray kept everyone at a distance save himself and his sister, Mrs. Hay (afterwards Lady Inverness) (see p. 60). In July, the date of his next letter, Mar was still in prison in Geneva.

---

[1] These four letters from Lady Mar, though taken from the manuscript at Windsor, have previously appeared in a publication of the Historical MSS. Commission. They are the *only* letters here given, which have done so—all the rest being later than December 1718.

Mar to the King, from his imprisonment, and detailing to the latter his correspondence with King George's minister [1]

GENEVA. *July* 3, 1719.

"You'll easilie believe, Sir, that I would take all the wayes I could which were faire, in my writing to Lord Stair to get out of my present difficulty which I foresaw would be no easie matter to compass. Having before sent the seals to Spain, I told him there was some difference betwixt my situation now that I had not the Seals a-keeping, and the last time I had askt leave to goe to Bourbon and was refused, upon account of my haveing them. I told him further that I had for some time been quite weary of business and that I was resolved to retire from it and to live quietly in some corner of France, if I could be allowed, without medling with anything, where I hop'd I might recover a little of my health. This I thought I might very fairly and safely say when I found that my health would not allow me to follow my Master to Spain where he was likely to reside for some time at least. . . . You know, Sir, I was resolved five months agone not to have keept the Seals had my Master gone to England. . . . I have long been weary of the post of Secretary and only waiting for an occasion of quitting it; in time comeing you are to look on me as a faithfull servant who is in a manner dead, but whose gost will ever doe you all the service that's in its power.

Without vanity I may say that I have served my Master and the intrest these four years past wt zeal and faithfulness and done what was in my power to please those who are or pretend to be his friends.[2]

By the last letter I had from Lord Stair a few days agone he tells me that he had laide my request of goeing to Bourbon before his Government.

---

[1] Portions of some of Mar's letters have been printed by the present Editor in a volume for the Scottish History Society dealing especially with "The Jacobite Court in Rome in 1719."

[2] He therefore himself dates the beginning of his Jacobitism in July 1715.

Allow me to mention one or two other things to you, which proceeds from a sincere intention to your service. It will be absolutely necessary for you to have one to supply the place I had the honour to serve you in—and you have not many to choice on this side the water—with submission I should think your best way were to desire of those friends in whom you have most confidence at home to find out and recommend one for that station. . . . This will do much to prevent all factions and envie amongst your people abroad. . . . I hope in God you will not want wherewith to maintain those whom you have done hitherto and who suffer now upon your account.
. . .

The particular people of yr suite are all so well known to you that it is needless for me to mention them. Allow me tho', I beg of you, to mention one who is too modest to speak for himself—it is Col. Clephan, who is old and has a great family.

Colin Campbell of Glendarule, if he can get away from Scotland would be a most valuable friend to have at Rome, because he knows all the Highlanders and was of great use to me in Scotland. Also John Paterson, now weary of service and perhaps not so willing to serve under another as he has done under me.

My Lady Mar will have the honour of waiting upon the Queen in Rome, as she now does, as farr as those about her will alow, until the heats be over when she is to come to me either here or in France as I shall chance to be.

I hope ere long Lady Mar will get of her own to keep me or any belonging to me from being a charge or burthen upon your My.

The Duchess of Mar (still in Rome, but anxious to rejoin her husband) to the King, at Montefiascone

ROME. *Sept.* 13, 1719.
Your Majesty's letter merits my earliest and sincerest thanks and if I don't express them as I ought tis not for want of being

truly sensible of the honour yr Majesty does me. Ye last letters I had from my Lord were from Geneva where he has been long confined with great strictness and at that time he saw no appearance of his releasement—taking the air attended by a guard was all ye liberty he could obtain. I hear from him once a week and he seems desirous I should come to him as soon as ye weather will permitt, but I suppose upon ye receipt of yr Majesty's letter he will write particularly himself in answer to yr commands.

Oct. 7. "My Lord writes me word to set out as soon as I can get ready, since he apprehends being kept all winter at Geneva and if I stay much longer, I cannot undertake so troublesome a journey. I have a pair of horses here yr Majesty gave him the money for, wh. I beg to know how I must dispose of. I have also two large Boxes under my care that he desires me to ask yr Majesty's orders about which I shall follow with the greatest exactness I'm capable of. There is another thing I must trouble yr Majesty with because its necessary I should know it before I leave this place. I can't perform such a journey by myself. I don't know who your Majesty can spare best to go along with me. My Lord thinks Mr. Paterson might be proper, if his going will be no interruption to anything yr Majesty designs."

The King to the Duchess of Mar

MONTEFIASCONE. *Oct.* 19, 1719.

Mr. Forster gave me this afternoon yrs of the 7. You will easily believe that the loss of yr good company att Rome this winter will be a mortification to us. . . . You have but to dispose of your horses as you think fitt and you will find here enclosed an order about the boxes under your care. . . . Cardinal Gualterio leaves us tomorrow, and the two rooms he lodged in will be ready for you whenever you please. Though your modesty makes you say nothing as to money matters and that they are at present very low with me, yet when you come here, I beg of you to tell me freely what you may want for your journey in which and everything else I shall ever be ready and desirous to make you easie and be as kind to you as depends on me.

A letter from Lady Mar of date October 14th says she will leave on Wednesday next, and she did visit the King and Queen and then proceeded to Paris where she remained with her husband until her mind gave way and she was removed to the care of her sister, Lady Mary Wortley-Montagu. She died in 1761—twenty-nine years after her husband. One more letter of hers, of two years later, to her father, shows how the stories of Mar's double dealings persisted.

The Duchess of Mar to her father, the Duke of Kingston
PARIS. July 9, 1721.

MY LORD,

Within these few days there has been a great many reports spread about here, which gives my Lord so much uneasieness that he beg'd me to write to yr G. about it. There has been many letters wrote from England that say he is soliciting his pardon and leave to go home himself. Your G. knows the obligation he is under of liveing quietly and entering into no business and he has done so and I hope given no cause for complaint to anybody since his being here, but these storys for wh he knows there is no ground are vexatious to him upon several accounts and I cannot imagine what has occasioned them. My Lord is very sensible of yr great kindness to him upon all occasions and begs the continuance of it. He will ever esteem it a happiness to him and is a very particular to me.

Yrs. etc.

After their wedding at Montefiascone and their return to Rome, James and Clementina were at first very happy, and the birth of the eldest child, Charles Edward Louis John Casimir Silvester Maria [1] on December 30th, 1720, was greeted with joy by Jacobites all over Europe. Before the birth of Henry Benedict Thomas Maria François Xavier [2] four years later (March 6th, 1725) the Queen had begun to show signs of that hysterical and jealous temperament which later caused so much trouble.

The main objects of her jealousy were—

John Hay and his wife (Lord and Lady Inverness)

John Hay, Lord Inverness, with his wife, Marjory or Marcelle, who was sister of James Murray, Lord Dunbar, played a very large part in the life of the Jacobite Court at Rome for the first eight years of the period covered by this book. He was the second son of Lord Kinnoull and she the daughter of Lord Stormont; the fathers of both having been among those suspected of Jacobitism in 1715, though not active participants. John Hay joined Mar, was made a Colonel and was at the capture of Perth and the Battle of Sheriffmuir, afterwards escaping via the Orkneys to France and Avignon. He remained a faithful attendant on his master, filling the office of Secretary of State resigned by Mar in 1719, and stayed in Rome until 1727 when the unfortunate jealousy of Queen Clementina caused his voluntary retirement to Avignon where he died in

---

[1] These are his *correct* names, as shown by his birth certificate, a finely illumined parchment in the British Museum, 2 English, 1 French, 2 Polish and 2 Sacred names.

[2] These are also his actual names, in his baptismal certificate at Windsor Several others were considered by his father who made a long list, including Alfred, Hemengildus and Aloysius !

1740. His wife long survived him and continued to live at Avignon with her brother till her own death in 1768.

The following letters show honest John Hay in many different aspects, the first being to Edgar (see page 190), and the next from his wife ; then that written by him to the Queen, endeavouring by all the means in his power to restore peace to the Royal Household ; others from his light-hearted brother-in-law, James Murray, at that time exiled to France, and another from a fellow-Scot, anxious, somewhat quaintly, to engage the King in business ; to this, unfortunately, no answer exists. One showing Hay as making the best of a stay in Bologna, and the last from his intimate friend on his death, also a later one from Lady Inverness when a widow, living in retirement and rejoicing in the good news of the Prince's successes in Scotland. Later, she received him when a refugee from France; she died before her brother, at their country home in Avignon, having left a small legacy to the King her master, of which Lord Dunbar writes in an *undated* letter to the King, "I am extremely concerned at the account you give me of your circumstances which make so small a sum as a hundred louis d'ors of consequence to you. At the same time I am extremely glad that my poor sister's legacy which you did not expect, gave you so seasonable a supply."

John Hay, writing from Paris, whither he had been sent by the King, sees plainly the tortuous policy of Mar, but was not in the least anxious to succeed him as Secretary of State. He was, however, compelled to do so in the long run, though only for a few years, until Clementina's jealousy forced his retirement.

To Edgar

PARIS. 16 *Dec.* 1720.

I have the honour of Mr. Knights [1] of the 24th. As Martel is not yet come to town, I don't know what Peter [1] wrote to him by the same post, but I expect him every minute.

I would gladly stay till nixt post comes in from Italy upon what you are pleased to say, but my passport is for so short a time and the roads so very bad that I am afraid I shan't get to the frontiers before my pass expire and in that case I must return to town to have it renewed and after all may find it difficult enough to get a new one. I am fully persuaded Martel has no thought of returning again to be about Peter in the way he was in formerly, and I can see plainly that people will never agree upon who is to succeed him. I don't think it would be for Peter's ease and tranquillity that one should be recommended in a hurry and by a few. It is better that folks on the other side should have time allowed them for a full meeting from whence a general report will be given ; than that a few should recommend one, and a few another, so that Peter's choice must necessarily disoblige one party.

I bring Sheridan [2] along with me, and am the fonder to do it, laying aside Peter's desire of having him which shall always be a rule to me, that I shan't be obliged to appear in anything of writting upon my arrival at Rome, since he will supply Nairn's defects. I'll persuade Peter that my way of thinking is right at meeting. After that I don't know what it is to disobey and despise those that have further views than what are consistent to Obedience. . . . I am to see Mar and Dillon this morning, so I shall certainly leave this place after dinner.

I pray God preserve Peter and partner.

The Hays were a most devoted couple, as shown by the following.

---

[1] Both these pseudonyms stand for the King.   [2] See p. 113.

Marjory Hay, afterwards Lady Inverness, to her husband in Paris

ROME. *Dec.* 10, 1720.

"Altho I have nothing to say to my Dear Body worth giving him the trouble of a letter except to complain of not having had the hapness to hear from you by laest post I don't know what to think of it—if it be not that your letters have come too leat for the post. I was once in doubt whither to write you my dear life or not today for I hope that this shall not find you att Paris and you know that returned letters give but little pleasure, but however I resolve to let this take its faite—realy the truth is ye deare body I love you too much for it is impossible for me to be easie when I am not with you if I was ever so much convinced of the reasonableness of it and the only devertion I can have is to writte to you ffor I imagine itt gives me ane opportunity to speak to you. Certainly there never was so dull a place as this, for news or anything else. We have none except for the victory the Spinards gott over the Moors which I suppose you will have att large in Paris, and the Pope's being better, neither of which I think imports us very much—the only thing that dous is that the King and Queen are in perfite good health ; her Majesty grows bigger every day. I believe we shall not get our Prince before the new Year. God Almighty preserve her. I tremble many times when I think of the danger she must be in, tho' I don't imagine her Majesty shall suffer more than other people do, but still upon these occasions there are more dangers than most people think of and when I look up on myself as the only body that is to have care of her it gives me all the pain in the world, for I shall be blamed if anything happens amiss, though I am sure I am not capable to neglect anything that may be for her Majesty's good however dair it may cost me. But the charge is too great for one body but since it is so I must do my best and with God's assistance I hope all shall go well.

. . . Love me alwais and we shall live and die the happiest

63

people in the world, but my dear heart I don't writt this to you for news—only to putt you in mind that I love you more than ever I could express. My dear body shoe yours for me by taking care of yourself upon your journey. My dear life I have wrote a great many times to make you remember the promiss you made me of your picture. If you don't bring it me indeed I shall be angrier than ever you saw me, for this is the only thing I have asked of you that I might not be troublesome to you, but I don't desire you to stay ane hour upon that account nather —for without compliment I love the original better than anie copie. My dear Angle, God preserve you. Dear body, adieu. I must bid you farewell for I have no more paper."

The King in writing to Hay at the same time, says, "Your wife is well. Mine grows as big as a house."

(*Endorsed—Mr. Murray, Rheims.* 1st Oct. 1723.)
To The Honourable John Hay Esqr at Paris
RHEIMS. October 1st, 1723.

DEAR JOHN,

As I conclude by the last letter you did me the favour to write me from Rome that you will soon arrive at Paris I have sent this letter to be kept for you by Mr. Waters to acquaint you in the first place that I have received one from home of the 14th of August in answer to what I wrote formerly on your affair. My father (*Lord Stormont*) says he is using all possible endeav-ours to prepare you money, which was never so difficult to be had as at present, and that as soon as he is sure of it he will inform me and be ready to pay it at Ed^r. It is therefore reasonable that you should have your thoughts how to dispose of it in the manner you formerly mentioned to me. I am also glad to prepare to my self by this the pleasure of seeing and embracing you. I don't know whither you intend to go after your short stay at Paris and therefore cannot make any pro-posal in order to meet you. But if this place be not considerably out of your road I could wish you might pass this way because in that case my brother Charles [1] may have the honour to see you also, but if that be inconvenient I will meet you wherever you please. By what I have heard of the situation of our polliticions at Paris I fancy you'll be confirmed in your design to make no stay there. I shall long with impatience to hear from you and am yours with all my heart.

As is but too well known, when her son Henry was only eight months old, on November 19th, 1725, Clementina in a fit of hysterical jealousy because her husband would not part with his valued servant, John Hay, at her bidding, left the Palazzo Muti, "retired with Lady Southesque to a convent" and spent two years there. The ostensible causes of this very unwise step were the action of her husband in dismissing Mrs. Sheldon, the nurse (whom he found to be an undesirable influence about the Prince and who also went into a convent,) and appointing James Murray, Lord Dunbar, a Protestant, as tutor, while the Catholic, Sir Thomas Sheridan, was the under-tutor and Lady Nithsdale was in charge of the infant Duke of York. The Queen had also taken a sudden distaste for Lady Inverness, sister to James Murray, of whom she had formerly been so fond that she wrote a personal letter to the Duchesse de Bourbon begging her to intercede, through the French Ambassador in London, for the release of Mrs. Hay, then on a visit to England and imprisoned in Newgate, as she (Clementina) earnestly desired the presence of Mrs. Hay at her approaching confinement, in 1725. (As Henry's birth was premature—she actually arrived too late.) The Queen's antipathy to the two Hays became unfortunately notorious and only too much was written at the time about the trouble in the

[1] The Hon. Charles Murray died unmarried.

65

Royal Stuart family at Rome. It is not an exaggeration to say that all Europe (at least that comparatively small part which received "News letters !") rang with it, and the enemies of the banished dynasty made much capital thereof, while echoes of unfounded accusations against the virtuous and well-meaning, if sometimes tactless, James Stuart persist to our own day and find their way into works of reference like the *Dictionary of National Biography*. A great deal of the contemporary correspondence on the matter was, no doubt wisely, burnt, but the letter written from John Hay to his Queen sent by hand (with the request that it might be returned and destroyed) when relations first became strained in the winter of 1722, has survived for 200 years as evidence of his good faith, complete trust in his wife and unbounded loyalty to the King his master, and by consequence to that King's unreasonable wife. There is no better definition of loyalty than "A sense of limitless obligation," and here was John Hay ready to break up his own home if necessary for his master's peace.

John Hay to the Queen

Undated, but belongs to a period sometime before the Queen left home.

A letter, Madam, which I received last post from Paris, occasions my giving Your Majesty this trouble. Severall expressions in it, deserve, in my humble opinion, your Majesty's notice, being write by a person of the first rank, whose attachment to the Royal family is not to be doubted and being persuaded that his view in writing proceeds chiefly from his sincere fervent wishes to see peace and union reyne in yr M's family, I can't doubt but yr M. will think a little time well spent in considering what I take the liberty to represent to you on ane affair that not only concerns Mrs. Hay's honour and my quiet, but yr Majesty's ease and the King's reputation. After a pritty long preamble showing the reasonableness of sending Mrs. Hay from Rome, the writer says *The Queen's dislike to Mrs. Hay is now known almost to everybody* and the letter runs so much upon the notion, as I cannot but construct it of a jealousie which people believe the Queen to have with relation to the King's conduct with Mrs. Hay, which is confirmed by another expression where he says *That the Queen should be made easy with regard to Mrs. Hay*, And I can assure yr My. I am entirely of that person's opinion, for my principles are such that I think myself obliged to do what may be never so disagreeable to myself, if I can imagine that it can contribute in the least to your Majesty and the King's ease, and you may be assured Madame that if Mrs. Hay's being at 400 leagues distance should be only insinuated by yr Majestie to be agreable to you, without asking any further reason, Your inclination shall immediately be followed and I'll, as soon as possible, go about falling upon ways and pretexts for sending her to her friends in England. I was not ignorant, Madam, even before your Maj^tle had been six weeks married, of endeavours then used to raise jealousie in yr Maj. as to ye King's Conduct in relation to Mrs. Hay. I was so much persuaded then of the King's virtue as well as of Mrs. Hays, who I did believe would not throw away her reputation upon any King or Prince in the World, and seeing yr Majesty's goodness towards Mrs. Hay continue, I then believed that those were only assertions and contrivances of some people by which they might be enabled to gett att their own ends and that they had no manner of impression upon yr Maj^te. But since the same story is renewed again, I beg yr Maj^te would lett me know what would be agreable to you yt I should do to remove uneasiness—that yr Maj^te may be perswaded that I am ready to sacrifice everything that is dearest to me for your satisfaction, since there is nothing that I'll stick at one moment to make yr union with the King flourish. I most humble beg of your Maj^ty that this letter may be seen by nobody, for a Lady's character is a nice thing to expose and as I have said nothing in Mrs. Hay's vindication which the design of it does not lead me to do, your Maj^{tie} may easily perceive that I have calculated my letter for *yourself alone*. To which I beg yr Maj^{tie} will be graciously pleased to send me two lines of ane answer. This is a subject the King is intirely a stranger to and I hope yr Maj^{tie} wont mention it to him. You'll do me a particular favour if you are so gracious as to return me the letter yt I may putt it in the fire. Had I been able to putt on a coat, I would not have dared to trouble yr Maj^{tie} with so long a letter, to which I shall only add, that the King has not these 6 weeks past mentioned the least thing to me of any family uneasiness.

Allow me to subscribe myself with all profound submission, Madame, Your Majesty's most dutifull, most faithfull and most devoted servant,

JOHN HAY.

No answer seems to have been received, and Clementina and Mrs. Sheldon both went off, as seen, into separate convents, while the letter, not having been returned to the writer, was found and duly filed by the industrious secretary of the King, James Edgar. There is no note to show whether the King saw it or not.

In the year 1727 John Hay, at his own urgent request, himself retired to Avignon, with his wife, and Clementina consented to return to her wifely and maternal duties. Curiously enough, at that moment James was on a journey, it was hoped of political import, owing to the death of George I, but nothing came of it. He got as far as Nancy, then returned to Avignon, where he wanted his wife to join him, but the French authorities, not permitting this, he returned to Bologna and then to Rome. Clementina also said she could not leave her children

—a very transparent excuse from one who had left them for two whole years !

That the whole story was well known in Paris is shown by the following letter, some time later.

(*Endorsed—Charles Forbes (of Brux) to Sir John Graeme* (see p. 198, recently made Secretary to the King)—*never delivered to him.*)

(Charles Forbes was a gossiping individual, and may have been making unpleasant insinuations against Hay, or more probably against Cardinal Albani who was supposed to have started the story. Cardinal Alberoni was also mixed up in it and later Cardinal Imperiali, who wrote to King James most impertinently.)

PARIS. 29 *Sept.* 1727.

DEAR SIR JOHN,

Your travelling has been the occasion I did not trouble you with a line long ago to congratulate you upon your preferment [1] and the share you enjoy of your Master's favour, the continuance whereof I wish with all my heart, both on your own account and that of all honest men, since most of your acquaintances are persuaded ye will disinterestedly study our Royall Masters honour as well as his interest, since the one is allways the support of the other. As the error of the Queens going to the Convent gave ane inexpressable grief to all disinterested people, so the reconciliation of the Royall family gave ane unspeakable joy to all the Kings true friends. It is with pleasure we all hope to see that harmonie renewed betwixt their Majesties, which is the ornament of a married life and will be among the best aids to the Common Cause, when

---

[1] Graeme was appointed Secretary of State in place of Hay to the great inconvenience of the King, who wrote "Hay knew all my business— Graeme has everything to learn."

they are once in others arms they will soon be convinced what cursed wretches were the instruments of their unhappy differences, who, tho' they should escape punishment in this world (as I hope they shall not) can never hope to do it in the next.

One more letter from Mar in the following year is in a curiously familiar vein.

From the Duke af Mar to the King

PARIS. *Aug.* 24, 1722.

I had a letter from John by last post telling me that you was that day setting out to join the Countess of Cornwall (*a thin disguise for the Queen*) at the waters of Luca. I am very glade of it for it will amuse you besides the pleasure it will be to you to see the Lady and I see not any inconvenience that can attend it. I hope too, that you will find good of the waters, they being as I hear very good against vapours. You will hear by this post of the Cardinal de Bois's being declared Prime Minister for which he has a patent that must they say be regestrated by Parl—which is thought will meet with no opposition. I suppose you'll think it fit to write him a compliment upon it. It is said that Mr. Bellisk will be made minister pour les affaires etrangieres. It is expected by most people that the D. of Orleance will very soon be declaird Lieut. General of the Kingdom and some talk of M. le Duc's [1] being Constable, but what ground there is for the last I know not. There was little news from England by last post, only a good deal of talk of several souldiers of the guards being taken up for disaffection to the Government. I saw a private letter which says they had found no papers of any consequence amongst Mr. Kellie's things which they had seased. [2]

[1] De Maine. Illegitimate son of Louis XIV.
[2] Kelly managed to burn his papers when arrested and taken to the Tower where he lay for eleven years.

There's a little fool prattling by me who will needs have me to offer her humble duty to you and the Countess, whose bounty she never forgets.[1]

That the King's entourage was seriously perturbed by what Mar was or might be doing is shown in their letters to each other.

James Murray, Earl of Dunbar

Of James Murray of Stormont, a good many letters have already been published. He was one of those followers who had a great influence on the lives both of King James and his son Charles. He was about the Court from the close of the Rising of 1715 till shortly after the collapse of that of 1745–6. He acted as confidential Agent for the King when the latter was absent in Spain, representing him at his proxy marriage. On the defection of the Earl of Mar, Murray carried on the duties of Secretary of State until the appointment of his brother-in-law, John Hay. Having become obnoxious to the Queen, he was banished to France for a while but returned to take up the duties of tutor to Prince Charles, aged 4½, and remained with him for nearly twenty years. He accompanied him on his brief campaign at Gaeta, and was also with him on the tours to Venice, etc., and assisted in the secret departure from France in 1744. In 1747 he left Rome and retired to Avignon with his widowed sister, Lady Inverness. They received the furious Prince when he was ejected from France in December 1748 and entertained him till he left, to disappear, in the following February. After that, Lord Dunbar lived on in Avignon for

---

[1] This was his little daughter, Frances, seen in the portrait. She was at this period about 6 years old. She eventually married her cousin, the son of Lord Grange, to whom the title of Earl of Mar was restored, though not the Aberdeenshire estates.

another twenty years, writing frequent but quite dull letters to Edgar—the only event of any importance being that chronicled by himself in 1751 when he joined the Roman Catholic Church—as had his brother-in-law and sister long before. See page 219.

At his death, in 1770, aged over 80, he left all his property to the Cardinal Duke of York (his will still existing in Avignon). A small legacy by his sister to Prince Charles then became available—as chronicled on page 61.

The first letters were written during his temporary exile from Rome (1721-4).

James Murray to his sister, Mrs. Hay

NANCY. *Aprile* 16, 1721.

DEAR SISSIE,

Having been here for some time, I can now pretend to give you some account of this Court. The Duke and Dutchess are the best people in the world and have the finest family of children that ever I saw. I have dined often with the Duke, and Mr. O Ruerk did me the honour to invite me to dine one day at his house with the young part of the family, which I was extreamly pleased with. The Dutchess dresses and undresses her head every day in publick, so that the usual time of making court to her is at her toilet. The Court goes, the latter end of the month, to Luneville and if I gett any sort of invitation to go there I will choose to pass summer at that place. So much for news from Lorraine.

I saw, since I came into this part of the world a letter that said that the D. of M. had at Paris a coach and six, with a number of servants and that he lived in the great house where the Emperor's ambassador was formerly. This letter bore also that he made and received visits frequently from the English Minister, Sir Robert Sutton and that Coll. Churchill on his return from Vienna came to his house when he arrived at

Paris and gallanted the Dutchess to the Opera. The gentleman to whom this piece of news was directed, asked me what I thought of all that, to which I answered not a sillable, but turned the discourse by asking him for a pinch of snuff, which I thought was all that was reasonable for me to do upon that occasion.

. . . I have not had any letters from Paris, so know nothing of our wise people's politicks there, but I'm in hopes by this time I'm forgott by them.

I suppose the cardinals will be shutt up again in such a manner that it is not reasonable to write to any of them, but if Mr. Hay has any way of corresponding with Cardinal Gualterio I beg the favour of him to assure him of my most inviolable respects.

On April 9th, 1724, Murray writes to Hay from Paris :

"I was told by a friend of Mr. Martel's (Mar), in relation to his pension, which he finds to be a load upon him in the opinion of the publick, that the proposal was made to his wife to his great surprise and that the moment she acquainted him of it he informed Mr. Dillon and his other friends of the matter and told them he was heartily sorry that such a proposal had ever been made because he foresaw that his refusing to accept it would draw a new storm upon him but that Mr. Knight should judge of the matter and decide what should be done upon it. Upon this the same person (who is a man in the secret) assured me that a full confirmation had been sent to Mr. Knight of the proposal and that he not only had directed Mr. Martel to enter into it, but that he wrote a letter acknowledgeing that all the steps Mr. Martel had taken in this affair were with his knowledge and approbation. I answered I was glad to hear anything to justify the nobleman concerned, for whatever bad usage I had received from him, I was one of those who never mixed my private resentment with public concerns, but that I would never for my part, have asked direction from Mr.

Knight upon a proposition of such a nature, and that if I had been near Mr. Knight and worthy to be honoured so far as to have my opinion asked, I never would have given it for approving a thing of this kind in any person whatsoever."

Hay's reply to Murray

"If Martel thinks there is anything wrong in his receiving a pension he ought not have done it, and who can hinder people from making their reflexions upon it. It is Martel's business to clear himself of the aspersions that and other things may have brought upon him and as our good Cardinal says 'Si quelqu'un s'attache à une planche pourrie, il tombe au fond.'"

James Murray to the King

PARIS. *June* 10, 1724.

"Forgive me Sir, if I endeavour to show you that Martel's receiving a pension by your consent, and remaining thereafter in the secret of your business, could not but be of the worst consequences to you in all the different suppositions one could make as to his views in manadging that matter. In general it appears that you can never gain but may lose by your ministers having correspondence with George's." (Which certainly seems obvious unless the Ministers were double traitors.)

A letter from Mar's son to his uncle, John Hay, who was about to go to Paris on the King's business, may also be given here :

(*Endorsed—Ld. Erskine. Sept.* 17, 1723.)
*Addressed to "Monsieur Hay," from Thomas, son to Duke of Mar
(his mother, Mar's first wife, was Hay's sister)*

GENEVA. *Sept.* 17, 1725.

SIR,

My father, in a letter I had from him on this day sesennight acquaints me that you were to be soon at Turin, and desires that I would consult some friend here whether it would be safe for you to pass through this place. I have spoke with one to whom I could intirely trust the nearest interests I have in the world, and who knows the thoughts of our Magistracy on that head perfectly well, and he assures me that you will be as safe here as in any place in Europe. I believe I need not tell you that when a friend of ours his father was arrested the more cool and sensible part of the Magistrats were against it, and the thing met with a great deal of opposition in the Council. They were soon very sorry for the ridiculous step they had made, and the returns of thanks they met with from England were much short of their expectation. The Comte de Marcie who resides here ordinairly as a kind of Minister from England, and who was the cause of our friend's being stopt, is now in France and will be there some months, and there is nobody here that supplys his place. Believe me you need have nothing to fear from Geneve, there are not the same reasons for your apprehension as there was in our friends case. Things are calm in England, the person whose province it was to enquire what British strangers arriv'd is absent, and Experience has made our Magistrats wiser. The earnest desire I have to see you makes me insist the more on the reasons for your safety in this place, which you may be persuaded I would not do had I reason to be apprehensive of the least danger. I beg a letter from you as soon as you come to Turin, and if you cannot be persuaded to pass through this town, let me know the route you intend to take that I may lay myself in your way, for I must see you. I wish it might not be very far from Geneve, not because I want health or any fatigue of the journey, but to let you into the true secret our finances just now are at a low ebb.

I am conscious to myself that I stand in need of long apologies for not having wrote to you since I have been at Geneve, but I can with truth assure you that my fault does not proceed from any want of that duty and affection I owe you, so I hope you will the more easily pardon me. I shall not trouble you

now with any account of my manner of living here.   That till
I have ye pleasure of seeing you I am
> Sir,
your most dutifull nephew and most obed[t] humble Servt.,
ERSKINE.

(This is the little boy in the picture at page 44.)

Mar died of apoplexy at Aix-la-Chapelle, where he had gone
for his health in 1732 ; he suffered much from gout and at times
from scurvy.   His lunatic wife had been removed from his
side in 1730.   His only son, Thomas, died without issue in
1766, but the attainted title was restored in the son of his
daughter, Frances, and her husband who was also Mar's
nephew, James Erskine, son of Lord Grange.

Both the Earl of Mar and Kellie, and his distant relative, the
Earl of Mar, are descended from these two.

Will. Erskine of Pittodrie, Aberdeenshire, writes to John
Hay, Lord Inverness, making a most peculiar suggestion to the
King.

HAGUE. 18 *Nov.* 1925, N.S.

MY LORD—

I should not take the liberty, not having the honour to be
known to your Lordship, to write you this letter, but that the
subject of it regards his Majestie's service, the case is this.

Two Jews, one here whose name is Costa and his Brother
Baron Schwartze at London have proposed t'me that if the
King will be pleased to act in concert with them for a few days
only they'l make the stocks in England fall twenty per cent and
thereby gain fourty per cent on a capital of five hundred
thousand pounds which they'll Engage themselves to lay out

that way—they reckon the profit will amount to nigh two hundred thousand pounds and are willing his Majesty have one half thereof. I am particularly acquainted with the brother that lives here and it is at his desire that I doe address myself to yr Lordship on this occasion. If the King approves of their project in general, as soon as I know it and have orders I will sett out for Rome and bring with me their Sceme and a letter from Costa to your Lop. he assures me the part his Maj[tl] is to act is easy and no ways derogatory and that he is fully persuaded the Execution of the project will be on many accounts advantaegous to his Interest as will clearly appear by the sceme when his Maj[tl] come to examine it.

Those people, the Jews, have a fair character in the world as to morals and 'tis well known they can, when they please purchase for much more than the sum mentioned in the Stocks. They pretend to be well affected to his Maj[tl] but I won't say that what they propose proceeds more from the motive of serving him than for that of private interest, whatever may be in that. They will give his Maj[tl] all the satisfaction can be desired for the performance of the Engagements that are to be mention'd in the Sceme on their part.

If yr Lop thinks proper to acquaint the King with this proposal and that his Maj[ty] orders me to go to Italy I will with great pleasure obey and therefore remain here two months In which time if I don't hear from your Lop I shall conclude the project is not relisht, but if it is and that yr Lop does me the honour of a letter you'l please to direct it à Monsieur de Lues au Maréchal de Turenne à la Haye.

I shall only beg leave to add that I am of the familly of Pittodrie, perhaps your Lop knows my brother or at least have heard of him. I am with the greatest respect.

My Lord Yr Lops most obedient and most hon. servant,

WILL. ERSKINE.[1]

[1] William Erskine died in 1774, aged 86. He was uncle to the then Laird of Pittodrie.

(Endorsed—Duke of Mar. 5th May 1727—Apparently the last he wrote to the King.)

CHATTOA. *May 5th*, 1727

R. P.

SIR,

How to be of service to your Majesty and the Royall ffamily, on which the intrest of my country depends, having been from my infancie the chife object of all my views and wishes, to be under your displeasure, as I have had the misfortoun (tho innocently I think) to be for these two long years, could not but be the greatest and most sensible affliction to me. All my consolation was that time would show and make plain to you the uprightness and sincerity of all my actions and intentions towards you, and how groundless were all the assertions and calumnies maliciously throwen upon me.

The ernest desire I have that your Majesty will be now graciously pleased to receive in good part this assurance of my constant devotion to your service, encourages me to ventur upon it, and to know that those unjust impressions which have been so industriously endeavoured to be given you of me, are effaced, would be a greater satisfaction to me than all that yr Maj. could give me, were you upon yr throne, as I hope one day you shall be.

The part I have acted ever since I had the honour to be first in correspondence with you, Sir, now a good many years ago and before I was actually in your service, as well as the time I had the honour to be employed by you, and ever since without the least alteration, notwithstanding all that has happened are proofs much stronger than words of my fidelity and inviolable attachment I have always had to your person and cause, and that I am incapable to tarnish (as time will show) the former part of my life with the small time of it that still remains, so all I shall farther take the liberty at present to trouble you with, is my earnest wishes that God in his good providence may

preserve and prosper you and yours, make peace and concord reign amongst you, grant you a numerous ofspring, and in his own good time restore you to the Throne of yr Ancestors for a blessing to your people, which wherever providence shall think fit to place me, shall always be the fervent prayers of
Sir,
Your Majesty's most obedient and most
faithfull subject and servant,

MAR.

Some historians have stated that Mar was definitely dismissed from the King's service in 1723, but none of these writers had studied Mar's own voluminous correspondence at Windsor. It has already been plainly shown that he himself considered that his term of office as Secretary of State was ended when the King went to Spain in 1719, and he took the extreme and some-what perilous course of sending the seals after his Master to that country. James, who hated all changes, did his best to per-suade Mar to return to him, even after the latter had acknow-ledged that he was in communication with Lord Stair as to his release from captivity at Geneva. A rather pathetic letter from the King to Mar contains this passage—"I have tired you, I am sure with this long letter, but it would be yet longer did I go about expressing to you the least part of my true kindness and friendship for you, for I shall not be easie till I know you are it, nor can I be, entirely, till you are with me." The King also made no appointment as Secretary of State for five years, hoping for Mar's return, and described himself during that period as acting as a "Commis" (clerk) that is writing his own most important letters, though he had two scribes in the per-sons of Francis Kennedy, who left him in 1726, and James Edgar.

In 1723 Mar sent to the King from Paris a curious memorial

on Jacobites considered to be actually treasonable and in August 1724 the King wrote to Dillon and Ormonde that he was "resolved to put a stop to Mar's underhand dealings and will have nothing more to do with the Duke," but will appoint John Hay to the vacant post. An anonymous writer from England comments on this, "The Duke of Mar's disgrace is now no secret in Britain." In 1726 the King was in Bologna.

Lord Inverness from Bologna to the Duke of Ormonde
Oct. 29, 1726.

Nothing has occurred since my last—the King has got into his own palace which is one hired from Senator Fantucci and has a noble staircase which most of the strangers that pass this way, come to see. There is but little conveniency in the house, but by a Communication that is made to another place, the royal family will be well lodged. I have got a little house, pretty near, built by a whimsical physician who has laid out so much money on it that he is obliged to quit it for the payment of his debts, to my no small ease. It is very like an English house, and if it were on the road betwixt Bristol and London I would make you an offer of it, but where it stands I should be very sorry to see you in it.

By the sharp weather that is already come in we don't doubt of feeling here a pretty severe winter, which will do well to season us that are used to a Roman climate and prepare us for colder weather which I hope we shall soon feel at home.

The first letter to be given, from the King himself, is to Cardinal Albani, recommending the interests of his eldest son's wet nurse and her husband to the care of the Pope, and shows as ever, the kindness of James Stuart for his dependants, but, at the same time, his sometimes fatal lack of any glimmerings of humour ! (The *placet* was a request for a favour of some sort.)

King to Cardinal Albani

DE ROME, *ce* 19 *Avril* 1722.

Je viens de sevrer mon fils et je suis trop content des services de sa nourice pour pouvoir luy refuser de vous recom-
mander le *placet* cy joint, vous priant instamman a vouloir
bien, ou faire ce qu'on demande ou obtenir quelchechose
du Pape pour le mary. Car vous scavez qui je suis pas en
etat de faire quelque chose pour elle.[1]

The letter of Prince Charles to his father written when
he was 6½, promising not to jump near his mother, has been
reproduced by Andrew Lang, and is well known, but several
others of a slightly later date may be given, as throwing
light on his developing character.

The one of the spring of 1730, to his father's faithful servant,
Daniel O'Bryen, afterwards Lord Lismore, displays a delightful
childish impatience, and the still earlier one from his fond
tutor shows the care that was taken of his health, and the
unwillingness of a healthy little boy of 8 to travel in a litter
like an old man !

The early letters to both father and mother are so much
better written and spelt than those of any other time of his
life that one fears they were only copies from Sheridan, or
perhaps Murray.

Very much later, when the Prince was in Paris, his father
is found suggesting that the old tutor should revise his letters !

To this period also undoubtedly belongs the following,
undated :

"Copie of the Oath to be taken particularly by all the
King's servants who are under the Lord Steward of his
Majesty's household.

[1] The accenting of the French letters is most erratic as well as the spelling.

You shall sweare by the Holy Evangelists and by the contents of this book, that you shall bear faith and true allegiance to our Sovereigne Lord King James the third and that you shall know nothing that may be hurtfull or prejudicial to his Majesty's Person state dignity or Government, but you shall give notice, with all speed that in you lyes to his Majesty or one of his Majesty's most honourable Privy Councillors and that you shall faithfully serve his Majesty in the office of . . .

And obey such orders as you shall receive from ye Steward of his Majesty's household or other yr superior officer according to ye rules of his Majesty's Household. So help you God and ye contents of this Booke."

The following letters refer to one journey :

Sir Thomas Sheridan, Under Governor to the Prince of Wales (James Murray, Lord Dunbar, being Governor) to the King

April 16, 1729.

SIR,

In obedience to your Majesty's Commands I design'd to have got every thing ready for H.R.H. to begin his journey on Monday next, but the Queen being assured that the Duchesse of Parma [1] will be here on Wednesday night, and being desirous she should see the Prince before he sets out, has made me put it off, till Thursday in the afternoon, when we shall not fail by the blessing of God to set forward ; and I hope to order it so that your Majesty may have the pleasure to see the Prince on the Wednesday following. I shall not fail to observe your orders on the road, but as to a litter, I am assured it will not be necessary, and besides I know not how the motion of it might agree with H.R.H., many People not being able to bear it. I have deliver'd Your Majesty's

---

[1] Clementina's aunt, another Princess of Neuburg.

letter to the Legat, who has promised me the answer for this evening.

I am with the Greatest Submission and Respect
Sir,
Your Majesty's most Faithfull Subject and
most obedient humble servant,
THO. SHERIDAN.[1]

Lady Nithsdale, Governess to the two young Princes, to the King
Docketed as received 21 April, 1729.

SIR,

It is noe small pleasure to me yt at ye same time yt I acknowlege ye honour of Your Majesty's letter, I have yt of assuring you yt his Royal Highness every day improves in his health and gathers both strength and flesh, he having been reduced very low ; he has not yet stirr'd out of his Appartment, but tomorrow if it be a tollerable day is to goe to ye other side to Mass, and a day or two after to take ye Air, in Order to prepare him for his journey, wch if he continues to mend as he has done, and ye weather prove favourable, I doubt not but that he will be in a condition of undertaking it at ye time yr Majesty appoints. now remains my most grateful and humble acknowlegments for ye great Favour yr Majesty does me in permiting me not only to bring my Daughter [2] but to allow her ye Honour of accompaning his Royal Highness, and humbly beg leave to have that of Subscribing my selfe with ye profoundest Duty and respect
Sir,
Your Majesty's most Dutiful obedient subject and most
Faithful humble Servant,
WINEFRED NITHSDAILL.[3]

[1] Other letters of Thomas Sheridan occur on p. 130 and 133.
[2] Lady Anne Maxwell, afterwards Lady Bellew.
[3] Lady Nithsdale remained in Rome till her death in 1749.

Sir Thomas Sheridan to Queen Clementina—a week later
April 23, 1729.

MADAM,

Notwithstanding the roughness of the roads and the bad-
ness of the Weather, His Royal Highness arrived here last
night before it was quite dark, and God be praised in perfect
health. He was well lodg'd in a Convent of Olivetan
Monks, has slept very well, and is this morning very gay
and brisk. He gives his humble Duty to your Majesty and
bids me inclose this Paper wch he cou'd not find before he
took leave off yr. Majesty. He charges me likewise to tell
you what is very true, that he has been very good and civil.
I hope I shall always have the same good account to give of
him. I am with the most profound Submission and Respect
Madam,
Your Majesty's Most Dutifull Subject and most
obedient humble Servant,
THO. SHERIDAN.

ICARICA L'ASINO,
Saturday, six in the morning.

Letters from Queen Clementina to her son, not hitherto
printed, show that she was not a perfect scholar in English
any more than in French, but they are very normal letters
from a Catholic mother to her child.

9th of May 1729.

I am overjoyed to hear that my dear Carlusu is safely arrived
at Rome : and I hope Got Allmighty will preserve you in
good health ; and I hope also to hear that youl Continue to
be as civil and good, as Sir Thomas writ to me you was on
the road :—Remembre well my lessons, which you know is
the only proof you can give me of your love ; and in doing
that, be sure of mine, and that Got Allmightie will bless you,

and prosper you in every thing, as I wish with all my heart, being truly your loving Mother,

C. R.

MY DEAR CARLUSU,

I received with great satisfaction your letter and the more, seeing in it the desire you have to please me. I don't doubt but you allways will do so and be good and obedient which will draw you the Blessing of God, and be certain of my constant and just love I always will have for my dear Carlusu for whom I have prayed with all my heart to day, and put you under the protection of the Blessed Vergine. God Allmighty Blesse and preserve you. I hope very soon to embrace you, with the tendernesse of your loving Mama,

C. R.

James to Clementina, who still remained away from Rome, but had rejoined her younger son.

ROME. *May* 11th, 1729.

I am mighty glad, Madam, to find by yours of the 4th that you and Hary were well, and sorry that the weather continued so bad, not only because it unavoidably delays your journey, but because I foresee that betwixt your finding the Roads practicable, and the hot weather, there will not probably be Interval enough for you to make the journey in. But there's no help for that, and you will be sure, either by coming over very early, or stopping in the heat of the day, expose yourself and the Duke as little as possible to the heat of the day. It was very natural for the Duchess of Parma to leave you both some kind token. This town, which is fertile in invention, had made her Regale you with great sums of money in her own and her Daughter's name. Carluccio was mightily pleased with your Letter and to Sir Thomas's and my great surprise, read it almost current without

much help. I saw him ride yesterday much to my satisfaction, and on the whole I am very much pleased with him.
He thanks you for your letter and presents you his Duty. I
have taken Goats-whey these 3 days, which had done very
well with me, and next week I am to begin a Course of
Steel. The weather is now here reasonably warm, and if
it continues I hope I shall be able to get to Albano in about
8 days, to stay there with Carluccio till you come here. I
pray God to bless Harry, and to send you both soon and safe
to me,

JAMES R.

James to Charles Edward

ALBANO. June 9th, 1729.

I am mighty impatient, My dear Carluccio, to see you
again, but the weather is so favorable for the Countrey, that
I shall stay here till Tuesday. Be sure you be very good when
I am away, and don't forget me, for I think very often of
you, and pray God to bless you and your Brother,

JAMES R.

James to Clementina

ffriday morning, June 10th, 1729.

I have had the satisfaction to hear this morning, Madam, of
your being come safe to Rome, where I hope this will find
you in good health, as well as our Children, to whom my
Blessing. It was almost cold here last night, and it is far from
hot today. The Pope left us this morning. I have taken
my walk and am just going to Mass. I am well enough in
my health, much as yesterday, which with my best wishes
is all I shall trouble you with at present.

JAMES R.

Charles Edward to James on the same day

DEAR PAPA,

I am glad you find the good weather at Albano so favorable to your health tho it hinders me so much longer from the happinesse off seeing you. Whether absent or present I hope you will allways continue your love to me. My brother is very well and so i is Dear Papa,

your most Dutifull Son,

CHARLES P.

Charles Edward to Daniel O'Brien, same day, expecting a present which has been promised to him, and ending with a beautifully turned phrase of thanks most certainly inspired by the Irish Tutor.

IN PARIS.

J'atten avec impatience un je ne scay quoy, que le Roy vous charge de m'envoyer. L'on ma tant vante votre bon Gout que je suis persuade que J'en seray fort content, servez moy bien ; je vous en remercie d'advance, et soyez asseure que ma reconnoissance durera plus longtems que le plaisir que je m'en propose,

CHARLES P.

James to Clementina

(ALBANO). *Monday afternoon, 12th June, 1729.*

I am very impatient to see Harry in his Breeches, wch will not be till Wednesday morning, Tho' I shall God willing be with you to morrow before 9 a'cloke at night. Dont come out to meet me, no more than Carluccio, to whom my blessing, as well as to his Brother. I continue well enough and am I hope to see you to morrow. I need say no more to yours of yesterday.

JAMES R.

Clementina to Prince Charles Edward—two years later
                                    ROME. *June* 13*th*, 1731.

MY DEAR CARLUSU,

I received with a great deal of satisfaction your letter, and the more because you tel me that you have been good at Mass, and that Sir Tomas has been pretty well contented with you. I hope you'l continue to be as good til I see you and that then Sir Tomas will be able to tell me, that he is very well content with you, having no greater satisfaction than when I see that you do your duty: hoping then that God Allmighty will bless you, as I pray him for and do wish it with all my heart, being sincerely your tender and loving Mother,

                                    CLEMENTINA R.

P.S. Your letter has done me mor pleasur being of your own composition than if it had been of another—it will be hard for you to understand my English. Give this to Hary.

*The same to the same, showing a curious economy of space in writing
    Benediction in two letters and using the sign for double con-
    sonants. She comments on the fact that her son's letter is well
    written. The same could hardly be said for hers.*

                                    16 *Oct.* 1732.

MY DEAR CARLUSU,

je suis tres satisfaite de votre obeissance et de l'esperance que vous me doné que je vous trouveré ben lundy. Ce que je souhaite de tous mon cœur et que vous continuer toujours de meme parceque cela vous atirere la B^n du Seigneur que je prie de vous maintenir en sa Ste Grace et je vous doñe de tous mon cœur ma B^n etant sincerement votre tendre et bone mere.

                                    C. R.

P.S. coñe je ne doute pas que henri soit R^n je lui doñe aussi de bon Cœur ma B^n. Votre lettre eté tres bien ecrite.

The King to Prince Charles

Friday morning, July 30, 1734.

I cannot, my Dear Child, let this day pass without sending my blessing, with all the tenderness I am capable of, & with it you will find an *Estuy* [1] which may be of use to you. Remember & practice all I said to you yesterday, & then you will I hope be one day both a great & a good man, which I pray God to make you, & that I may have good accounts of you, which will be the greatest comfort I can have during your absence.

JAMES R.

King James to the Prince—(during his Neapolitan campaign, [2] *July–Sept. 1734)—in his own writing*

The Duke is better today & I hope the worst is over, the possibility of the small Pox made the Doctors the more willing to bleed him yesterday, and it hath certainly done him good : I shall expect you on Saturday about four thirty : your letter to me was well enough writ & spelled, a little practice would make writing easier to you. The Pope is

[1] Etui.

[2] The long account by Lord Dunbar (James Murray of Stormont, q.v.) of Prince Charles's brief experiences at Gaeta in 1734 has never been printed in its entirety. It is particularly interesting to remember that these few days in the camp of the King of Naples under the guardianship of his admiring cousin, the Duke of Liria, now become Duke of Berwick (and when he was only 13), constituted the whole of the military experience of the Prince who landed in Scotland eleven years later with his seven followers, and in the months to follow assumed the commander-in-chiefship of a considerable Highland army and flouted the advice of experienced soldiers, like Lord George Murray, who served him.

King James's anxious letter, and the Prince's very brief, schoolboy replies make rather pathetic reading. They foreshadow only too well the future relationship of the two. King James, affectionate, conscientious, but invariably tactless and too much concerned with trifles, and Charles, airy and detached, already feeling quite capable of managing his own affairs, breathing in every syllable of these few lines the pettish exclamation, "Do not fuss so much."

well. The last French post brought no great news, but I have seen since the speech to ye Parliament in which I dont mark any thing very material more than commonplaces. I hope Ld. Dunbar & Sir Thomas are well, Adieu, my Dear Son. God bless you.

J. R.

Lord Dunbar to the King
MOLA. *Thursday, August 5th,* 1734, *in the morning.*

SIR,

The Duke of Berwick having writ to yr. M tuesday night after the Prince's arrival by the extraordinary, I did not think it necessary to trouble you, nor could I write by the ordinary who set out early the next morning, but I begin this letter in the intention to dispatch Camillo tonight. The Prince arrived, blessed be God, in perfect health and was less fatigued than most of the company, the Duke carryed him directly to court where he received all the hon^{ry} invitation to the guards etc. due to the Prince of Wales and Comte St. Estevan met him on the head of the stairs, where H.R.H. made him a compliment thanking him for these marks of respect but desiring, as he was incognito, that he would order them not to be performed any more. When the King arrived the Prince went to the sale des gards to meet him and there made a compliment very prettyly and without the lest embarras after which he followed H.M. into his room and spoke to him with the same ease as he used to do to any of the Cardinals at Rome. He presented Sir Thomas and me and told the King in doing it, that he had great obligations to us, which was much remarked and has done him vast honr. The King answered him something to his first compliment, and inquired if Y.M. and the Queen were well afterwards, when the Prince made compliments from Y. My to him ; and, if after that the reception he gave the Prince might appear cold to those who are not acquainted with the bashfulness of his temper, yet he certainly meant to receive him kindly and therefore Y.M. may reckon that he did so. Count Montemar sent to excuse his not waiting on H.R.H. the night he arrived on account of his courier, but came next morning: some time after mutual compliments had passed between H.R.H. and him, he took the Prince aside into the Balcony and told him he had received precise orders from the King of Spain to ask H.R.H. in what manner he would be pleased to be treated and to give him all the distinctions due to the Prince of Wales if such was his pleasure. In answer to this the Prince expressed his acknowledgements to the King of Spain for the honr he did him and thanked Mr. de Montemar for his obliging attention, and said he desired to be incognito. While the Prince was at supper the evening he arrived, the King sent him compliments by one of the first Gentlemen of his bed chamber to know how he found himself after his journey etc. which is all that past the first night which merits Y. My attention. On Wednesday morning at 10 oclock the Prince went again to court and was invited to Dine with King, as I was likeways and Sir Thomas, and he dined there accordingly: In the afternoon we went by sea towards the Camp and from thence to a house from whence the King is used to view the batteries but where he runns but little danger, yet they persuade him it is the post of the General officers who are ordered to be there at the hour he gos, which seems is a joke to the whole army. To imitate him in this conduct would not turn to H.R.H. accompt. On the other hand it is certain that the Spaniards will be mortifyed extreamly when they see the Prince do more than he dos : However the Duke of Berwick who is the most competent judge of this matter, thinks that as the King has not invited the Prince to go along with him, since he gos by himself, he is at full liberty to do what he pleases, and therefore intends to carry him today at eleven a clock to view one of the batterys where he says he will run

little or no risque; he choses that hour because he says the
Ennemy dont fire at that time of the day, which is all I can
write to Y.M. at present on that subject but shall give Y.M.
an account of what passes. In the meantime I can assure
Y.M. with truth that the Prince has behaved himself extreamly
well and that he is much admired by all, as well courtiers as
officers. Mr. de Bissy told me the King asked him "s'il
avoit vu le petit Chevalier" adding "il est vif, et charmant."
Mons. de St. Estevan after making his *éloge*, told me he had
writ an account of him to the court of Spain the very night
he arrived, he made me an excuse at the same time if he did
not come to wait on him, his employment not permitting
him to leave the King's person (which seems to me a very
extraordinary etiquette) but said that H.R.H. might command
him in every thing that could be for his pleasure or satisfaction,
after which he sent his son and son-in-law to wait on H.R.H.
It is very certain that it is his intention as well as Mr. de
Montemar's to shew the Prince all civility's and therefore I
submit it to Y.M. whether it might not be proper for you to
get the Bishop of Cordova to write in order to thank the King
in the first place in Y. My's name for the civilitys he has
shewed the Prince and also to acknowledge an obligation to
Count St. Estevan and Montemar for their good offices with
ye King and attention towards H.R.H. I'm apt to believe
that some such thing would have a good effect. It is not
known when Gaeta will be taken but I do not believe it will
happen very soon. The King returns immediately after to
Naples and the D. of Berwick told me he had already insinuated that the Prince had a mind to profit of this occasion to
see that town, adding that he had a house in view where he
would be conveniently lodged. I answered that it was
Y. Mys intention H.R.H. should lodge in the same convent
where you lodged yr. self, to which he said that he had actually sent to borrow the house from the Duke of Matalins
for him self and yt H.R.H. would he hoped allow him to

receive him in it as a place belonging to himself. As there is time as yet to think of that matter I thought it proper to say no more but wait Y. Mys command and dont doubt but you will write to the Duke what you judge fit on this particular. This is the most agreeable situation can be imagined for passing the hot weather, which we feel very little, since there raises a westerly wind regularly every day at ten a clock, which lasts till the evening, by the means of which we find it cool and set all the day long with the windows open, and I dont believe there is better air in Italy : I'm sure I never felt any so agreeable in summer. The Prince is invited to dine aboard the Capitans Galley on Sunday next by Prince Campo Florida's brother who is General of the Galley, and this particular makes me remember to tell Y.M. that, tho there was a considerable motion in the sea, H.R.H. was not the least sick.[1] We are lodged in Cardinal Cibo's house from which we have a full prospect of Gaeta and see every bombe or cannon that is fired either by night or day. Sir Thomas, I thank God is pretty well and seems not to have suffered by his journey, he presents his most humble duty to Y.M. Thus, Sir, I have mentioned to Y.M. all the particulars which deserve your attention just as they occurred to me, but without order, for which I beg Y. Mys excuse and will add what may be further necessary after we are back from the Camp. I have just now received a message from the Duke of Berwick who is in the trenches importing that they had been obliged to break a certain communication in the night to draw some cannon yt way and therefore the Prince could not go there today so that it is likely that I shall not dispatch Camillo till tomorrow night at soonest. I cannot but inform Yr M. how much you are obliged to Mr. de Buonioni the King's phycitian who is a man of learning, good nature and good sense and has I'm sure a sincere affection towards Yr.

[1] In later life, viz. on his voyage to Scotland, the Prince was not so immune. See p. 133.

M. and yr. family: He has given me several hints by which
the Prince may speak in a manner pleasing to the King and
assures me that he has already a real inclination towards him,
I therefore think it very proper if Y.M. approves it that you
desire Monsr. Lysrote to write to him of purpose to make
him a compliment in yr Mys name and to thank him for his
attention to serve the Prince. He speaks familiarly to the
King and therefore I think he may be of vast use. I cannot
conceal from Y.M. that he asked me what was the meaning
of the Prince's bringing two frayers (friars) along with him,
saying that this particular was much blamed by all men of
judgement here, adding that we would see it published in the
Dutch and English papers "et che questa era una delle piccole
cose che faccevano perdere regni." [1] I endeavoured to excuse
it as well as I could but he said it was a thing which was no
ways approved, that he was a frank man and told me in confidence not only his own, but the sentiments of others on this
occasion and so ended our conversation as to this particular,
on which Y.M. will be pleased to make your own reflections.
After writing what is above, the Prince went to court when I
can assure Y.M. that he did himself great honr. by his behaviour and discourse. Count St. Estevan told me the King
had commanded him to let me know that if the Prince would
come & dine with him every day he would do his M. great
pleasure, but that he left him at liberty to do in that what
might be most for his satisfaction, and as I might judge it
proper for his health. I made a proper compliment in return
to this and concluded that the Prince "profiteroit des faveurs
de sa Majesté sans en abuser," and therefore we intend to
carry him to dine with the King to-morrow and that he
should go dine with him hereafter about twice a week.
The Duke of Berwick and I having made reflections on the
consequence of the Prince's going into the trenches—though
the King has never been there, think it is necessary to come to

[1] (And that this was a small thing which might lose kingdoms.)

an explanation on this matter with Mr. de Montemar [1] before
he gos, in order to persuade him that H.R.H.'s situation
is very different from that of the King of Naples, and that
in his case he is under an obligation to act in a manner which
may do him honr. in the english army, having no fortune in
the world but what he must gain by the point of his sword.
If we can persuade him not to be against it, all will go well,
otherways, we cannot I think do what might risque at once
this court and that of Spain, by which yr. My's interest would
suffer more of one side than it would gain of t'other. I will
inform Y.M. when we have talked with Mr. Montemar of
what passes, and I own I shall be grieved if H.R.H. cannot
go at all into the trenches, because I'm sensible that he would
run little or no risque by the wise precautions the D. of
Berwick proposes to take by carrying him at a certain time
of the day etc. so yt. he would get in a few days a great reputation at a very cheap rate, and the Prince himself is teasing
both the D. of Berwick and me every day to shew him these
trenches of which he hears so much discourse. However
he went this day to the same place as yesterday, where the
enemy fired five cannon shot a quarter of an hour before he
arrived and the Duke of Berwick actually left the house
upon it, and went back with the Prince to the same place
some time after when he came there.

Aug. the 6th.

I hear this minute that the Major of the place is come out
with offers to capitulate and that they are treating of the
articles of capitulation which probably will be agreed on and
the place evacuated tomorrow. In the mean time least they
should not agree, the Duke of Berwick is of oppinion that
we should still speak to Mr. Montemar least they should still
happen to fire for some days and his Grace and I are to speak

[1] The Neapolitan General.

with him accordingly this afternoon, but we dont think it necessary to delay sending Camillo our Courier.

It is probable that the King may set out for Naples in a few days and the Prince must go at the same time since he is to go in one of the Galleys which naturally ought all to set out at the same time. The Duke of Berwick to whom I have spoken again upon the subject is still of opinion yt the Prince should not lodge in the Convent but in the other house. But I suppose if Y.M. insists upon it he may be there on his own expense, in which case, his Grace would no doubt lodge elsewhere. If this be Y. Mys intention you will be pleased to send off Joseppe, with a cook, immediatly who if they are dilligent may arrive yet before the King leaves this and in all events I should be glad to have your orders soon by somebody.

Monr. de Bury assures Y.M. of his most humble respects, he makes the Prince *éloge* [1] in all companys and told me he would not only give ane account of what he remarked in him to the court of france, but that he would write on this subject to all the french ministers in all the different courts of Europe. This surely deserves that Y.M. should take notice of it in some shape or other for it marks a particular affection to yt interest and may do H.R.H. considerable service. The Prince is just now writing his letters to Y.M. and the Queen. He has dined today at court and really never gos there without saying something which raises the admiration of those people. Y.M. knows I never flattered you in my way of talking to you of H.R.H. and therefore I'm sure you'll believe me when I tell you yt I'm extreamly satisfied with him and if he had a compange of six months before him in the way he is of conversing with the public here, and of being more familiar with some pretty Gentlemen whom the Duke of Berwick has thrown more particularly in the way of his acquaintance, I'm persuaded Y.M. would

[1] Eulogy.

96

see him come back quite another thing, for people say of him here already "que c'est un homme formé," and one thing is very sure yt he gives a great dele of surprise to the King of Naples by his way of talking, and receives none from him, tho he has behaved with all respect. Today at court his cockade fell from his hat and Mr. de St. Estevan took it up and the hat in order to put in on, but was plaising it wrong, upon which the King put it right. The Prince immediately told him that he would keep that cockade as long as he lived because H.M. had done him the honr to touch it. Yesterday morning the King asked him how he did and he immediately answered that ever since he had the pleasure of dining with H.M. the day before, it had cured him entirely of what he had till then suffered by the fatigue of his journey. In short in the train he is I cant but regret that he is to pass so short a time amongst these people who already admire him very much. I never saw him se well in his health in my life, and I can assure Y.M. that he eats more here in a day than in two at Rome. I write these things confusedly to Y.M. well knowing that they will be of satisfaction to you and that you wont mind the unnaturaleness of the stile which it would be hard to amend in the midst of the noise and bustle which surrounds me while I write. But I can say at least that I have mentioned in some shape or other every thing which Y.M. would be desirous to know.

P.S. The courier is dispatched about four a-clock supposing he may not be detained, waiting for the order for posthorses.

DUNBAR.

King James to Prince Charles while in the camp—(and the Prince's brief replies)

ROME. *August 7th*, 1734.

I was mighty glad, My Dear Child, to hear you were safe arrived at the Camp, and am very impatient to have some

97

good accounts of you from thence, which will be the case, if you are docile and obedient, as I hope you will be, and as I earnestly recommend to you, and to have a particular care of your dyet, for it would be a foolish and vexatious thing should you fall sick there, by eating trash, and so not be able to do and see what is fit for you. I pray God to bless you and embrace you with all my heart.

JAMES R.

Prince Charles to King James

Aug. ye 12, 1734.

SIR,

I am very glad that you are contented with me. I have been very good and hope with the Grace of God to continue so and umbly ask your Blessing.

CHARLES P.

Prince Charles to King James

Aug. ye 21, 1734.

SIR,

My Lord Dumbar has excused me for not haveing writ to you hetherto.

I have been very good and humbly ask your Blessing.

CHARLES P.

Prince Charles to the King (the year after his first military expedition)

ALBANO. *June ye* 1st 1735.

DEAR PAPA,

I cannot be so long without assuring you of my Duty and letting you know that my Brother and I are, God be praised, in perfect Health. We long very much to hear that you are so, and more to see it. In the mean time we humbly begg your Blessing.

CHARLES P. (*aged* 14).

Prince Henry to the King (same day)

June the 1st, 1735.

MY DEAR PAPA, the impatience I am in to see you makes me write this letter which I hope will be acceptable, being I writ without any assistance, by your most dutiful Son,

HENRY (*then* 10).

(Much better written than that of his brother.)

The King to Prince Charles

ALBANO. *June* 30*th*, 1736.

I am much pleased, my dear child, with your letter of yesterday, and am as impati'nt to see you and your brother as you can be to see me. I beseech God to bless you both and make you good and I hope I shall have a good account of you when I see you which will be God willing on Munday night. My kind compliments to Ld. Dunbar and Sir Thomas: Cardinal Comadini is just come, adieu Dr. Carluccio I embrace you and Henry with all my heart.

JAMES R.

The letters of King James to Queen Clementina, never before printed, which have been given, show his patient affectionate character, much occupied with detail, most of which would be somewhat boring to the ardent young Princess who had hoped to share his throne.

To his children when young he was a most tender father, and like many others, found it very difficult to realize that they had grown up.

Charles in particular threw over parental authority very largely from the time when (as has been seen), as a schoolboy of 13, he went to war in Naples, and most of his correspondence shows this. From the time he left his father's roof in

January, 1744, just after his twenty-third birthday, until the latter's death twenty-two years later, his letters are very rarely intimate, and though always ending with the stock phrase "humbly asking blessing," the impression they leave on the reader's mind is that Charles valued his father's opinion very lightly, was quite sure he himself knew best, and made it almost a habit to do a thing first and tell his father about it afterwards, if at all ! The King's letters show him as endeavouring conscientiously not to impose his authority (he realized very soon that, in any case, it was no use to do so), and to see things from his son's point of view. But at times he felt called on to make a solemn protest, as for instance before the '45, when the Prince openly boasted to him of how he was tricking Sempill and Balhaldy, and the King pointed out with dignity that such conduct was becoming neither to a Prince nor a Christian, and again in the immensely long letter of February 3rd, 1747, printed by Browne, and an earlier one of December 16th, 1746, protesting against the outrageous manner in which the disappointed Prince was treating the French Court, after his return from Scotland.

And another of December 4th, 1748 (also printed), in which he actually lays his paternal and royal commands on his son, to obey the orders of the French King and leave France before he was turned out. Orders which, unfortunately, the headstrong Prince continued to disobey.

At the time of the Queen's death, a number of letters were written to the King, a few of which will be given. Though during her life she had been hysterical, jealous, and moody, after her death no one remembered anything but her virtues, and her conscientious husband reproached himself for not having been able to make her consistently happier.

His own life was one long series of hopes deferred, and regrets that he had never been able to place her beside him on a throne and give her the position she longed for. It was not his fault, nor was the fact that he was fifteen years older, of a very different temperament, and almost morbidly a slave to the duties of his immense correspondence.

The Dutchess Dowager of Melfort [1] *to James*

PARIS. 8 *Feb.* 1735.

May it pleas your Majesty.

the grat los that your M: his mad of our lat gratius sovran the queen is a sensible affliction to all your loyal subjects, and to none mor than to me who wod be incolable for your M ; afliction if I did not know the Cristien use that your M. maks of all your crosses, and the grat consolation your M. has in the prince and the Duk, thye ar the admiration of all thos that sees them or hears speak of them that they may live to be your comfort and that your M. and they may be comble with all the blissings of hevene and all the prosperety and hapinesse on erthe that your M. so justly deserves shal be the constant prayers of the person in world that is with the most dutiful zeale and the most profound respect,

May it pleas your Majesty
your most faithful most dutyfule and most
obideant and most humble subject and servant,

EU: MELFORT.

---

[1] Euphemia Wallace, second wife of the 1st Duke of Melfort, died 1763, aged 90.

The Duke had died so long ago as January 1715. He had been one of the advisers of King James II as to his policy in Scotland 1685 to 1688 and his advice had invariably been fatal, as the great Dundee saw clearly.

Robert Arbuthnot, the Banker in Rouen, to Edgar

BOULOGNE-SUR-MER.

Feb. 10th, 1735.

DEAR SIR,

I have the favour of yours of the 8th Janry, last post brought us the Dolefull newes of the death of our good Queen wch much afflicts all his Majesty's loyal subjects, I heaertily grieve for her Majesty's untimely death, of so virtuous and devote a princess, our King's comfort, and mother of our royall hopes. God preserve them all three. My Brother the doctor's [1] illness bereaves me of my best correspondent in Eng^d, and gives me great greiffs, for he is in danger, and I fear more than they tell me, when I have any thing worth while I shall not faill to write either to my Lord Dunbar (to whom the inclos'd) or to you, I am ever and ever yours

R. A.

Sir David Nairne (the King's old secretary) to Mr. Edgar at Rome

PARIS. *7th March,* 1735.

DEAR SIR,

Besides your share in the generall affliction which we all had for the death of our dear late Queen—I suppose you have also had your large share of writing upon that sad occasion, so I do not wonder that I have no letter from you since that time, tho I flatter my self that if you had any news to send me of my son I should have heard from you before now, so not having heard from you I conclude you have got no account of him as yet. Pray let me recommend to you to continue to enquire about him for I am very uneasy upon his subject and not without reason.

I recommend the inclosed to you for M. l'Abbé Stuart and desire you'l make my compliments of condolence to Mrs.

---

[1] Dr. Thomas Arbuthnot, physician to Queen Anne, friend of Pope and Swift, author of *John Bull.* He died in this year.

Fitzgerald and Mrs. Massy upon the great loss they have had of the best of mistresses, As I allways had an esteem and concern for them I should be glad to know how they are provided for.

My daughter [1] is in a convalescent way and gives you her kind service, and I am

Dear Sir,

your very obedient humble servant,

DA. NAIRNE.

Two years later

James to Prince Charles, who was then on a tour through Italy

ROME. *May* 18*th*, 1737.

I cannot express to you, My Dear Son, how pleased I am with your two letters of the 5th and 7th May, because I take them as marks of your taking some satisfaction in writing to me, and of your endeavouring at the same time to improve yourself, so that I hope on your return, you and I will be better friends than ever, and for that you know what is necessary and will not I hope be wanting on your part. You did very well to confess to The English Penitentiary at Loretto, the other father not being there, and I understand from Sir Thomas you behaved very well at your Devotions there, and I hope you will be exact in not letting the hury and diversions of your journey, hinder you from performing those duties of a good Christian, which I recommended to you. Make many kind compliments from me to Sir Thomas, to whom I have nothing to say in return to his letter of the 7th, more than he will find in this letter, which you will show to him. Your Brother writes you a long letter, and is I thank God very well. We reckon to go on Tuesday to Albano, I believe Abbé Fitzjames [2] will go with me there, and to continue his journey to Naples on Wed.

---

[1] Who married the Chevalier Andrew Michael Ramsay (for a short time the Prince's tutor) and had a pension for many years.

[2] Third son of the first Duke of Berwick.

(The next part is in James's handwriting.)

I understand you have behaved very well in all respects on this journey, I hope you will continue to do so, and that I shall find you quite a man on your return to me. God bless you, my dear Child, and make you as good and as great a man as I wish you to be.

J. R.

(The King hardly seemed to realize that Charles was then 16, and felt himself a man. He had already taken to a grown-up wig, and to shaving.)

The young Duke of Perth, James, born 1713, died 1746, had sent presents of a kilt each to Princes Charles and Henry, who thus acknowledge them.

The Prince to the Duke of Perth

ROME. *Feb.* 17, 1740.

"Your kind and obliging letter came to my hands in due time and I profit with pleasure of this occasion to let you know how sensible I am of the sentiments you there express for me. Mine I assure you for you and your family and in particular for your brother,[1] are such as you could wish, and my thanks for the fine present you make me of a complete dress are very sincere. The value and esteem I have for my friends like whom I shall be dressed, will make me wear it with satisfaction, and it will be a great one to me to have occasions where I can show you the kindness and friendship I have for you— etc."

---

[1] Lord John Drummond, second son of the 2nd Duke of Perth, succeeded his brother, James, the 3rd Duke, who died on his way back to France after Culloden. John 4th Duke died unmarried in 1747 and was succeeded by his uncle John.

The Duke of York to the Duke of Perth—same date

"I thank you most kindly for your obliging letter, and for the book of Country Dances and for the dress you are to send me. I shall be glad to wear it for your sake and for the sake of others I have a great esteem for. Do me the favour to make my kind compliments to all my friends and to be assured yourself of the real friendship with which I am etc."

These two letters exist only in the copies (or more probably original drafts) in Edgar's handwriting. The style and phraseology are his. It is interesting to note that in both letters he used the Scoticism I *will* be dressed and *will* be glad—which is crossed out and corrected to *shall* in the King's own hand !

After the death of the Queen, the next eight years—1735 to 1743—passed for King James in a perpetual if mild ferment of Jacobite plans, and more than one Scots Jacobite travelled to Rome to lay projects before the King, and to indulge in sentimental raptures over the young Princes. Of the former the most important were Gordon of Glenbucket, 1737, and MacGregor of Balhaldy (known as Drummond) in 1740, of the latter John Murray of Broughton.

In 1741, the seven Scots Lords presented to Cardinal Fleury the famous memorial giving the numbers of Highlanders ready to rise and join a French landing in favour of the Stuarts. (Of these seven "Lords"—Lovat, Linton, John Stuart (his brother), Lochiel, Perth, Lord John Drummond (his uncle), Campbell of Auchinbreck as well as Balhaldy—only Lochiel and Perth did anything when the time came !)

Had Fleury (formerly so well known as the Bishop of Fréjus) not died in January 1743, something might have come of it. In any case, it led at least indirectly to the invitation from

Cardinal Tencin which brought Prince Charles secretly and in much haste to the French capital which he reached on February 10th, 1744. The romantic departure from Rome and the hurried journey have often been described. There followed a dreary time of waiting in Paris for something to happen.

Henry, Duke of York

Of Cardinal Henry Benedict several lives have been written and a good deal of space devoted to his engaging childhood when his father doted on him, when he played and sang and danced so charmingly and the Earl Marischal greatly preferred him to his brother.

Of his later life, after he became a Cardinal at the age of 22 and thereafter made his home entirely in Rome, and usually at his father's side, also much is known, not to mention his own voluminous correspondence in the British Museum, but from the period when he flung his little sword from him, in fury, because at the age of 9 he was not allowed to join his brother in the camp near Naples until he appears as welcoming his brother back from Scotland in 1746, very little has been given to the public. This very curious picture of the mentality of the future Cardinal at 17 is certainly worth preserving.

Account of H.R.H. The Duke of York, written in 1742, by Lord Dunbar

"After examining in the most exact manner Mr. Constable and Mr. Turner both together, we have supplied the particulars of which I had not myself perfect knowledge, I offer to yr Majesty the following account of the manner in which the Duke used to spend his time.

He is called by special order, a quarter of an hour before six

106

in the morning, rises at six and sometimes says some prayers in his bed during this quarter of an hour or a little more. He commonly spends about three quarters of an hour in washing his face and hands and putting on his shoes and stockings, for he does not dress till afterwards. After this he employs ane hour at prayers of which one half in his little closet and the other in walking in his bed chamber. Always says them aloud, so that when he is in his bed-chamber with the doors shut, they hear him in the next room. Next to this, he takes his breakfast, which lasts about half a quarter of ane hour or ten minutes.

Father Ildefonso comes about half ane hour after seven and always waits a good half hour during his prayers and the time of his breakfast. He stays with him generally ane hour, sometimes ane hour and a quarter and sometimes, but seldome, ane hour and a half. When Mr. Dicconson dictated to him on a day that was not a holy day and when he did not ride, this lasted about half an hour at this point of time, after which he danced and fenced, but sometimes when the dancing master was in the way, he danced two little minuets with him before he began with Father Ildefonso which lasted but a few minutes, because he has lost the inclination he had to that exercise. When he rid a horseback he went out immediately after his lesson with Father Ildefonso. Then he dressed and went to Mass of which he heard two and sometimes three on holydays and Saturday last four—to wit two with yr Majesty one with the Prince and one by himself. When he hears Mass with the Prince he stays at prayers in the Chapel about a quarter of an hour thereafter when the hour of dinner permits it. Since Lent he has heard sermon always twice, sometimes thrice and once four times in a week, but of this last they cannot be absolutely positive.

When dinner is over, he waits a certain time with the watch in his hand and then goes into the chapel where he stays at his prayers as in the morning about $\frac{3}{4}$ of ane hour and sometimes a little more. Then he goes abroad and generally goes to church (but sometimes he does not) where he remains about half ane hour. I have remarked it by my watch and have observed sometimes 7 or 8 minutes less and sometimes 3 or 4.

He comes home about 4 hours, goes to his chappel again where he remains always ane hour and some times ane hour and a half. It is to be remarked that in reciting or reacting his prayers he puts his mind in agitation, pronounces his words aloud, and crowds them with great precipitation one upon another and I often remark him when he goes abroad after dinner with a blackness about his eyes, his head quite fatigued and his hands hot and the same thing when he comes from his prayers at night. What effect it has upon him in the morning, I have not observed, but probably it will have so much. I forgot to mention Father Ravillos who comes twice a week, and takes his time after Father Ildefonso.

It is observable that the Duke is the whole day in constant inquietude for fear of not having time for all he ought to do and very often has his watch in his hand on that account. His temper and inclination is so far changed that to propose to carry him of ane evening as next Sunday to ane assembly, in place of doing him a pleasure it gives him paine and he seems to have no pleasure in anything.

It deserves serious attention that he undergoes much greater application of mind than his delicate health can bear, yet there is little of it directed towards forming his judgement or adorning his mind with knowledge of things suitable to his station. His small study with Father Ravillos may be reckoned of this sort, and though Father Ildefonso teaches him a language yet as he reads a little history in that language by which he may form sentiment, I also comprehend it. But this is a small matter and though he has always a perfect goodwill to apply while he is with him he is often unable to do it otherways than with interruptions of 10 minutes at time.

During the rest of the day he never reads a word on any subject nor could he probably do it, so that were not the course

Prince Henry, aged 15

From the portrait by Domenico Dupra

he is in noxious to his health, as it certainly is, he would arrive at the age of 22 without having cultivated his understanding or acquired a reasonable degree of such knowledge as is the chief duty of station at present both towards God and man.

In this manner, the first capacity in the world with a wonderful memory would be lost, and this I take to be a very great evil and what wants a prudent and ane affectual remedy. I will add to this that when he is not employed as above he is always singing, which I am far from thinking indifferent in regard of his breast.

I have read over to Mr. Dicconson what is above who declares that all the facts are according to the most exact truth.

I take it for granted that the Duke's only pleasure is in the exercise of his devotions in which he is employed, that it is become a passion and that the contradicting him in it will have a very violent effect upon him and therefore this matter I think is very delicate and required to be considered very maturely."

This interesting document does not appear to have been seen by any of the biographers of Cardinal York ; it is certainly not without significance as regards what seems to have been his narrow-mindedness in later life (cf. p. 164.)

Henry Benedict seems in many ways to have been curiously young for his years, and the letter from Foligno to his father in Rome of January 15th, 1744 (two years after the date of the last letter), written when he had just been made aware that his brother had started on the great adventure to Paris and Scotland, without a word of warning to him, is very childish, as is the one a month later to his brother in Paris. Both of these have been used by Lang and others, but of his own progress to France when he had at last persuaded his father to let him start, no letters have till now been given.

Henry to his father about his being kept in the dark as to the Prince's hurried journey to France :

The Duke to the King

FOGLIANO.   15 *Jan.* 1744.

SIR,

I am very much obliged to your Majesty for the honour of your two letters.   Your goodness has really been very great in giving me reasons for not revealing to me sooner this affair. You may be very well assured Sir that I can never be anxious to know anything but what you think fit I should know, and that also but when you please. . . .   I have had a good deal of anxiety while at Cisterna for I really did not think it a good air in this present conjuncture, but now that we are, Thank God, at Fogliano as I think out of all harms way and that I perceive by your Majesty's letter that all things continue quiet at Rome, I am very happy, but at the same time very impatient to hear news of our "dear Traveller."   I shall stay here with a great deal of pleasure as long as your Majesty will think fit, were it to be of any use.   In this occasion I would really be locked up very willingly in an old Tower till Easter . . .

Begging your blessing I am yr most dutiful son,

HENRY.

The King to Francis, Lord Sempill [1]

IN PARIS.   *Jan.* 2, 1744.

"I received on Tuesday yours of the 16th Dec. and have since had the pleasure of hearing from Balhady who I hope may be with you before the end of the week, and will have told you, be sure before you get this, all the measures he took on the road to facilitate the Prince's journey with which I have been much

---

[1] This letter proves conclusively that the Prince's dash from Rome was *not* without his father's knowledge, as it so often said—also that Balhaldy was *not* with him on the journey.   Lord Sempill was an inveterate intriguer, very distasteful to the Prince.   See pp. 3, 121, 125.

taken up these days past. We have at last settled all that relates
to it ; and after having weighed everything very maturely, I
have fixed on the road of Genoa and Antibes as the least
exposed to danger and accident. On the whole, I am well
enough pleased with the plan we have layd, and bar accidents,
the Prince will probably be at Antibes about the 20th of the
month for he is to part from hence Tuesday the 9th before day.
I did not forget that the day named for his beginning his
journey was the 12, but I thought I might take upon me to
anticipate 3 days to make a party of chase serve the more
naturally to cover the real journey—besides the journey being
once determined and settled, the sooner it is executed the
better. . . . The King of France has called for the Prince,
and he shall part.

. . . I take the case to be now or never in relation to France,
and therefore we must all act accordingly . . . I don't remember I have anything more to say but the assurance of my
constant kindness to you and Balhady."

Of the period when the Prince was in Paris (February 1744–
June 1745), just before he left for Scotland, a number of letters
have already been printed. One or two new ones are, however, here given, and one from Sir Thomas Sheridan which
is humorous. There was an interval of seventeen months
between that breathless arrival after the romantic dash from
Cisterna before the Prince got off for Scotland, and as during
all that time he was not officially recognized by the French
Court, his position was anomalous, and his finances always in a
precarious condition.

In February 1744 Sir Thomas had been sent for to join him
and allowed to do so by the King, though somewhat un-
willingly. James, it seems, distrusted most of his son's chosen
friends, and Sheridan, though devoted heart and soul to his

former pupil, now his young master, was certainly not always a judicious adviser. In the letter, on page 118, to O'Bryen he appears as the anxious housekeeper.

Things were being made very difficult for the Prince by the fact that those of his immediate circle thoroughly distrusted Balhaldy and Sempill, who were nominally managing the Scots affairs.

Sir Thomas Sheridan writes to the King soon after his arrival in Paris.

June 8, 1744.

"The Prince is lodged in a pretty little house near Montmartre where the Prospect and air are very good. He has all his conveniency and room enough for so small a company as his. I found him in very good health and he seemed to me both taller and broader than when I saw him last. He is certainly increased in bulk, but for his height, when I seemed surprised at it, he let me into the secret. He showed me ye heels of his shoes which he weares now of the usual size, whereas before he wore them remarkably lower than other people.

In fine, he has altogether a much more manly air than he had when he began his travels. His sentiments towards yr Majesty are such as could be wished."

After the sad fiasco, from Charles's point of view of the magnificent expedition under Maréchal Saxe, designed to invade England in 1744, the Prince with characteristic optimism persisted in regarding the design as only postponed. The truth was that of the numerous transports, ready to carry 15,000 men across the Channel, many were total wrecks, and the others so badly damaged that it would have taken six months to put them again in order for use. Meantime, of course, the element of surprise would have been lost ; the English Fleet temporarily absent in the Mediterranean would have returned and the coasts of England put in a posture of defence. Saxe put this position of affairs quite plainly before the Prince, and himself returned to his Continental wars.

Thomas Sheridan

The letters from Thomas Sheridan are, of course, legion.

He writes a very small and not very legible hand, and though he spells better than his pupil, Prince Charles, his letters, either French or English, are by no means impeccable.

It was tacitly understood that his mother, whose name is never given, was one of the illegitimate daughters of King James II and married Thomas Sheridan, the King's secretary.

The younger Thomas very early entered the service of his grandfather and fought at the Battle of the Boyne, being at that period about 16 years of age. He then went to St. Germains where he became page to the Queen, and was later attached to the household of King James III (his uncle, though so much younger than himself). He took some small part in the '15, but does not seem to have gone to join the little court at Avignon. Later, he was sent on various missions about Europe, but was brought to Rome in 1725 (by John Hay), and when King James decided to "put his son among men" at the age of $4\frac{1}{2}$ years and appointed the Protestant James Murray of Stormont as Governor, he gave him as assistant sub-governor, the Catholic, Sheridan. At what period Sheridan adopted this faith is not known ; he may have been baptized into it by his mother's wish, but his father was a Protestant.

Several early letters of his, showing curious glimpses of Prince Charlie as a little boy, have been already given, but the more interesting are of date after he had joined the Prince in Paris, just before the '45. King James had not wished his son to have his old tutor with him for several reasons ; Sheridan was over 70 and in poor health, he had already had more than one shock, fit or slight stroke, as chronicled by several correspondents, and the King wrote—"le pauvre Sheridan n'est pas en état de s'appliquer beaucoup." Moreover, he was as wax in the hands of his headstrong and fascinating pupil and therefore of no use as an adviser, but the pupil got his way, and Sheridan arrived in Paris five months after the Prince, having had one more "shock" on the way. When there, he had his hands full with a great many various occupations, not the least that of keeping the Prince quiet, fairly content, and at least outwardly polite to his French hosts.

During this weary time of waiting actually to get off for Scotland, Sheridan did his best to keep the King's accredited agent, O'Bryen, fully informed, rather against the wishes of the Prince, who distrusted all those who were in communication with his father.

Sempill, meanwhile, continued to write to Rome that he "feared the Prince had some thing extraordinary in view," but he did not know what it was. He told the King that he had interrogated Waters whom he believed to be in the secret, but "could draw nothing from him." This of course was in accordance with the Prince's own strict orders. Sempill adds that he himself was in "such a ferment" that he did not feel it wise to write much, though he was far from keeping to this wise resolution, and his letters are very numerous. A great many were printed by Browne and they are full of schemes of his own, none of which came to anything. He was quite without influence on the fortunes of the "Forty-five" except in so far as his officiousness irritated the Prince and made him more than ever secretive ! He did not go to Scotland.

On July 19th, 1744, Sheridan wrote to O'Bryen from the little country house that he was hoping for a pretext to come to Paris, but that the Prince would not hear of it at present.

"Cela m'ennuée fort et comme ailleurs je ne me porte pas tout a fait bien, le spleen, ou si vous voulez le Chagrin, commence a prendre diablement le dessus sur moi, et je ne sai si j'y pourrais resister longtemps."

He seems then to have consulted his doctor !

Letter to Sir Thomas Sheridan from his doctor in Rome

(It is to be noted that this was written six months *before* he undertook the campaign in Scotland with the Prince, and shows how precarious his health already was.)

ROME. *Jan. ye 26, 1745.*

DEAR SIR,

I am favoured with yours of the 4th Inst. and am glad to hear that you have had no more fainting fits and have felt but very little of that deep melancholy you formerly complained of. I am persuaded that you shall be no more troubled with either if you can keep strictly up to the Diet I formerly mentioned, which I reckon will be the easier for you to do seeing you have already brought yourself near to the quantity desired, tho' I wish that you exceed not that quantity of flesh meats (without descending to weights and measures). Yet I can see no good reason for all the Infusion of Quinquina to deprive you of a light breakfast, yea, I think that it would be beneficial for you to take both breakfast and supper providing they be without any kind of flesh meat, but of grewels and such light foods as I specifyed to you on the 8 Dec. For as young folks should gradually come from children's food to such as men use, so should every bodie at our age return gradually to feed oftener and on less and lighter foods than formerly, but with this difference that the young may exceed in the quantity with less danger than we, because their Tubes are always increasing in their dimensions and ours are allways decreasing even many of them cease to be tubes and become impermeable solids and the more so as our years increase and we stop ym up by undigested food. No bodie, that has not observed exactly, can well imagine how small a quantitie of food will suffice to support our bodies in health and vigour. I hope that you have got free of the headaches you complained of, by the power of diet but if you have not, I expect that you shall by 8 or 10 days use of the pills, to clear yr obstructions, help yr digestion, prevent headache or any blooding of the nose . . . If you will give credit to me, you should go on resolutely with yr diet, even to be uneasy from hunger at the end of yr greatest meal, for I am affraid yr dinner is not low enough when you are drowsy after it, and I believe if you go on rightly and persevere that you shall sleep longer and more kindly in the nights and be more lively all day.

Yr obed. hum. servt.

ROBT. WRIGHT.

The King to Prince Charles

December 15, 1744.

"I thank God I am better and about as usual, the Doctors tell me my ails are not dangerous, yet they increase with age (56) and I cannot apply as I could have done even a year ago, for as for reading or writing myself I can do very little of either, because the least fixing of my eyes gives me some sort of giddyness in my head. So you see my dear Child that you are likely to have but a useless old father in me, but still I thank God my heart is good and if its being all yours could be of any help to you, that will never fail you."

(Waters about this time sends a nightcap of Virginia wool, to make the King sleep!)

The Prince to his Father

PARIS. *ye 28 Feb.* 1745.

SIR,

I have received yours of ye 1st and 7th Current. As I have been so much hurrid between Balls and business, I shall refer to my next. It would be a great comfort to me to have real business on my hands, but I see little of that at present as I shall explen in an other. It is something surprising to me not to have heard from Lumley (*Lord Sempill*) this to weeks and even he owe me an answer of one of mine of that standing, but I esely conceive the reson on't, which is that after making such a noise of his being able to do a great deal, he dos nothing— or he dos not care to lett me in the confidence of his manedg-ments, which I believe has happened before now, to more than he, for I see here everybody thinks himself to be the wisest man in the world.

I lay myself at your Majesty's feet, most humbly asking blessing. Your moste dutiful son

CHARLES P.

King James writes on March 1st : "It is really a grievous thing to me to see you all in pieces amongst yourselves and that I can do nothing to ease you or to serve ourselves."

Sheridan had written, soon after his own arrival in Paris the previous year : "I find the Prince has been strongly prevented against Cardinal Tencin, O'Bryen and Lord Marischal, which prejudices I shall make it my business to remove as farr and as fast as I can." The jealousies among the various Jacobites made prompt and secret plans almost impossible.

Balhaldy on his side writes to King James

APRIL 26, 1745.

"We judged it not advisable to move until such time as Sir Thomas were out of the way. The Pr. sees clearly enough now the mistakes he has been led into, as appears from his complaining to one *Sullivan* who is with him, that Sir *Thomas* before parting had engadged *him* by repeated promises and assurances to call for him so soon as he arrived here. But however that is, it is to be feared that the Prince's good and tender heart will never be able to resist the tears and fainting fits [1] upon the least refusal or seeming indifference to what is urged by that proud man, so far as to see that he means only to govern him and all under his influence—the consequence of which has often been extremely hurtful to yr Majesty's affairs here. [2]

Thomas Sheridan, to O'Bryen, revealing a pathetic state of affairs.
The Tradesmen of Paris were unwilling to deliver provisions at the house of the incognito Prince and Sheridan was unwilling to be seen carrying a dead fowl

4 Mar. Jeudi, 1745, *a huit heures du matin.*

Nous voice, Monsieur dans un nouvel embarras. Il n'y a point de Traitteur qui veuille nous donner à manger en gros. Si on veut aller chez eux, il nous en donneront tant que nous voudrons. Mais vous jugez bien que cela ne nous convient

---

[1] Sir Thomas's strokes.

[2] The King had written somewhat earlier (in 1741) that he regretted to "observe a want of harmony among my well-wishers and I am sorry Cardinal Fleury should have any reason to remark little jealousies," and again, "I am heartily sorry to find there should not be that confidence and good understanding that were to be wished amongst those concerned in my affairs at Paris."

To Sempill he wrote a little later, "A proper subordination of the Prince to me and of other people to us both would make everything go better and more smoothly than it has done for some time past." This condition of affairs was *never* achieved!

pas, et l'on n'ose traverser la Rue seulement avec un poulet. Ainsi je vous prie d'obtenir un ordre de Monsieur de Marville pour que le nommé Nancierre à l'hôtel Dauphin Rue Croix des Petits Champs, puisse apporter à manger en gros au Baron de Ziveebach autrement dit de Renfrew et la Compagnie à l'hôtel de Bretagne dans la même rue. Je profite volontiers de cette occasion pour m'informer de la santé de Madame d'Obryen. Monsieur le Baron revint hier au soir de Versailles en bonne santé et il n'est pas encore levé.

J'ai l'honneur d'être etc.

SHERIDAN.

—docketed "répondu le meme jour," so it is to be supposed that someone was found to supply the incognito Prince with provisions.

Letter from Prince Charles to John Murray [1] *(docketed "to Barclay," in Kelly's hand)*

Before June 1745.

You may very well remember when I saw you last, I had no great hopes of procuring any Succours from the French and asked you what we should do, if we could obtain none. Your answer was that then we should trust to Providence and see what we could do for and by ourselves—upon which I gave you my word to do so and pay you a visit this summer. It being at the same time agreed that this resolution should be kept as secret as possible and particularly from the King and Lord Marischall, the latter being never like to approve of or the other consent to any such thing. I am now resolved to be as good as my word and to execute a resolution which has never been a moment out of my thoughts, since I first took it in your presence. Had I received the several pacquets you

---

[1] John Murray of Broughton, who had visited him in Paris, and became his Secretary in Scotland, and afterwards a traitor.

sent me, the one by the Coffee house, the other by sea, things might have been better concerted—as it is, I venture myself and hope to find friends enough among you to do the same and I am persuaded if we can make ourselves Masters of the Highlands, and of both or even one of the Castles you mention, we shall be able to make such a stand as will encourage those abroad to give us the succours we want. I am promised a good ship to be ready before the end of the month, so that some time in the next you may depend upon my being landed, and therefore I would have you be in what readiness you can and lose no time to seize the Castles and whatever money you can find in the country by fair or foul means. It is above *two months* since I writt to the King to have the jewels pawned, but not being willing to let him into the secret, he made some difficulties, which will subsist no more after he hear of the resolution I have taken with which I shall not acquaint him till I am actually on board, and then I doubt not but he will send me whatever money can be raised on those jewels and a large sum which has been ready these many years past for such an occasion.—I have besides strong hopes of obtaining succours of one kind or another from France and Spain, for then I can employ many people and particularly Lord Marischall to sollicit openly for what I dare not hint at before to the very people I must now employ and depend on, having kept my resolution within my own breast and that of two other people [1] whom I intend to carry with me. Had I done otherwise it would have been the Town Talk of Paris and Madrid, and consequently never have come to anything, and whilst the matter was debating in such council the SUMMER would have been spent and perhaps a treaty set on foot, to facilitate which I should have been desired to take a trip to Rome, which rather than see again, I shall choose to leave my bones among you. I shall bring with me broadswords and a few other arms with some powder and ammunition but little

[1] These were apparently Sheridan and O'Sullivan.

money. For the same reason I can only send a hundred pounds to the person you mention in your letter to be in particular want of it. Had I known sooner of his circumstances I would have endeavoured to help him better.

I send you along with this the blank Commissions and letters you desire for different people, and acquaint Lord Aboyn that there is such a one for him, which I think better than sending it to him.

I think it likewise better for the sake of secrecy to bring the Duke of Atholl with me, than to propose to him what you mention,[1] for he shall know nothing of the matter until he is on board or at least on the point of embarking ; but send you in the meantime one for Johnson,[2] who is to command the Athol men till his arrival.

I send you with this my declaration which you must get printed and published at the moment hostilities are begun. That and my Commission of Regency must be printed together. Sir H. McL.[3] whom I lately sent with despatches to you has informed me that the Isles of Mull, Terybol Uist or Barrow are the best places to land in. You may therefore expect me at one or other of them and I would have you pre-pare accordingly for my reception and to let me know what measure I am to take immediately after my landing.

You may be assured that neither Lord S. nor Malloch [4] shall ever know anything of my dealings with you nor of this matter until it becomes no more a secret.

There is a short letter to Lochiel (copy on same sheet), "To M. Dan" :

"I had the several pacquets and letters designed for me come safe. You had heard from me before now and consequently

---

[1] That Tullibardine be told the plans !—This was *not* considered wise.
[2] The Chevelier Johnstone who wrote *Memoirs of the '45*.
[3] Sir Hector Maclean (who was already in prison !).
[4] Sempill and Balhaldy, whom the Prince thoroughly distrusted.

been better informed of everything that relates to me. I have now, in mine to Barclay acquainted him with my last determination, towards which I expect the concurrence of all my friends. Among the principal of these you may be sure I reckon upon you, and you may depend accordingly upon my friendship. When we meet I hope shall find opportunities to convince you of it."

From Undated Papers

Memoir written by Prince Charles for Murray some time in 1745

My Lord Traguair must come to London in order to concert with the English.

To see Dr. Barry [1] and talk to him about Money, and at the same tell him that it is the Prince's pleasure he shall acquaint nobody of his royal Highness's intentions but those agreed upon between him and Lord Traguair. The Prince's resolution of going to Scotland without Forces to be keept private from the King, Lord Marischal [2] and the Court of France, but at the same time to acquaint those in Scotland who may be trusted.

Silence to be recommended to Lord Elcho and Sir James Steuart with reference to Lord Marshall.

To endeavour to procure a considerable sum of Money for arms and in as short a time as possible. And to recommend to some particulars to have as much ready Money as they can upon the prince's landing.

Letters to the Prince to be addressed to "Mr. Burnet" sent to Clark Smith and forwarded by him to Mr. Waters.

The properest place for the Prince's landing to be considered and his Royal Highness acquainted of it as soon as possible.

To recommend to the Gentlemen with Highlands to provide as many broad swords as possible and to endeavour to get a number of Kilts. To desire the Highlanders to provide targets

---

[1] An English Jacobite agent in London.
[2] The Earl Marischal did not go to Scotland in 1745.

during the winter. To desire the low country gentlemen to provide as many horses as they can without suspicion.

If Money is got to purchase the arms let the gentlemen that give it pitch upon one to go to Holland and transact the affair.[1]

Added in the prince's handwriting :—to speke about Lord Panmure [2] and Lord Craford.[3]

Mr. Carnegie [4] or somebody to come about the arms.

To speke and agree with Mr. Moore about the correspondence and that it should be safe.

Barclay for Murray and *Burnet* for the Prince (all in Prince's hand.)

Of the other persons mentioned in this letter, the following details are interesting, Lord Traquair, Charles, 5th Earl, was the man who as Lord Linton signed the letter of the "Sept Seigneurs écossais" to Cardinal Fleury in 1741, which certainly was one contributing cause of the Rising of 1745. The assurances which these lords gave to His Eminence the French Minister that Scotland was ready to rise in favour of the Stuarts if a French expedition was sent over to co-operate with them certainly induced the French Court to invite Prince Charles to France in 1743, which invitation he accepted in January 1744. Traquair was one of those who did not fulfil his promises, he

---

[1] It is known that one John Blau was sent by the Duke of Perth on this affair and successfully bought the arms in Holland.

[2] Lord Panmure, nephew of the Jacobite peer of 1715, being second son of Harry Maule of Kellie. The peerage, which was attainted, had been revived in his favour but became extinct.

[3] John, 20th Earl of Crawford, fought at Dettingen and Fontenoy. Like the Lord Panmure of the period, he was never a Jacobite.

[4] Probably James Carnegie of Bonnymoon, who distinguished himself at the capture of the Hazard in Montrose Basin, and also later by escaping from the hulks in the Thames, where the Jacobite prisoners were kept under such terrible conditions, after Culloden.

failed to deliver letters [1] and "Mr. Evidence" Murray, even, was able to gird at him for "hiding his dirty head" instead of joining the Prince when the latter did come. He, Traquair, was eventually arrested in England and confined for some time in the Tower where he and his wife Theresa made the life of the Governor of that fortress a burden to him. He was released and died in 1764.

Clerk Smith was Charles Smith, a banker in Boulogne.

Prince Charles to his father, dated from FITZJAMES (*the house of his cousin, the Duke of Fitzjames, seven posts distant from Paris*).

12 *April* 1745.

SIR,

I have received yours of the 23rd March. I am very sorry to see by it that Strickland [2] has given you again occasion of mentioning his name. I can't but do justice on this occasion to Obadiah (*Strickland*) in saying that hitherto he has given me all reason to be pleased with him in every way, which makes me fiere that some people have done him injustice towards you. What I know for crrtain is that sume people here have sed that I had nobody at all about me that was discreet. I don't realy remember that Kely [3] or Morrice (*Sempill*) said

---

[1] Lord Traquair not only read and destroyed a letter of John Murray's which he had promised to deliver or send to the Earl Marischal, but having undertaken to send a packet from England to the Prince, kept it for some weeks and then returned it to Murray, saying he had been unable to find anyone to convey it from London to France. This was merely because he would not pay the expense of a messenger. Murray blames him entirely for the Prince's unexpected arrival, as the undelivered letter would have explained how unready the Scots were to rise.

[2] Francis Strickland, the only Englishman among the Prince's little band of seven to land in Moidart. He had been Prince Henry's tutor, as his father had been King James's, but was distrusted by the King. He died in Carlisle, January 1st, 1746.

[3] Probably Balhaldy.

anything particular. I know them to be dangerous people, and might certainly do a great deal of hurt if disgusted. I am very young and it is very hard for me to foresee many things, in which all I aim at is at leste not to do harm, not being able to do good.

I lay myself at your Majesty's feet most humbly asking blessing and remaining your most dutiful son.

CHARLES P.

Prince Charles to his father

19 *April* 1745.

My want of experience is what I two much know & would fain get as soon as possible, for to be able to serve you & our country more effectually & to purpose, which is all that I am putt in this world for. It would be endless for me to write & for you to rede, if I were to enter into all the little Malice and douings of Lumley (*Sempill*) & Mallock (*Balhaldy*) & sum others. It is certain they both never say to me anything to the purpose. I believe because they have nothing to say, which makes them both avoid seeing & writing to me as much as possible. You see by this what they are—& that their heds are filled with nothing but malice & spite. I lay myself at your feet.

Sempill and Balhaldy were the two Jacobites in Paris, with the exception of his own special representative, Daniel O'Bryen, whom King James trusted the most.

Sempill had all along been working more or less in opposition to the Prince, certainly to his Irish advisers, and writes on July 13th, voicing his own horror and annoyance at "the resolution the Prince has taken and executed without my knowledge," i.e. the secret expedition to Scotland and adds "I am afraid there is little room to hope he will succeed." One feels that he probably did not even wish this enterprise, undertaken entirely on the Prince's own, with the aid of his Irish friends, to be a success !

Prince Charles to Edgar, ten days before he started for Scotland

NAVARRE (*a seat of the Duke of Bouillon,
the Prince's cousin*).

12 *June* 1745.

Having writt a long letter to the King, I chose to refer some particulars to be added to yours, which are these. I owe Waters about 60 thousand livres part of which went to the payment of my debts last winter which the F.C.[1] did not think fit to complete. Young Waters has advanced me a hundred and twenty thousand livres and promised to pay several other things which I had referred to him : it will be absolutely necessary to remit the two sums immediately and young Waters desires that his money may be sent by Beloni [2] directly to himself, without letting the old man [3] know he made any such advance and whatever other money may be remitted for my use the best way will be to send it to the young one for the other I believe will be glad to be eased of that trouble. All this money I have employed in my present undertaking having bought 1500 fuses eteen hundred broadswords mounted, a good quantity of powder, Balls, flints, Durks, Brandy etc. and some hundred more of the fuses and broad sowards of which I cannot at present tell the exact number. I have also got twenty small field pieces two of which a mule may carry and my casset will be near four thousand louis d'ors. All these things will go to the frigate which carry's myself. She has twenty odd guns and is an excellent sailor and will be escorted by one and perhaps two men of war of about 70 guns each. It will appear strange to you how I should get these things without the knowledge of the

[1] French Court.   [2] The King's banker in Rome.
[3] His father, Waters senior.

126

F.C.   I employed one Rutlidge [1] and one Walsh [1] who are subjects.

The first got a grant of a man of war from the F.C. to cruise on the Coast of Scotland & is luckily obliged to go as far north as I do, so that she will escort me without appearing to do it. Walsh understands his business perfectly well & is an excelent seaman ; he has offered to go with me himself, the vessel being his own that I goe on board of ; he has also a man of war that will likewise go with me if she can be got ready in time & a frigate of 44 guns which he took lately from the English & is manning to be sent out with all expedition.   He lives at Nante & I expect a courrier every moment from him with an account that all is ready & then I must lose no time to get there & go directly on board.   If there be no danger of being stopt or discovered I shall write from there.   Adieu friend.   I hope it will not be long before you hear comfortable news ; in the meantime be assured of my constant friendship.

CHARLES P.

P.S.   I send you here also enclosed an authentick copy of what is to be printed & dispersed at my landing.   I have forgot also to mention that I intend to land at or about the Isle of Mull. I enclose you here also five letters and one open to yrself, all from Sir Thomas.

I here enclose you the King's and Duke's letters, one for Lord Dumbar and another for B Tencin.   if the bearer be one Piere I know him to be very honest and a good servant, Mac donald is his master, whom I carry with me [2] so the servant deserves to be taken care of.

Sheridan to O'Bryen (Daniel O'Bryen, the King's Agent in Paris, afterwards Lord Lismore, who had been so long in Paris that he was practically a Frenchman.   Sheridan here describes the

[1] Walter Rutlidge, who brought the vessel Elizabeth, and Antony Walsh who owned the Du Teillay. They were Irishmen.

[2] Aeneas Macdonald, the banker.

Prince's arrangements whereby his letters to his father an-
nouncing his departure for Scotland were to take so long upon
the way that there could be no possibility of a reply reaching
him. The messenger was to go via Avignon and invite the
veteran Ormonde to join the Expedition. Also the Earl
Marischal. And Henry Stafford was sent into Spain on a
mission which was to produce money but no troops and, like
the French money, it arrived too late to save the Cause)

12 *June* 1745.

Le Prince envoie un Courier pour Rome, avec ordre de
passer par Avignon pour y remettre diverentes lettres. Il
écrit à Mylord Marishall pour qu'il se rende d'abord à Paris et
lui envoi une lettre pour le Marquis d'Argenson. J'ai laisse
chez Monsieur Waters un memoire cachete [1] pour vous etre
rendu des que vous le demanderai. Vous jugerai s'il peut-
être de quelque usage. Je crois que Monsieur d'Argenson l'a
déjà vu. Le Prince a encore écrit au Duc d'Ormonde pour
l'engager a se rendre à Paris mais a dire vrai l'on doute fort
qu'il soit en état de le faire.[2] S'il l'entreprend je n'ai que faire
de vous rien dire pour le manière dont il en faudra user avec
lui. Le Prince a écrit a leur Majestés Catholiques pour leur
demander des secours et il a envoye Stafford en Espagne avec
ces lettres qu'il doit consigner au Chevalier Geraldin. Je me
flatte que Madame O'Bryen (a qui il fait bien des compliments) voudra bien employer son credit en ce pays la pour lui
faire obtenir une reponse favorable. Il est vrai qu'il n'en peut
guère espérer des Troupes, mais il demande du moins qu'on
lui envoie des armes, des munitions, de l'argent et des officiers.

Nous emmenons avec nous le duc d'Athol qu'on demande
forte dans ce pays-la. On a trouve moyen d'embarquer avec
nous de quoi armer deux milles hommes avec de la Poudre,
du Plomb etc., et provision, on nous a aussi promis une
vingtaine de ces petites pieces qu'on appelle vis de mulets, et

[1] This memorial is at Windsor.
[2] He was nearly 80 years old, and died in November.

que nous appellons, s'il vous plaît, autant de pièces de "Canon." Nous avons aussi quelques peu d'espèces tonnantes. Pour la personne du Prince elle est assez bien équippée et il ne lui manque rien de ce qui lui peut-être necessaire.

Letters of the Prince just before starting for Scotland

The Prince to O'Bryen

NAVARRE. 16 June, 1745.

I have received yrs of ye 13th Cur. and in it the news of ye Battle.[1] It is not esy to foresee if it will prove good or bad for our affairs. I find the situation & country here so agreeable as also the People's here procuring me all diversions possible that has made me prolong this first gant of mine here. I expect a distincter account of this Battle which if you geat, you will send it to me under cover to Mr. Kelly as I mentioned to you in my last.

CHARLES P.

My compliments to yr lady.

In the next letter to O'Bryen of June 20th from the same place, the Prince says he has received O'Bryen's of the 18th ; (the latter seems to have been a very good correspondent, but his letters are now somewhat illegible). The Prince says, "I design to go today to a party of pleasure that I have which is to see a little of the country hereabouts as La Trappe, near by Rowan," and that he returns to Paris in a few days ; this was, of course, a blind as he went privately to Nantes where his chosen followers joined him singly within the next few days.

The following letters were written after the Prince had left Nantes and while he was waiting at Belle Isle to sail for Scotland.

[1] Fontenoy, May 11th, 1745, where Maréchal Saxe defeated Cumberland.

The Prince to Edgar

26 June 1745.

I write you this for to make my excuse to Grevill & Hicks [1] for not writing to them this poste. Howell [2] is going up & down seeing the Country and at the same time doing sumthing very much for Gerard's [3] interest which I cannot explain at present but shall as soon as I can in safety and it is this that hinders Howell from wryting this Poste as he would wish. I am, thank God in perfect health and having nothing more that I can add at present, shall remain.

ISHAM.

On 28 June, old Sir Thomas shows himself full of glee that they are at last " nearly off " and promises to write again as soon as they shall have reached Scotland, though he wonders, not unnaturally, how the letters will get back from there. It was in fact, another fortnight before the expedition really left French shores.

Thomas Sheridan to O'Bryen when they had actually started for Scotland

A NANTES. le 28 Juin 1745.

Je suis persuadé, Monsieur, que vous aurez été surpris d'avoir été si longtems sans recevoir de mes nouvelles, mais par mes deux autres du 12 de ce mois que vous recevrez en même tems que celle-ci, vous en verrez bien la raison. Celle que vous m'avez fait l'honneur de m'écrire du même jour, le 12, me fut remise avant hier par Mons. le Baron qui était arrivé ici le soir précédent, en parfait santé. Quand il s'y seroit rendu plûtot cela n'auroit servi de rien le vent ayant été toujours contraire. Nous en espérons maintenant quelque changement,

---

[1] The King and Duke of York.   [2] Himself.
[3] Scotland.

et nous croions être à la veille de notre depart. Nous avons un petit bâtiment qu'on nous assure être un très bon voilier et nous sommes escorter pas un vaisseau de Guerre de soixtane et six pièces de Canon, parfaitement bien armé. Vogue la Galere. Dès que nous serons debarquis, je ne manquerai pas de vous en faire part, mais Dieu sait comment les lettres vous parviendront. J'espère pourtant, que l'on trouvera de tems en tems des occasions de maintenir la correspondance."

In Prince Charles's handwriting to Edgar

30 *June* 1745.

I write you in this manner again to make excuses in Mr. Howell's name for not wryting to Grevill and Hicks, he being so very busy. Do not be alarmed if even you do not heare from me next post—or may be to, at firthest. You may be shure of my impatience to let you no more fully the reason of this hiding of Howell's which you may possibly happen to no before this but imperfectly, by not being writ by him and by consequence not so distinct as when it will cum from himself, which if not before will arrive very soon after you receive this ; in the meantime for Gods sake let none of his Correspondants be in pain, for he enjoys perfect good health and is in high spirits. Adieu Friend.

(sig) JENKINS.

The Prince then actually set sail for Scotland, with his seven companions. Sir Thomas Sheridan, Sir John Macdonald, John O'Sullivan and George Kelly—all Irish ; the Marquis of Tullibardine and Aeneas Macdonald—Scots ; and Francis Strickland, the Englishman. There were also with him, the Abbé Butler as Chaplain, Duncan Buchanan, clerk to Aeneas Macdonald, Antony Walsh, the owner of the ship, Michele Vezzosi, the Prince's faithful valet, who had already escaped from Scotland nearly thirty years before, with Lord Nithsdale,

Donald Cameron, a retainer of old Lochiel to act as pilot, and three others of the Prince's household. A slender force indeed with which to set out to conquer Scotland as was very nearly accomplished.

Prince Charles to the King

ST. LAZAIRE [*sic*] AT YE MOUTH OF YE LOIRE.

ye 2nd of July 1745.

SIR,

The contrary winds that have been blowing hitherto have difered my Embarking which will be this afternoon at Sevem for to go to the redevau of ye man of war of 67 guns, and 700 men aboard as also a company of sixty volonteers all gentlemen whom I will probably geat to land with me, I mean to stay which tho' few will make a shew, they having a prety uniform. The number of Arms are just as I mentioned in my last of ye 12 that goes with this, except they augmentation I was in hopes of is of a hundred or to less than I expected which is no ods.

I keep this open and do not send it until I am ferely set of from Bell Isle, Idest, the Randevous so that I may add a note to it iff being sea sick does not hinder, iff it does Sir Thomas will suply in mentioning what more may uccor. It is a mortification to me to want so many of ye Packets which are lying at Paris becase of ye daly expectation of parting. We have nothing to do now but to hope in ye Almyties favouring uss. And recompencing our troubles which as you may see by the nature of ye thing were not small. I hope in God my next will bring comfortable news. In ye meantime I remain, laying myself at your Majesty's feet most humbly asking blessing your most dutiful son,

CHARLES P.

(The original of this letter was removed from among the Stuart papers by the Librarian, Richard Holmes, by the orders of Queen Victoria, March 29th, 1873.)

Prince Charles to Edgar

St. Lazaire [*sic*] *ye 2nd July* 1745.

This being the Laste note I shall write this side of ye Seas, I not faill to give you adieu in it, making my compliments to Lord Dunbar and to as many of my friends as you shall think convenient & proper. I enclose here to letters for King & Duke which will go together with the great packet of the 12th last, as soon as I am freely sailed off from Belle Isle. I hope in God wee shall soon meet, which I am resolved will not be but att home. In ye meantime I remain all yours,

Charles P.

Belleisle à la Rade ye 12 *July* 1745.

After having waited a week here, not without a little anxiety we have at last got ye escorte I expected which is just now arrived, *Id Este* a ship of 68 gun & 700 men aborde. I am, thank God, in very good health but have been a little seasick & expect to be more so, but it does not keep me much abed. I find the more I struggle against it the better. Pray make my excuses along with my most humble duty to the King for not writing, not having anything more particular to add but what is here, I reckoned it would suffice. My excuses also to the dear Duke with many compliments. My compliments again to all friends and give you adieu with nothing more to add, & being in a great hurry

C. P.

This is actually his last letter written before leaving France.

Sir Thos. Sheridan to Dan. O'Bryen, same day

De la rade de Belleisle le 12 *Juillet* 1745.

Voici Monsieur la quatrième et, comme je l'espère, la dernière lattre que vous recevrea de nous jusqu'à notre debarquement. Vous savez de quoi nous aurions alors besoin.

133

Monsieur Walsh après nous avoir débarqué, compte se rendre à Hambourg et de là à Amsterdam et à Dunkerque. Vous pourrez lui écrire par les addresses suivantes. On cas que vous veuillez envoyer quelques secours, il est homme à tout entreprendre. Il prend le nom de Granville.

A Mons. Mons de Grandeville
    chez Messr. Gran et Michel, Négociants à Hambourg
    chez Messr. Grae et Libant, Négociants à Amsterdam
    chez Messr. Rutledge et Compagni à Dunkerque.
J'ai l'honneur d'être etc.

Prince Charles to the King, after arrival in Scotland, asking for a title of Count for Walsh

Abord du vaisseau le du Tellier à l'Ancre dans la Baye de Loughaylort

(The correct name of the vessel was Du Teillay, after the Commandant at Nantes. In Scottish records she appears as "La Doutelle" !)

le 2 Août. O.S. 1745.

SIRE,

J'ai reçu des services si importans de Monsieur Antoine Walsh qu'il n'y a rien que je ne me croie oblige de faire pour lui en témoigner mon agrément. Ainsi je lui ai promis d'emploier tout mon credit auprès de Votre Majesté pour lui obtenir le titre de Comte d'irlande.[1] Il est issu d'une fort bonne famille, très en état de soutenir la dignité de ce nouveau titre et n'est pas besoin d'autre chose. C'est la première Grace qui je vous demande depuis mon arrivée dans ce pai ci. J'espère bien que ce ne sera pas la dernière, mais en tout cas je vous supllie de me l'accorder. Je la regarderai comme une obligation particulière accorde a votre très obéissant fils.

CHARLES P.

[1] This was granted in the same year.

134

Prince Charles to O'Bryen, sent by the Abbé Butler
(Sunday)

LOUGH AYLORT, *ye 4 August* 1745.

SIR—I am thank God arrived here in perfect good health but not with little trouble and danger as you will hear by the bearer who has been along with me all along, that makes it useless for me to give my accomptes and particulars on that head. I am joyned here by brave people as I expected as I have not yet set up the standard I cannot tell ye number, but that will be in a few days as soon as ye armes are distributed, at which we are working with all speed. I have not as yet got the return of ye message sent to ye lowlands, but expect it very soon. Iff they all joyn or at leste all those to whom I have sent commissions to at request, everything will go to a wish.

Butler's Own Account

Not much has been written about the Abbé Butler. It is known that he was a relative of the Duke of Ormonde and made one of the party which sailed with Prince Charles for Scotland on June 22nd, 1745. Both Sheridan and the Prince testify to his usefulness on the voyage. He did not apparently *land* in Scotland, but remained on the ship with Walsh, and with him returned to the Continent, first to Amsterdam, and then to France.

Sheridan to Edgar

AT ANCHOR IN LOUGH AYLORT.

Aug. the 2nd O.S. (1745).

A Mons. Edgar à Rome.

DR. SIR,

The Bearer of this, Mr. James Butler, has been chaplain on our ship in his passage hither and has been in many ways very

useful to us. He is otherwise a man of very good life and conversation. The Prince therefore makes it his earnest request
to his Majesty that he would be pleased to obtain for him some
simple benefice in ye Province of Brittany where he has been a
great while and is very well known. He will tell you all the
particulars of our Voiage which I have not yet had time to doe.

I am etc.

Ye most obedient and humble sevt

THO. SHERIDAN.

*Copy of a Letter wrote by Abbé Butler to his Grace the Duke of
Ormonde, his relative (some say his father).*

(The Abbé puts no day to his letter, it probably took several
days to write.)

Aug. 1745.

As I was charged by Mr. Kelly to give your Grace a full
account of what passed in our voyage to Scotland along with
Prince Charles I hope your Grace will permit me to honour
myself in giving you ye full particulars. We parted Belleisle
the 15 Juy. last—little winds to calm till on ye 20 we met
an English man of war in Lat. 47.57N. 8 39 leagues from the
Lizard. The Captain was called Brett and the ship the *Lyon*
of $5\frac{1}{2}$ Guns from Brest, armed by particulars to serve as a
convoy. The Prince and his retinue were on board a small
frigate of 16 guns, the English man of war attacked us about
$5\frac{1}{2}$ in the evening and the battle continued till 10 at night
with valour and fire on both sides. Its true the french man
continued firing a $\frac{1}{4}$ of an hour longer than the Englishman.
I was on board the small frigate with the Prince. Mr. Walse
who was owner and chief on board did not think it proper
to fire our guns or engage in ye battle for fear the Prince
might come to any mischance, however as the Englishman
sailed better and doubling the French man of war, fired first
his chace gun at us, and, as he passed by, his stern gun, but

136

caused no damage but what we received from his musketry that pierced our sails. With much ado we could gain on the Prince to retire—so seeing his resolution and for fear of any accident we retired entering until the battle was over and then bore down and spoke to ye French ship who told us they had about 300 men killed and wounded, and consequently were obliged to go back to Brest. Seeing their interest, we took our leave choosing rather to dye than return that way and committed ourselves to Providence who after several allarms from the different ships we met with, conducted us to the Island of Barra in Scotland, when thinking to get some Intelligence of what passed in Scotland we met nobody we could confide in, so we got a pilot on board and resolved for the Main land—but unfortunately at one in the afternoon perceived a Man of War—at least we took her such and immediately got in again between the Isle of Barra and Whyst. And as she followed us closely, we put the Prince and his company on shore being a very wet dirty night and the wind not favourable for coming in, the Man of war kypt off and on about 2 leagues from the entrance of ye harbour, which induced our Captain to send a person to pray Ye prince and his company to come on board but the weather was so bad and the seas so high without that bay that it was impossible. Next morning (*July* 21, *O.S. Aug.* 4 *N.S.*) one Mr. McDonald (*Boisdale*) came to visit ye Prince and after his compliments, assured us all the matter was discovered, and insisted upon our returning back, saying positively he had such orders from all of ye Prince's friends. We all came on board and held council upon this information to see what was to be done. The Prince declared he would rather die than depart upon so slight a motive and that he was resolved not to return till he had seen his friends who as he was perswaded had a different opinion of the affair. This concluded, our difficulty was how to escape the ship that lay cruizing off and on for us and after deliberation we resolved at all hazard to goe for Scotland and accordingly got under sail when it grew dark, tho' the other was in sight of us at sunsett. As fortune was pleased that we got into a bay on the mainland called Loughanou right opposite to the Isle of Egg. There we announced the arrival of ye Prince and told them that as he risked on their account he expected they would adhere and correspond with their promises. All those that then appeared answered that their lives and fortunes were at his disposal and that he may depend upon their attachment and fidelity and entreated that he would remain quiet and keep alle secret untill they had advised all their friends. This he assented to and immediately Mr. McDonald of Killough (*Kinloch Moidart*) parted for Edinburgh and the low country to communicate his arrival (*July* 26. *Aug.* 6). In a little time after the Camerons, the Stewards and the Scots with all ye McDonalds, with many others I don't recollect, came to assure H.R.H. that they were ready to march and follow him whenever he thought proper. Mr. Clan Renolds who made the same offer parted for the Isle of Skye with design to engage Sir Alexander McDonald and Mr. McCloud into the party. In a few days they despatched a messenger to know if the Prince had a power signed by the King his father. Having assured them he had and having shewed it to ye Bishop of ye place it was the common opinion they would shortly join ye rest who are determinedly resolved to die or conquer. Mr. Murray who was agent in the affair before our arrival was hourly expected and with him an account how matters stood in ye low country. All the arms and ammunition we landed were to be divided in a few days time. What the people complain of Mostly is that the prince did not bring arms and money enough. I assure your Grace both articles would be very requisite. We left them 18 small field pieces as they designed Fort William in their way. The affairs have a very promising look, and numbers crowding daily to offer themselves. They complain they have no man of note but the prince to head 'em which greatly dispirits 'em. Provisions were also very scant, the moisture of the year having occasioned a very late harvest but God seems to favour them in all things, for the very day we parted we met three English ships loaded with oatmeal, amounting in all to about 400 tons we took 'em as prizes and despatched 'em to the Prince which will sufficiently supply for some time. As much as I can perceive things could not be in a more smiling attitude. The Prince shows a vast deal of resolution and undauntedness which prodigiously pleases the people, and we supposed the disaffection Sir Alex McDonald and Mr. McCloud shewed was but a feint to know if the Prince was stedfast and determined and as they find him to their wish there is no doubt but they will soon joyn him. The Prince was pleased to assure the people that he hoped by their bravery and fidelity to surmount all difficulties and that for his part he would give them daily proof of his love and tenderness. The people were charmed at his goodness and declared they'd forgoe all earthly concerns to sustain his right. Sir Hector McLean was taken prisoner at Edinburgh and conducted to London, the Motive of his detention was some letters that were found at his lodgings. This accident imperilled the Prince's party before his arrival but as the Government could make no sense of what they contained immediately after his first tryal which was a little before we parted Scotland, he was remitted to the Tower till further information.

About two days before our departure—they made an attempt to seize the Duke of Perth,[1] but he luckily escaped in Highland dress—all this was upon Suspicion—not one of ye opposite party knowing of ye Prince being in ye Country. I expect some time after our departure the affairs were made public as they had three thousand choice men ready to march with the Nobility at their head. They could have had double the number but wanted arms. It is evident and

[1] See p. 104.

moraley probable that the least assistance from France or Spain at the present happy conjuncture would entirely terminate our misfortunes and crown the glorious attempt with success, and are persuaded by the situation of affairs in Europe and the divisions and dissatisfaction in Great Brittain a very small supply would be sufficient. We arrived in Scotland the 3ᵈ of Aug. N.S. and parted, ye Prince and his company in perfect health the 19ᵗʰ and after a very difficult journey arrived safely at Amsterdam the 3ᵈ of 7 ᵇᵉʳ N.S.

Edgar to Abbé Butler

8 Nov. 1745.

The occasion for my writing to you is to desire you would be at the pains to write in French as particular an account as you can of all you know of the Prince personally from the beginning of his expedition to the time you left him in Scotland, mentioning the small number of Gentlemen & servants that embarked with H.R.H. & every little Circumstance relating to him you can call to mind. That you may do this the better I shall tell you in confidence the use proposed for such a paper, Mr Voltaire the famous poet is I hear desirous to make a poem on H.R.H. & his enterprise & wants material to go upon and you can furnish him with these better than anybody I know. Pray set about it without loss of time and take care that it be very distinct. When you have done it send it to Col. O'Bryen unto whom you may write under Mr. Water's cover & I shall be glad you send me a copy of it that I may see the poet's art in cooking it up when the Poem comes out.

The Abbé James Butler to Edgar

NANTES. 5 Jan. 1746.

SIR.—I take the liberty of sending you the enclosed, according as you were pleased to order me (*this is the English account of the voyage to Scotland, already given)* [1] & pray you will be so kind as to accept my best wishes upon your prosperous & happy New Year, As also to the rest of your Gentlemen in general. We have all the expectation possible of our dear Prince's conquest in England this year, & have so many flying letters of late that wee cannot tell what to think of them. Some doe assure us the Prince has bet Ligonier & routed all his army—& that hee tooke the Duc of Cumberland & remitted him prisoner to the Towne of Liverpoole, which he is now Master of, as also of Chester, all which merits confirmation. We also had an account that the Duc of Richelieu parted from Dunkerque along with 8000 men the last ultimo & that the Duc of York & the rest were to part from Boulogne the first of this month, others say they are countermanded—but it's certain all letters agree about the Prince's great success.

After the arrival in Scotland

Thos. Sheridan to O'Bryen, announcing the landing and the adherence of the Highlanders to the Prince, though giving no details of the voyage. Being more concerned with the help O'Bryen is to send. The Prince himself wrote to King Louis.

Le six Août 1745.

Nous voici Monsieur arrivés enfin en Ecosse. Je n'ai pas le tems de vous marquer les particularites de notre voiage, quoiqu'assez intéressants et en débarquant je ne trouve rien de nouveau à ajouter à ce que je vous avez écrit avant que de partir. Nous avons trouvé des amis qui nous promettent de tout risquer avec nous et c'est maintenant le tems de travailler pour nous faire avoir au plutôt du secours. Je ne doute point que vous n'aier déjà commencé à vous donné des mouvements pour cet effet. S.A.R. m'ordonne de vous faire bien des amitiés de sa part et de vous faire savoir combien il compte sur votre zêle et votre attachment pour lui. Il écrit par cette occasion au Roi T.C. et j'écris par ces ordres

[1] The account in French must have been written later, and is not extant.

à Mons. d'Argenson. Vous avez ici une lettre pour M. le C-l de Tencin. S.A.R. m'ordonne d'ajouter qu'il persiste toujours dans sa résolution de vaincre ou de mourir ici.

Ten weeks later

Thos. Sheridan to Edgar

HOLYROOD HOUSE. Oct. 25, 1745.

DR. SIR.—The pleasure of dating a letter to you from this place, & least you should forget my hand, or think I have forgotten you, are the inducements for me to write you this. I had begun a journal of all our proceedings which I intended to send you but could never find time to finish or copy it. For publick news about us, I suppose you will find enough in the Gazettes—for politicks the Gentleman who transmits this will take care to inform you and for what relates personally to the prince I have written fully to Ld. Dunbar, so I shall only desire you to make my compliments to all friends, particularly Ld. Dunbar, Dr. Robert, to whose brother I am much obliged. If I had time I should write both to him and Vinciguerra, but you cannot conceive what a hurry I live in, & I believe it will scarce be otherwise till we meet at London. In the meantime I am as ever, Dr Sir,

> Yrs most sincerely,
>
> T. S.

Early in the following year, he was less cheerful.

Sir Thos. Sheridan after Falkirk to Col. O'Bryen. In this he speaks more plainly and voices his disillusionment, comparing the Prince's expedition to an old man ready to die, but trusts O'Bryen will be able to send the wherewithal to keep it alive. The miserable inadequacy of what had been sent roused his ire.

21 Jan. 1746.

Venons maintenant, monsieur, au fond de nos affaires. Il n'y a pas longtemps qui je vous écrivais ce que j'en pensois.

J'espère que vous avez reçu ces lettres. En tout cas je vous le répéte ici en deux mots. Nous sommes justement dans le cas de ce viellard qui disoit, Je me porte bien, Graces à Dieu, mais je mourirai bientôt. La différence est qu'il ne tient qu'à nos alliés de faire changer la dernière partie de cette sentence et de mettre fin à toutes nos craintes. Mais il ne faut pas perdre du tems, surtout à nous envoyer de l'argent.

Ce sera un cordial qui nous poura soutenir quelque tems et sans quoi nous creverons quelque beaujour comme un vieux.

Mais il ne faut pas s'amuser à la moutarde.

Pendant qu'on envoie des millions en Allemagne et en Italie, on crois faire beaucoup pour nous en nous envoyant cent mille écus. C'est nous donner l'aumone. S'il nous était permis de faire la quête dans les églises de Paris, je suis persuadé que nous en eussions ramassé bien davantage. Si l'on eut ajouté deux mortiers avec quelques centaines de bombes au petit Train d'Artillerie qu'on nous a envoyé vous ne saurez croire l'avantage que nous en aurions tiré.

. . . Dans l'état ou nous nous trouvons—obligé de risquer tout, avec la vie précieuse de notre Prince, sur le sort incertain d'une Bataille. Si nous le perdons, tout est fini pour nous, si nous le gagnons c'est pour avoir quelques semaines de relache et puis recommencer sur nouveaux frais contre un Monarque encore maître de deux Royaumes entieres. Pensez bien, Monsieur, à tout cela et faites le bien sentir a qui il appartiendra.

Sheridan to O'Bryen, six weeks before Culloden. Again he is sarcastic over the late arrival of the consignment of money from France which did actually fall into the hands not of the English but of the Whigs of the north under Lord Reay. He makes the suggestion that the French would do better to send larger ships. Apparently the frigates which subsequently brought the

143

Loch Arkaig gold were able to give quite a good account of themselves in a two-to-three fight

INVERNESS, *le 2 Mars* 1746.

Monsieur. Vous apprendrez de M. Warren, à qui S.A.R. a donné un brevet de Colonel, et qu'il a fait depuis un de ses Aides de Camp, l'Etat de nos affaires que je n'ai pas le tems de vous expliquer en détail. Nous apprenons bien qu'on nous a envoyé des secours de France, mais on s'y est pris un peu tard—l'Ennemi nous ayant enlevé tout la côte où ils pouvaient aborder. Ainsi nous craignons fort qu'ils ne soient ou retourner ou tomber entre les mains des Anglais.

De tout ce que l'on a envoié il n'est arrivé que six-vingt hommes du Regiment de Fitzjames et une petite cassette d'or qui a été débarquée et enfoncée en Terre, d'ou Dieu sait si nous la retireront jamais. Nous comptons avoir dans peu de jours une autre bataille à livrer. Si nous la gagnons nous redeviendrons Maitres de la Cote. En attendant il faut que les vaisseaux viennent débarquer au nord de l'embouchure de la Speye. L'argent est la chose dont nous avons le plus de besoin, quoique tout le reste nous soit nécessaire.

Si au lieu de petits Batimens on envoiait des Vaisseaux de 30 ou 40 cannons, ils pourraient se défendre, car les l'Anglais n'ont pas encore envoyé de gros, dans ces passages. On dit qu'un officier de ceux qui ont débarqué de la dernière fregatte parle d'embarquement fait à Brest pour l'Ouest de l'Angleterre —mais comme nous ne l'ayons pas encore eu, l'on ne sait ce qu'il en faut croire, tout ce que crains qu'on n'est pas encore perdu entièrement de vue la grande entreprise qui devait se faire dans le voisinage de Londres. Mais envin il en sera ce qu'il pourra. Le Prince a du moins tenu plus qu'il n'avait promis malgré toutes les difficultés qu'il a eu à surmonter. La Providence lui a jusqu'ici tenu lieu de tout et j'espère qu'elle continuera jusqu'à la fin. J'ai l'honneur

of absolute necessity for mine and the Prince's service that I should have some free discourse with you, and so give you occasion of explaining many things to me, for I am unwilling to think that you are alter'd towards me, and should be sorry to have reason to be it towards you, after all the pains you have taken in the service of a Son so dear to me, and to whom I shall write about your coming here, that he may not wonder not to find you in France, and when you go back to him, I am sure both he and you will thank me for having sent for you. Mr. Waters has my order to give you 1,500 Livres for your journey when you call for it.

Sheridan's own defence of himself came three weeks later, not of course in answer to the letter from the King just given, but to the previous one received by him on August 12th.

It is evident that the King had reproached him with various derelictions of duty. First for not warning him of the Prince's intention to start for Scotland. Without doubt he had been prevented from doing this by the express commands of his young master. Secondly, in not preventing Strickland's forming part of the Prince's household and expedition to Scotland. For this, according to O'Sullivan, he really was responsible, and, thirdly, for having left the Prince after his defeat. The poor old man took all these reproaches very much to heart, and we can picture his sad journey through France and Italy apparently alone, each step taking him farther from his beloved Charles, wherever the latter might be, and ending in a somewhat cool reception by Charles's father and friends, who now only viewed the expedition to Scotland in the light of its ultimate failure, never having tasted the joy of its glorious beginning and brief heyday of glory.

Sheridan only survived for another three months, dying of apoplexy in Rome November 23rd, 1746, leaving as his heirs two elderly sisters who drew pensions for many years afterwards.

The letter about to be given is really one of the most pathetic in the whole collection. The old tutor almost apologizes for not having committed suicide. He wrote at the same time to Prince Charles, and, after his arrival in Rome, one more letter of tender affection, on the news of the Prince's safe arrival at Morlaix reaching Rome.

(*Endorsed "Sir Thomas Sheridan" to the King.*)

NAVARRE. *August 14th* (1746).

SIR,

On Thursday the 12th I received the honor of your Majestys commands with which I shall not fail to complie. Yesterday I came hither to acquaint His Royal Highness the Duke with them and to know if he had any orders to give me on this occasion. Tomorrow I intend to return to Paris and shall set out from thence towards the end of the week. The pleasure of laying myself at your Majesty's feet wou'd make the journey more agreable to me were I not like to continue all that time under the cruel uncertainty in which I have so long been as to the Prince. This has been the only reason of my silence, for having once given an account of all I knew concerning his Royal Highness, and how I came to part with him, which I did in my first letter to Ld. Dunbar, I cou'd not find any thing else to say, that I cou'd think worth yr Majesties notice; and it has not been without reluctance that I have ever seen any of my acquaintance here or writ a line to those of them that are elsewhere. If it had been possible I cou'd have content to be so long buried alive.

As for Mr. Strickland I know nothing of his conduct here.

When he was sent for, the Prince did not know that he was fallen so far under your Majesties displeasure and when he was known to be arrived at Avignon and to have thoughts of settling there: the Prince, who by this time had heard farther from your Majestie, began to flatter himself with the hopes that the letter by which he was called to Paris had miscarried. So that it was a very disagreeable surprise when he notified his arrival at Paris, where the Prince declined seeing him, and only ordered him to attend him at Nantes. There, to the best of my remembrance, he saw him but once before we embarked, and that in the company of five or six Persons. Upon our first landing in Scotland we separated and went to different places at several miles distance from one another; so that Strickland never was with the Prince but when the whole retinue was together. On our march to Edinburgh he grew so ill, that he was forced to remain near Stirling and we really believed we shou'd never see him more. However he overtook us time enough to have a share in the Battel of Gladsmuir, and seemed for some time after to be in a fair way of recovery. During our stay at Edinburgh and our March for England he had the care of the Prince's equipage and table,[1] for which there was no body so fit, but that gave him no place of intimacy with H.R.H. who upon reading the Letters wch he received from you at Edinburgh, resolved to send him into France whenever he cou'd meet with a proper opportunity. By what time we got possession of Carlisle he was again fallen so ill, that it was impossible for him to advance farther. So he remain'd there till our return, where we found him reduced to a perfect Skeleton and ready to be tapt for the second time the day we left it. However he lived long enough to fall alive into the ennemies hands, and perhaps the ill usage he met with from them, might hasten his Death by two or three days. This, Sir, is all the account I can give of him. What he might do during the short time he re-

[1] He became the Master of the Household.

mained at Paris I know not, All I understood was, that he saw but very few People, and those chiefly such as were privy to our affairs and concerned in them.

I must now, Sir, in the humblest manner begg leave to tell your Majesty that I cou'd not without the greatest mortification observe something in your Majesty's letter, which looked as if you had conceived some umbrage against myself. Upon the sevierest recollection I can find nothing that cou'd give occasion for it, but my having concealed the Prince's design of going to Scotland. This is the only action of my whole life with relation to your Majestie on your affairs, which can give me the least scruple, and of my conduct in this I took the liberty to give you the best account I cou'd before I left this Country; and I was then in hopes that either success wou'd justifie the undertaking and the Prince at London intercede with your Majesty for my pardon, or that I shou'd perish in the attempt. I now think that tho' the event has proved so fatal, our first successes were sufficient to shew that they might have been compleat had they been tolerably seconded from abroad. As for my own Person, I never shrank from any danger which might have put an end to my days, but cou'd not find an opportunity of perishing unless I had either shot my self with my own hands or wilfully thrown myself into those of the Ennemy, of neither of which expedients I believe your Majesty wou'd have approved.

I had writ thus far when Sr. John Graeme came to my room and took occasion from his finding me writing to your Majesty to tell me that he had some time since received a letter from you, wherein you seemed to wonder at my silence and to believe it proceeded from that very apprehension which I have been just now mentioning. The favourable expressions which Sr. John told me you were pleased to make use of on this occasion make me more and more sensible of your Majesties great goodness, of which I have already received so many proofs. That I may still have the happiness to enjoy your good opinion is next to the Prince's safety the sincerest wish of

Sir,

Your Majesties

most humble, most obedient and

most dutiful Subject and Servant,

THO. SHERIDAN.

To Prince Charles also he writes much good advice, before his own departure for Rome.

Sir Thomas Sheridan to Prince Charles

Aug. 19 (1746).

SIR,

Notwithstanding a very long letter which I took the liberty to write to your Royal Highness some days ago, and wch you will receive at the same time with this, there are many things which have occurred to me since, and with which I think it is my duty to acquaint you. I shall begin with an account of my own departure from Scotland which was in the following manner.

Upon the receipt of your last letter dated April the 23rd. which was deliver'd to me by Mr. Hay together with one for the chiefs, I repaired to the side of a Lough where I found Mr. Murray and Loghiel with his Brother the Doctor, Major Kennedy and S^r. Stuart Threpland. I shewed Murray and Loghiel yr letter to the Chiefs, and whilst we were deliberating how to draw the remains of our broken forces together, an express from Ld. John found me out, and brought me letters from Abbé Butler and Nick Brown giving me an account of their arrival on the coast with some Arms, Ammunition and a considerable summ of money, none of which they said they wou'd consign to any body but me, conjuring me withall to make all the haste possible, for otherwise they shou'd be obliged to make off, for fear of being blocked up in ye Bay by the English Shipping. Upon perusal of this letter, Lochiel and Murray both desired me to make all the haste I cou'd to get the Cargo put on Shoar, and then to go on board my self in order to follow you, and in case I shou'd arrive before you to represent their condition to the Duke and to the Court of France.

Accordingly I went to the Seaside, where the first thing I saw were three English ships making for the Bay. That evening I got the money put on Shoar,[1] the Arms and Ammunition having been landed already. By this time I found the news of your departure was become publick, and every body was persuaded you were already in the Orkneys; but it was judged entirely wrong to go to look for you there, as I had a mind to do, for it was alledged that that wou'd be the way to draw all the English Shipping after us and by pointing out the place where you were supposed to be, render your escape impossible if you were not already gone off. Besides our Frigatts were foul, and, as it was alledged, began to be short of Provisions. So we resolved to go immediately on board as we did a little before break of day. Within half an hour the English Vessels bore down upon us, and an obstinate fight began, which lasted till noon when the English thought fit to bear away. After that engagement the reasons which had prevailed the night before, for making the best of our way to France, were become much stronger. Our Ships had suffer'd considerably, and were now in a much worse condition than before, either for fighting or sailing. So the rest of the day and the following night were spent in repairing them the best we cou'd, and early in the morning we set sail. The winds proved generally bad, and with much difficulty we reached Nantes after a voyage of three and twenty days.

Within two or three days after my arrival at Paris, Obryen

---

[1] The Loch Arkaig treasure, said to be 36,000 livres.

came to me from Flanders, where he had been to wait upon the Duke. We went together to Versailles, where I saw the Ministers, and gave them the best account I cou'd of the condition matters were in when I left Scotland, and assured them the cause might still be supported were sufficient succours sent in time. All the answer I got was that till they knew what was become of your Royal Highness, for whose safety they expressed a great deal of concern, they cou'd come to no resolution ; but the truth is they were so bent on the hopes of a Peace that they seemed to think little of taking any rigorous measures towards renewing the War. They have since sent several Ships from different places and by different ways to endeavour to bring you off, of all which you will have sufficient accounts from themselves, Obryen, and others. But I must not omit to inform you that the Cardinal had told me, *que nous avions fait plein de fauttes*, one thing which he instanced was that you had sent too many Agents and particularly wondered what occasion there was for sending Sr. James Stuart.[1] I replied that there was nothing more natural than when we were in the hands of the Scots and had found so many friends among them, to send one of themselves and a gentleman of such distinction to take care of your affairs here ; besides when the King of France had sent you a Minister, had you sent none in return wou'd not that have been cryed out upon as an unpardonable omission. I was likewise inform'd by several persons, and among the rest by Obryen, that his Eminence had found great fault that you did not write oftener to the King of France. To this I replied that shou'd I write myself to the greatest Prince in Christendom and that several times ; and not only receive no answer from him, but not the least acknowledgement from a Secretary or a Commiss to ye receipt of any of my letters, shou'd I not

---

[1] Steuart of Goodtrees. It was no doubt true that the Prince employed too many different persons in his secret affairs, many of whom did not work together.

have reason to conclude that they importuned him, and that both in Prudence and good manners, I ought to cease writing. But not satisfied with having represented this, I got the Duke de Bouillon to know of the King himself whether he took it ill of you that you had not writ oftener to him, and his answer was "*Bien loin de cela, ses lettres me flattoient et m'embarassaient parce que je n'y pouvois pas répondre comme je l'aurois voulu.*" Obryen likewise asked the Cardinal in my presence, whether if your Highness had privately acquainted the Court of France with your intention of going to Scotland, they would not readily have furnished you with all necessarys for such an expedition? But to this the Cardinal answer'd with great earnestness—*vraiment non on l'en auroit bien empeché.*[1]

I took occasion to tell Count d'Argencon that as there wou'd probably be a good many of yr. friends that wou'd be obliged to retire out of Scotland and for whom you wou'd be obliged to provide in some shape or other, I thought it cou'd not be better done, than by forming two new Scots Regiments, to which he answered, that there most certainly (would) be some Provision made for such People, and that he wou'd do all in his power to facilitate the matter.

I must now begg leave to tell your Royal Highness that I think you wou'd do well immediately upon your arrival here to send for Lally and employ him in yr. negotiations with the Court of France. He is very well acquainted there, and no body is more zealously affected for you. Bulkeley, by all I can hear has likewise behaved himself extremely well on this occasion, and I think your Royal Highness ought to shew a particular regard to him. Ld. Clincarty is certainly full of zeal for yr. service, he will wait on you as soon as he hears of your arrival. He is by his birth a man of ye greatest distinction in Ireland where he has lost an immense estate by the Revolution. He has passed all his life in England

[1] Which was honest, at least.

where he is very well known and has great relations. He has been so active during embarcation that I believe he cannot think of returning any more home—at least for some years.[1]

THO. SHERIDAN.

The very last letter Sheridan wrote to Prince Charles

ALBANO. 3 *Nov.* 1746.

SIR,

I hope your Royall Highness will give me leave to congratulate your safe arrival in France, after all the Dangers and Hardships to which you have been so long exposed. I should not have been obliged to do it at this distance, had I not received the King's positive Orders to attend him here. I shall not trouble your Royal Highness with representing to you the cruel anxietys under which I have labour'd, ever since the unfortunate day that tore me from your presence. I flatter myself that you will more easily imagin than I can express what I have suffer'd, and I am sure if my behaviour for so many years past, do's not convince your Royal Highness of it, all the expressions I cou'd make use of on the occasion, would prove superfluous.

That your Royal Highness may long enjoy the Reputation you have so justly acquired, and one day reap the fruit of yr. labours is the sincerest wish of

Sir,

your Royal Highnesse's most humble, most dutiful and

most Obedient Servant,

THO. SHERIDAN.

This was written only three weeks before his death.
And to this may be added Charles's last mention of Sheridan

---

[1] Lord Clancarty being rough in manner, and of somewhat disreputable appearance, having lost an eye, was not a very good envoy to send to the French Court, nor did he effect much; some said he was a traitor.

155

whom he was not to see again. It is dated three days after Sheridan's own letter was written, and is addressed—

To Edgar

FROM CLICHY, *ye 6th November*, 1746.

I enclose you here a Letter for ye King. My kind compliments to Lord Dumbar and all my Frends there. I say nothing to Sr. Thomas because I am in hops he is already set out for to join me,—My wanting of him gives me a great deal of trubble, for tho I have a very good opinion of Kelly, and must do him the Justice of saying I am very well pleased with him, yet neither he, or anybody else much less I wou'd absolutely trust in my secrets as I wou'd in Sr. Thomas, which occasions in me a great del of toil and Labour.

I remain at present assuring you of my Constant Friendship,

CHARLES P.

James Edgar to "Les Dames Sheridan," the poor old man's sisters
ROME. 28*th Nov.* 1746.

MESDAMES,

I am very sorry by this to give you the melancholly news of yr Brother Sir Thomas Sheridan's death, on the 23rd. I write now the particulars of it to Mr. Kelly, and send him an account of the money and effects found in his custody, he will no doubt inform you of what I say on those head. Not to encroche upon your grief, all I shall further say is that the King is graciously pleased to direct Mr. Waters to continue to pay the pension he gives you as formerly ordered . . .

King James, writing to Prince Charles from Rome, says that Sir Thomas died of apoplexy and "I had him buryed with all decency in our parish." And Edgar wrote to the Earl Marischal in the following January, "Sir Thomas came here, before the Prince arrived in France, and died as he was setting out to joyn H.R.H. in two days illness." The theory that he died of a broken heart at James's reproaches is not borne out by the above letters.

After the Prince had started for Scotland, his father wrote frequently to Paris, and, later, *after* Culloden, continued to write regular weekly letters to his eldest son, at the moment being hunted "like a partridge upon the mountains." They never, of course, reached the Prince until he returned to Paris in October 1746, when he writes to his father for the first time for six months and allows (somewhat quaintly) that he has not had time to read all the latter's letters, *yet*.

Some specimens of these weekly paternal epistles, not before published, are given later. Copies of all were kept in Rome. It seems unlikely that the Prince would ask for duplicates of those of any date which missed him, so it is possible that some of those here given were never read by him at all.

The King to the Earl Marischal on first hearing that the Prince had actually gone to Scotland

ROME. *Aug.* 11, 1745.

I received yours of the 27 of July only last Thursday, and it was only by the same occasion that the Prince informed me of the project about which he writ to you. What I know of it is very imperfect, but enough to show me that if I had been acquainted with it in time, I had certainly done my best to prevent its being executed. If it was rash, I cannot but say it is a bold undertaking and the courage and sentiments the Prince expresses on this occasion will always do him honour.

The King wrote on the same day to Colonel O'Bryen in Paris, saying that it was only on August 6th that he had known of the Prince's resolution to start for Scotland with his few followers. The letters which Charles wrote from "St. Lazaire" [sic] on July 2nd took therefore over a month to reach Rome—this was certainly intentional as shown in O'Sullivan's account of the expedition.

On the same day also his Majesty wrote to the Duke of Ormonde (who died three months later).

In both letters is to be noted the natural pride of the Father of a gallant son who has taken a rash resolve and executed it, struggling with King James's more usual caution and pessimistic expectation that the worst will probably happen. To Ormonde he says "Without a French landing in England is soon made, it will be impossible for the Prince to succeed."

To O'Bryen he speaks more plainly of his "surprise and agitation" at knowing that his son had actually sailed, and urges his faithful agent to do everything possible to see that French help is sent to Scotland. He says he encloses letters for the French King for the two brothers d'Argenson, for Cardinal de Tencin, for Monsieur de Maurepas, and Monsieur Orrey, and for the Maréchal de Noailles.[1] He certainly did all he could for his son, from his distant exile. The letters to Ormonde and to O'Bryen have been printed by Browne. (The latter, being in French, is printed with *many* mistakes.)

Prince Henry was then allowed to follow his brother to France. He left Rome secretly with Sir John Graeme on August 29th, 1745 (Charles had just marched over the Pass of Corryairack at the head of his Highlanders), and came to Avignon, where he stayed with the Duke of Ormonde and was laid up for two months with fever.

[1] All of these were powerful noblemen at the French Court, the younger Argenson, Comte Marc Pierre being Minister for War.

Prince Henry to his Father

GENOVA. *Sept.* 3, 1745.

SIR,

I arrived here about one and a half in the afternoon. I chose that time on purpose that I might find few people in the streets and from the place where I lay last night it was impossible for me to gett here as early in the morning as would have been requisite for the same purpose. So I have taken my party to keep close and stay here all to-night and tomorrow ; at the opening of the Gates I shall sett out for Savona, where I reckon I shall be 2 or 3 days before the news of my departure from Rome reaches this place. I must not omit to tell your Majesty that as wee passed by Pogibonii the post-master had liked to have obliged us to pass by Florence, as all courriers must do and had it not been for the Cleverness of my courrier I believe we never should have escaped that useless and troublesome detour for, as it was, I perceived he somewhat suspected our *bona fide.* After that we arrived at Pisa at a very untimely hour for it was just about four and twenty, all the world abroad and flocking about to ask news of the *Pretendente.* Wee were very anxious to get away as you may well believe and, for all the sights of that town pleased me extreamly, yet I was not sorry to find myself well out of it. I have been enchanted with the sights of Genoa and the Coast about it, but I cannot say the same of the roads which realy are much worse than ever I could have imagined and yet I think they deserve to be passed once for curiosity's sake. The Post master in a village betwixt Sarzana and this, where I lay a night, as soon as he had seen me told the courrier that the young Gentleman was very licke the Prince of Wales whom he had seen there as he passed on his way to France. I was much surprised at this for I never thought we had been like one another. I am now

159

pretty well rested and as I have nothing more—Humbly asking yr Majesty's blessing,

I remain

HENRY.

Paul Kearney [1] *to James Edgar from Leghorn*

Sept. 6, 1745.

"I must acquaint you with another piece of news flying here which makes great noise, that at the Forna-cette, 17 miles and somewhat more from this town, a young man in Abbot's dress pass'd by that way last Wednesday and it was Cardinal Aquaviva's Courier with him, who was the same sent from Rome with H.R.H. I am told that the Procurator of Florence, by name Fenzi, has declared this to be true and that the person soe dressed was undoutedly the Duke of York on his way to France. This news with the taking of Ostend and Tortona makes this town ring. I hear a person or two are arested here for speaking about the Prince of Wales. It is late, so I cannot learn what persons they be till tomorrow and then I believe the gentlemen merchants will give out their news from England of the Prince's landing in Scotland. The gentlemen your friends are brave and merry here upon their good news and make you their compliments."

First news direct from Scotland of the battle of Prestonpans:

O. Heguerty [2] *writes from Paris to the King*

21 *Sept.* 1745.

"Two English smugglers arrived at Boulogne the 16th and 17th of this month, brought the most agreable news of General Cope's defeat by his Royal Highness body of troops, that besides the Slain, about 1700 of the Enemy's were made Prisoners—all the toune of Boulogne gives creditt to it. May it be true in the name of God !

[1] British Resident in Leghorn—an Irishman.
[2] A Jacobite resident in Paris.

We see Mr. Walsh daily. He proposed to M. de Maure-pas [1] the manadgment of the troops passadge over to England and even to be their Guide in fisher boats if stormy weather —but if fair wind to gett over, he engadges to land them in 12 or 14 hours at furthest.

If a man rich with millions dread not the storm in a fishing boat a soldjer ought not to dread it and yett sir I greatly fear disobedience amongst the french soldjers when they be commanded to embark in stormy weather.

Walsh to the King, returning thanks for his patent of nobility

14 Sept. 1745.

SIR,

Je regarde comme le plus beau jour de ma vie celuy qui ma mie en état de marquer mon atachement plein de respect à votre Majesté dans la personne du Prince de Galles, votre fils. Je l'ai conduie à travers les hazards de la mer, Les eceuils et les risques respectifs de l'enemi, à Boradel ou une partie de ses fidèles écossais sont venu lui jurer qu'ils étaient resolues de mourir à ses costes ou de le conduire au pieds du trône reservé à Votre Majeste. L'intrépidité de son altesse royale répond à leur résolution et ne nous laise aucune doutte du plus heureux succès. . . . L'abbé Butler qui a eu l'honneur de Compagner son altesse royale jusqu'à son débarquement en Ecosse et qui est revenu avec moi se dispose à partir pour se rendre auprès de votre Majesté. Il vous rendra un compte exacte, sire, des details du voyage de son altesse royale et des disposition ou il a laissé la noblesse et les peuples des montagnes d'Ecosse.[2] J'ose assurer votre Majesté etc. etc.

WAILSH.

He does not say where he writes from, presumably Amsterdam.

[1] Jeane Frédéric Maurepas, Minister de la Marine.
[2] See p. 136 for Butler's full account.

Autograph letter from Louis XV, A mon frère le prince Charles Edouard, when sending his unofficial ambassador, Monsieur D'Eguilles, the letter is strictly non-committal.

MON FRÈRE

Sept. 24, 1745.

"L'interest véritable que je prends à ce qui vous regarde m'engage à vous envoyer le Sire M. d'Eguilles que j'ai chargé de vous expliquer mes sentimens pour vous. Je compte que vous ajouterez toute foi et creance à ce qu'il vous dira de ma part. Je ne lui ay rien recommandé plus particulièrement que de vous faire connoître combien je suis disposé à vous donner en toute occasion des temoignages de mon affection pour votre personne. Sur ce je prie Dieu qu'il vous aie mon frère en son Sainte et digne garde. Ecri à Choisz le 24 Sept. 1745.

votre bon frère LOUIS."

Even before the news of Prestonpans had reached him, but after hearing that Prince Charles had safely landed in Scotland and had met with some measure of response, the French King sent off this remarkably friendly letter and a French envoy, not actually dignified with the name of Ambassador, but charged with all sorts of encouraging messages and accompanied by a few Frenchmen and a welcome supply of money and ammunition as well as some weapons, which this envoy, the gallant Alexander de Boyer, Marquis d'Eguilles, a lawyer of Aix en Provence by profession, actually helped to carry ashore on his back.

Prince Charles to his Father—with the account of Prestonpans

Sept. 1745.

"Adam [1] has sent me a gentleman (who brought me your letter) to stay with me for to give notice of anything I may

[1] The French king.

162

want, which he says will be done immediately. Accordingly I am sending off three or four expresses all to the same purpose so that one may arrive—what is sed is very short, pressing to have succor in all heste by a landing in England for that as matters stand, I must either conquer or perish in a little while. Thank God I am in perfect good health, but longing much for the Happy day of meeting."

King James to Daniel O'Bryen, a little disappointed that more details were sent to Ormonde than to him

Oct. 4th, 1745.

". . . Enfin, Dieu merci, nous sommes sure de l'arrivé du Prince en Ecosse, J'ai receü Une de ses lettres du 4 Août Je suppose vieux stile, et Edgar a eü. Un mot du Chev^r Sheridan, l'une et l'autre envoyé par Mr. Welsh [sic], qui se rapporte à ce que nous apprendrons de l'Abbé Butler, *mais si ce n'avait été pour une copie de la lettre de ce dernier au Duc d'Ormonde que le Jeune Waters envoya ici, j'aurais été bien peu instruit de la situation presente du Prince* . . .''

There are three letters of King James to his younger son while the latter was waiting in France for the chance which never came to join his brother in Scotland[1] and one from Henry to O'Bryen. It will never be known how Henry Benedict would have acquitted himself as a soldier, for the opportunity was denied him in Spain, in Scotland, or in the Low Countries with the French armies, though he actually did join the camp of the latter for a very brief space in the following year, and saw the siege of Antwerp.

According to the accounts of *some* who knew the two Princes in their youth, Henry was then the more spirited and passionate of the two—the one who showed most plainly

---

[1] At the head of the promised French force.

his Sobieski blood. The account written by Lord Dunbar of his habits at 17 hardly bears this out, and the letter on page 166 shows him as rather peevish at being kept waiting and somewhat lacking in dignity and self-control.[1] As an older man, we have the celebrated remark of the Pope Benedict XIV that "if all the Stuarts were as boring as the Cardinal, he did not wonder the English had driven them out !"

King James to the Duke of York

ROME. *Jan. 4th,* 1746.

I hope in God, My Dearest Harry, this will find you in England and therefore I shall say the less in return to your packet of the 13th Dec., with wch I received one of Sir John Graeme's of the same date, one of Patersons [2] to him, and one of The Prince's to you. I have also now by me two letters of Lord Marschalls, two of Lord Sempils and two of Balhaldys, with the papers the last sent inclosed. But in the situation matters are in just now, and not knowing where any of you may be, I shall write to none of them myself at present, if they are, as I take it to be probable, all three with you, let them know their letters are come safe to me, and the reason why I dont write to them and make a kind and proper compliment to each of them in my name. It is a great comfort to me to see things in such a forwardness for the English expedition. The persons lately come from England and Scotland will, to be sure, yet more hasten the execution, but till that is done and that I know you once safely arrived in England, you may imagine my anxiety for your Brother and you. In the mean time it is a great comfort to me to receive such good accounts of you as I do, from the Card[1],[3]

[1] Charles definitely accused him of cowardice in not making a dash across the Channel some dark night, but this was later on, when their relations had become strained.

[2] John Paterson, formerly Mar's secretary.   [3] Tencin.

Sir James Stewart [1] and indeed every body. I am glad you are pleased with me, and I believe there is little danger of our ever being otherwise than satisfyed with one another.

I now write to The Card[1] that he may express my acknowledgements to the King of France for his goodness towards me, and shall add no more here but that my blessings, my prayers, and my most tender love and affection will always accompany you wherever you are.

King James to the Duke of York (after the battle of Falkirk of which he must have heard, but still gloomy)

ROME. *March 29th,* 1746.

The French post did not come in till yesterday and brought me yours and Sir Johns of the 4th. By all I can remark I am affray'd all is lost in Scotland, and really all things considered it is a greater wonder that did not happen sooner than that it should be the case now. My chief concern at present is for The Prince's person, and as I find you and Obryen are not less anxious about this important point, I am persuaded all proper measures will have been taken to afford him means to leave Scotland, when he can do no further good there. I am in great doubts whether what lately went from the coast of Flanders will come in time to be of use to him, and I much fear that his present situation may put a stop to any project of an expedition into England,[2] tho' that might possibly yet retrieve our affairs. But in all events what is I think of the greatest importance is to use all possible means to preserve The King of France and his Ministers in the good disposition they are towards us, and to conceal with care our being sensible that The Princes miscarrying in his present enterprise is manifestly owing to their being so long in assisting him. It is to be hoped The King of France will make it a point of honour to be kind to your Brother and you whatever may

[1] Goodtrees.   [2] As it did.

happen. If the War lasts, he will certainly do his best to send us home, and if Peece is made before we are there, his friendship and protection is our chief concern, and even in that case he may do so much for us both in respect of our politick and personal intrest, so that it greatly behoves us to manage and court The French Ministry in this juncture. I could not but say this much to you on this subject, tho' I am persuaded you think upon it as I do, and any thing I could say on other politick matters from hence at present would be useless, and so I shall conclude there being little time betwixt the receiving and answering of this week.

The Duke of York to O'Bryen, complaining of inaction while waiting to join his brother, rather unnecessarily occupied with his own boredom and need for exercise. The poems referred to are not extant, so it is not known if they were of his own composition or not

BOULOGNE SUR MER, *ce* 19 *Mar.* 1746.

Je vous ai écrit une assé longue lettre le 9. de ce mois. Je suis en paine de savoir si vous l'avez reçu. Elle contenoit les raisons qui me faisoit regarder ma demeure icy comme assez inutille. Je ne peut que vous repeter qu'il faut nécessairement que ma santé souffre si je continue à rester dans un pays où il n'est pas possible de me dissiper ou à pied ou à cheval. Je m'resens déjà et ça ne peut pas être autrement ettant toujours accoutumé à faire de l'exercise et ettant a cette heure obligé de garder la maison continuelement, sans le moindre amusement. Je ne me plaindrai pas, même à vous, si je voyasse le moindre bien pour mon frère dans ma demeure icy mais en verité c'est se moquer du monde de croire que pendant que M. de Richelieu [1] est tranquillement à Paris,

---

[1] Armand de Richelieu, grand-nephew of the Cardinal, and Maréchal of France, died 1788. He was the Duke who was nominally to command the French expedition to Scotland.

ma demeure sur la côte peut donner la moindre jalousie et pour ce qui regarde ce port icy et Calais, comme je vous ai dit dans ma dernière, nos enemis scavent mieux que nous que nous n'y pouvons rien faire pour l'Angleterre.—Enfin fait tout ce que vous pouvez pour me tirer de ce vilain trou, mais que je ne paraisse pas le soliciter moi même—Vous m'entendez. Si la Cour ne veut pas je m'approche de Paris, qu'on me laisse au moins la liberté d'aller dans quelque endroit en flandre pas loin de la côte—enfin vous verrez ce qui peut me convenir, mieux que moi, qui est au bout du comte. Qui peut resister à rester dans un endroit comme Boulogne, trois mois avec des nouvelles et des évènements si affligeants et après tout cela avec des gens comme les notres ? Je n'en pu plus.—

J'ai une fluxion sur un oiel qui m'a empeché de vous écrire aussi distinctement que j'aurois voulu et qui m'oblige de finir. Adieu mon cher O'Bryen—je vous embrasse de tout mon cœur. Envoyé quelquesunes de ces exemplaires de vers à Milord Dunbar de ma part. Elle sont très bonnes selon moi.

HENRY.

Two months later, he was a little more cheerful, having something to do.

Duke of York to King James

GHANT. *Mai ye 20th*, 1746.

SIR,

Your Majesty must pardon me the hurry and shortness of this letter, but realy I have not one moment's time having just gott leave to go to the Army under C^t Clermont's [1] ordres that is a goeing to Besiege the Cittadelle of Antwerp. I part in a few houers. The affliction and anxiety I am in

---

[1] Louis de Bourbon, Count of Clermont, the French general in Flanders.

for my dearest Brother makes me enjoy the pleasure of this leave much less than I wou'd have done had things gone better in the North than I fear they do. My constant attention shall be for the Prince's personal safety that I thinke is the chief point at present. Most humbly begging Your Majesty's blessing I remain with the utmost respect

Your most dutifull son,

HENRY.

The King to Prince Charles

ROME. *April 12th*, 1746.

I will not deprieve myself of the satisfaction of writing to you at least every week, My Dearest Carluccio, tho' I am still without that of hearing directly from you. We have been all much concern'd that the succours lately sent to you returned without your profiting of them, tho' the truth is, it is very hard for any thing or any body to come to you, now that you are upon your retreat, and that it is not known where you may be ; and after all, some small assistance sent to you would not do the work, without a powerful landing in England. By all I can remark, the French are seriously thinking of that or of a Peace, and probably one or t'other will soon happen, but they are so disgusted, and it is no wonder, with the odd doings of our people in France, that I plainly see they will not speak out either to The Duke or me, tho' I have at the same time all reason to hope and believe that in all events they will be mindful of you and kind to me. My chief concern at present is for your personal safety, but I trust in God he will always preserve and protect you, whatever may happen. I hear no more of the money sent you from Spain, but it is to be supposed that those who were charged with that affair have done their best to serve you in it.[1] (*The next sentence is in James's own handwriting.*)

---

[1] This arrived in the Isle of Barra before Culloden, and the Prince sent Aeneas Macdonald to collect it.

Adieu my D^{rst} Child. God Almighty bless and direct you. I heartily embrace you and am all yours,

JAMES R.

The same to the same

ALBANO. *May 30th,* 1746.

I must always write to you, My Dearest Carluccio, tho' without any matter to write upon, which is the present case. I have had no particular accounts of you by my last French letters. Since that there are reports of your having had another Battle, but they were so confused that they only serve to increase my anxiety and impatience to have further accounts about you, which I hope in God will be good when they come, tho' in the mean time I shall pass a melancholy time of it. You will have heard to be sure from Your Brother of his having seen The King of France at Arras, but he has not yet got his last answer about his Campagne. What else may be doing in Flanders or in Britanny you will know it sooner than from me, at present we are much in the dark as to all these matters. We have a fine season of it here this year. The Pope returns to Town next Monday, but I shall stay till towards St. Peters. Adieu my Drst. Child. God Almighty bless and protect you. I heartily embrace you and am all yours,

JAMES R.

The King to the Duke of York

ALBANO. *May 30th,* 1746.

It was Friday morning before I received My Dearest Harry's of the 6th May, with that of Sir John's of the same date. Sure next letters will let me know the decision about your Campagne. There is something incomprehensible in the conduct of the Court of France in that particular that I am tyred of thinking of it and I shall say no more of it here,

169

but that I still hope you will be allowed to make it, if you are not better employed, and that in all events, after all that is past, all the world must see that you have done your part, and in that respect we may rest satisfied.

I hear that the Brest Fleet is parted, but where they are gone is the question, and there are letters at Rome that speak of a battle in Scotland, but what I have heard of it is so confused that one can make little of it, and it only serves to make me more anxious to have further accounts, but as it is pretended the Battle was fought on the 27th Aprile,[1] if the Prince had had the worst, I should think one would have had but too certain an account of it by this time, by the pains The Court of London would surely have taken to publish such a fact, and with this reflexion I endeavour to quiet myself till more letters come. By what I have again heard from Sempil [2] I find he continues to negociate by virtue of the authority he pretends to have, but I don't intend to write to him this post at least. I am mighty glad to find you are so well in your health. Mine I thank God is not worse than usual, and the weather here is pretty good, tho' not so warm as it was. We have very little here, but from Rome or Frascati I have almost every day some company here with me. I remember nothing particular I have further to say to you this post and so Adieux.

The King to Prince Charles

ALBANO. *June 13th*, 1746.

I cannot express to you, My Dearest Carluccio, the anxiety l am and shall be in for you till I know how all goes with you in Scotland after the late Battle, or rather till I know you are yourself safely returned to France, where I trust in God this may find you, for I don't see what you can do more in

---

[1] April 16th, Old Style, the day of the fatal battle of Culloden.
[2] See p. 114.

Scotland, and by returning to France you may be able to retreive your affairs if the War lasts, and if it does not, you will be better able there to be of use to yourself and your Family than you could be any where else. I am persuaded The King of France will do what he can both for you and in favor of The Scots that have adhered to you, at least nothing is or shall be neglected to that effect. You will know Your Brother is gone to the siege of Antwerp. I shall enter into nothing else here, neither can I at present almost think of anything but your safety, and till it pleases God I hear of it, I cannot have an easy moment. In the Interim and at all times I beseech God to bless and direct you. Embracing you most tenderly, my Drst. Carluccio, I am all yours,

JAMES R.

The Same to the Same

ALBANO. *June 20th*, 1746.

What can I say to you, My Dearest Carluccio, in the obscurity and anxiety I am in as to yourself and what relates to you. Still I must write to you every French post, tho' I can say nothing that can be of use to you, but it is at least of some ease to me to express now and then in writing my concern and tenderness for you. Your Brother and our other friends are always attentive to do what they can to serve you, and I am comforting myself with the hopes of hearing every French post of your being safely arrived in France, for till then I shall have few easy moments in the light matters appear to me. You will have known Your Brother has been at the Siege of the Cittadel of Antwerp and I hope he will have had leave to make out the Campagne. I am going back to Town in a few days. I cannot bragg much of my health, but my chief ail at present is my concern for you, which does not allow me to say any thing more here of other matters or news. God Almighty bless and

171

direct my Drst. Child whom I tenderly embrace and am all yours.

JAMES R.

The Same to the Same

ROME. *June 27th*, 1746.

Being still without any certain or direct news of you, My Dearest Carluccio, you may imagine my situation and the pain I am in for you. But I comfort myself a little with the reflexion that the honor and intrest of France is so much concern'd in your safety, that at least nothing will be neglected for that, in case your affairs cannot be retrieved, which I fear is the case.

You have to be sure from France all the lights can be given you, if they can but reach you, tho' for my part I know not what to make or what to think of publick affairs at present, whether there will War or Peace ? What this Brest Fleet is designed for ? or whether it has any fixed destination at all ? What I know is that your friends in France will do their best to serve you and that I shall do what little I can from here for the same end. I am here again since Friday and thank God tollerably well. Adieu, my dear Child. God Almighty bless protect and direct you. I heartily embrace you with a heart full of love for you and confidence in ye divine providence over you.

I am all yours,

JAMES R.

The Same to the Same

ROME. *July 4th*, 1746.

I must always write a few lines to you, My Dearest Carluccio, tho' without knowing where this may find you, and amidst the anxiety and uncertainty I am in as to all that relates to you. For tho' I hear Lord John, now Duke of Perth,[1] and Sir Thomas are both come to Paris, I have not yet heard from them, but shall, I suppose, next post. I am glad indeed to find you were endeavouring to provide for your own safety, and I suppose you took the best measures you could for that effect, but till I know you once safe on this side of the sea, you may imagine the situation of mind I shall be in. In the meantime all I can do is to beseech God to bless, protect and direct you. You will know to be sure from The Duke all can be said to you from France, where I would fain flatter myself this may find you. Adieu, Drst. Child. I beseech again and again God Almighty to bless you. I tenderly embracing you am all yours

JAMES R.

The Same to the Same

ROME. *July* 11*th*, 1746.

I trust in Providence, My Dearest Carluccio, that this will find you safely arrived in France, but till I know that you are so, my pain and anxiety for you cannot cease, and till then I shall write but short letters to you, neither can I say anything of moment from hence. I am affrayed you have received but few of my letters, tho' I have never missed a week writing to you. I wish at your leisure you would let me know how many you have received, because there are some of which I might be glad to send you duplicates. You will know all The French have done for your personal safety, for which they deserve all our acknowledgements, and if we have reason to complain of them in other matters, it behoves us to conceal our thoughts as to that, since we stand

---

[1] Lord John Drummond, with his brother, the Duke of Perth, who died on the voyage, Sir Thomas Sheridan, Lord Elcho and others, escaped on the French frigate from Nantes, the Bellona, which brought the French gold, buried at Loch Arkaig—too late to save the campaign and afterwards the source of so many disputes.

173

so much in need of them. When I may have the comfort of knowing you in France, I can then write safely, freely and fully to you, and before I can do that you will know all that is material from your Brother and Obryen, and so at present I shall add no more. God bless you, my Drest. Carluccio, I tenderly embrace you and am all yours

JAMES R.

The Same to the Same

ROME. *July* 18, 1746.

I must always write to you, My Dearest Carluccio, tho' were I sure my letter would soon come to you, I should be at a loss what to say. I was anxious about you last week in relation to the dangers of your leaving Scotland, and now I am more uneasy since it would appear by the publick news that you were still there, tho' I am always in hopes you will find at last ways and means of getting you thence, and our friends in France will, I can answer for it, do all they can to assist you in that respect. It is useless now to write anything to you on what is passing on this side of the sea, and were it otherways, I should not know what to say, for the French Politicks and Conduct are become incomprehensible and no body knows any more what to make of them. God Almighty bless and preserve you, My Dearest Child, wherever you are and soon send you to a place of safety, where we may at least hear from one another. Adieu, my D^{rst} Carluccio. I tenderly embrace you and am all yours beseeching God to bless you,

JAMES R.

The Same to the Same

ROME. *July* 25th, 1746.

How great soever my pain and anxiety are at present for you, My Dearest Carluccio, it must not hinder me from

174

doing all I think may be of use and service to you. And therefore I now write this letter to you, and send it to Obryen that he may keep it by him till it pleases God you arrive safely in France, and then send it, or deliver it to you as soon and as safely as he can. Tho' I have never missed a week writing to you, yet a number of my letters have to be sure miscarryed one way or another, and it matters little whether you ever see most of them, since I could say little to you from hence of any importance. But on recollecting on those letters, I thought it was fit you should see a long letter I writ to you of the 19th Aprile, because, being informed of the chief contents of it cannot but be of use to you at all times. Since what is said there of Sir James Steuart,[1] he informed me of the remittances from Spain, and would have put the management of that particular into Obryen's hands. I writ him back word that it was well in his own, but that it was necessary he should concert with Obryen what related to the debursements he made of that money and the uses he employed it to, so that no body can inform you of that particular better than himself. There was a good deal of the money I sent from hence lay'd out upon the officers who were going to joyn you, and there yet remains a little of the fund in Young Waters hands, who can inform you of all the payments he made, and you will see that it was all layd out so immediately for your service, that there has been none of it even applyed to your Brother's personal use. I don't remember there was much of it sent to you in Scotland, because the minute France and Spain undertook to supply you, you did not want so small a help as that would have been, and I was glad to be always master of a little fund at Paris upon an extraordinary and unforeseen emergency which might fall out for your service. I remember even Sir Thos. Sheridan writ to Obryen to send you no more of that

[1] Sir James Steuart of Goodtrees, sent by the Prince from Scotland in October 1745, and since established as an agent in Paris. See p. 153.

money, and I myself writ to the last after that to keep apart 450,000 Livres of it, and not to touch any of that sum without my particular order. And then when I saw affairs in Scotland were lost, I ordered him to return that money to me here, as soon as it arrives. I shall with it redeem yours and your Brother's Jewels which were put in pawn, by which I shall save the expence of paying the intrest for the said money and the Jewels themselves will always be at yours and your Brother's disposal.

You will I am sure be surprised when I tell you I have not had a line from Sir Thomas Sheridan since his arrival in France. He has writ, that I know of, but one letter here, in which I am not named, and that to the person of all at Rome he knew to be the least agreable to me.[1] I am sure he does not act in this by your order, and I know not his reasons for acting in such a manner, and informing me so little of what relates to you and our affairs, but there is something so odd and mysterious in this that I could not be at ease without writing to him to come and joyn me here out of hand, for I think it equally for your service and mine that I should be fully informed of all these late transactions, besides that it will be a satisfaction to me, which I am sure you will not grudge me, and especially since I don't deprive you of him, because he is not now with you and that I shall send him back to you again whenever you please. I own sincerely to you that I am affrayed Strickland [2] has imposed upon him and God grant he may not have endeavoured to poison many others, My Dear Child, you did not know that wicked man, but whenever your eyes are opened as to him, you wont I am sure allow a disciple or prosolite of his to come near you. I have I am sure neither personal grudge agaist nor

[1] This letter is not at Windsor. It is presumably the one Sheridan *says* he wrote to Lord Dunbar, then out of favour with the King.

[2] Poor Francis Strickland had been dead six months when this was written, which shows how slowly any news from Scotland reached Rome.

partiality for any body, but should you be directed by such people, I can easily see that it would be your own and our Family's ruin, and that you will soon lose the honor and reputation you have got in Scotland.

When you are once in France, I hope you will let yourself be advised by Cardinal Tencin and Obryen. The first is the only sincere friend we can absolutely depend upon amongst those Ministers. You know my good opinion of the last, and as he is agreable to and has access to them, no body is better able than he to serve us effectually at the French Court. It is impossible for me, My Dearest Carluccio, to say all I would to you by writing, but what I have chiefly to recommend to you consists in three points. The first is to be always kind and loving to your Brother and never to allow anybody to do the least thing that may tend to sow discord betwixt you. The second is to behave with prudence and moderation in relation to the Court of France, on whom we are forced to depend, and from whom we must endeavour to get at least what we can.

And the Third is, to keep our own people in a due subordination, without allowing them to break your head with accusations and invectives against one another, but showing them that you are Master, and will act your own way,[1] without being unkind, much less unjust to any. And after all, with all our misfortunes, we may if we please be more Master of our own people on this side of the sea than most other Princes, because when we do not transgress the rules of justice and prudence, we have no political considerations to constrain us in such matters, for except a very few who have really suffer'd for us, and may be hereafter of use to us, the gros are people who owe us a great deal, while we owe them little, and who expect a great deal from us, while we can expect little from them. Could you see my heart, you would I am sure, my Dearest Carluccio, be satisfied with it.

[1] This Charles *never* failed to do.

In whatever situation I am myself I shall always endeavour to
do you what service I can and shall never cease to pray God
to bless and direct you, that you may never faill in what you
owe to him in the first place, and myself, your Brother and
our Countrymen in the second. I tenderly embrace you
and am all yours, my D^(rst) Child,

JAMES R.

Duke of York to the King

NAVARRE. *July ye* 31*st*, 1746.

SIR,

I have received yesterday the honour of your Majesty's
of the 11th. You may be very sure that I shall be particularly
attentive to every thing you are so good as to say concerning
my conduct with Humphry, (the Prince). It was allwais my
intention to act so, and I am sure there is nothing in this
worled [*sic*] I wont do for to cultivate a love that is so dear
to me. God send I may soon have occasion to convince
him of the respect, deference and tender love I have for him
not only by duty but by inclination. I flatter myself that
will not be a hard matter to do, and that in the midst of so
many misfortunes wee shall both be very happy to gett
together again. As for Sir Thomas, I did not enter into
many particular detaill with him about any thing when he
came at my first arrival here, and I have not seen him since.
I am well enough pleased to see the gazettes make no mention
of the Prince. I think wee may take it for a good Sign. It
is a cruel thing, these fregattes are so long a going, I am sure
it is not for want of pressing.

My halth is some what better now, but it was far from good
for a few days after I writ my last. The Post is just a goeing
a way, so most humbly begging your Majesty's Blessing, I
remain with the utmost respect

Your most dutifull son,

HENRY.

178

King James to Prince Charles

ROME. *August 1st*, 1746.

I writ you last week, My Dearest Carluccio, a long letter
and sent it to Obryen to be kept for you till you might come
into France, and now I continue to write to you as usual,
without knowing where this may find you, or without matter
to write upon, for till you are once known to be in a place
of safety, and can let us hear from you, all business must
necessarily be at a stand, neither can we indeed any of us think
of anything else at present but your personal safety, and till
that is secured my anxietys for you cannot cease, and even
daily increase the longer you remain in the dangerous situation
you now are, but I trust in God that he will protect and
preserve you, and shall never cease beseeching him to do so,
and to bless and direct you on all occasions. Adieu, D^{rst} Child,
I tenderly embrace you and am all yours.

JAMES R.

The Duke of York—addressed "To the King alone"

August 7th, 1746.

SIR,

What made me enter into no sort of particular with S. T.[1]
about any thing when he was here was that for all my kind
waise of acting with him, I did not see any Disposition to
open to me on certain matters for what regarded Stric (Strickland) personally. I never wou'd have cared to have spoken
to him and think it more prudent never to touch that string
myself. But what I remarqued particular was that haveing
occasion of speaking a good deal at different times of the
siege of Carlile, he never once made the least mention of
that person. I am much of your Majesty's opinion that it
wou'd be of very great consequence for us both to know what

---

[1] Sir Thomas Sheridan.

meneges S——[1] had with Humphry (the Prince) before is
going to Britt (Scotland) and by what canalls, but as it is a
matter that requieres a great deal of nicity and prudence to
find out I am persuaded it will be hard enough. Since I am
a writing it is good your Majesty shou'd be informed that
when S. T. was here the attentions and kindness I shou'd
him were so great, that I believe rather to much by the half.
I told him over and over again that he was master to come
and stay with me when and as much as he pleased, and that
it wou'd allwaise be very agreable to me. I desired him to
bring as soon as he cou'd to me one Mr. Hay [2] (not "Long-
Willy") that came over with him and for whom he told me
the Prince had a particular kindness. I charged *him* also
with the kindest invitation in my name to S. T. S.[3] and
show'd I wou'd have a particular pleasure if any of our people
in general wou'd come to see me. All this I saide as your
Majesty may believe for no other reason but that of policy.
Now, since this time which is six weeks ago at least not
a soul of those people have ever come near me or offer'd to
do it. . . . I take little notice as I can of all this, but I am
sure your Majesty will think it as well as I alltogether a very
singular way of acting. Leopold (*Mr. Obryen*) that is upon
the place, must know and hear a great many more particulars
about all that Click than I can, so I leave him to inform your
Majesty of them tho' I do know by him some things now
and then.

I am sure it goes against my heart to be giving subjects of
displeasure to you in any time much more in one so melancholy. But besides your own orders to me, you know the
motive that makes me more attentive to inform you of every
wisle (whistle) in this present time, and it is a motive I own
that lies very much to my heart. Most humbly begging

[1] Strickland.
[2] John Hay of Restalrig, who succeeded John Murray at Secretary.
[3] Sheridan.

your Majesty's Blessing, I remain with the utmost respect and submission to every thing you think fitt,

your most dutifull son,

HENRY.

King James to Prince Charles

ROME. August 8th, 1746.

Every letter I now write to you, My Dearest Carluccio, may find you in France and I hope in God that may be the case as to this. But in the mean time my anxiety for you cannot but daily increase, especially since the accounts we have received by the return of Messrs. O'Bryne and Linch [1] from Scotland. It grieves me to think of the situation you must have been in in all respects since the last unfortunate Battle and that you should have missed the opportunity of coming into France in the Ships that brought over Sir Thomas, but there is no help for what is past. In the uncertainty where this may find you, I shall add nothing else here. God Bless my D^{rst} Child whom I tenderly embrace and am all yours,

JAMES R.

The Same to the Same

ROME. Aug. 22nd, 1746.

So many precautions are taking My Dearest Carluccio, to get you out of Scotland, that I hope in God one or t'other will succeed, but I own I am affrayed that a just and right caution on your own side to keep as private as you can and not to discover yourself but where you are morally sure you can do it without risque may render it difficult to find you out, and

---

[1] Two of the Irish soldiers of fortune who had gone over to join the Prince, and had been fortunate in escaping capture both going to and returning from Scotland. Letters from old Sir Thomas Sheridan, recommending these two returned wanderers to O'Bryen are at Windsor.

181

perhaps prevent your profiting of an occasion to come off, but Providence will I hope direct both yourself, and those who are gone in search of you, so that I may soon have the comfort of know you in a place of safety, for till then my anxiety cannot cease ; In the mean time no business of any kind can be thought of, and anything I can say from hence is of no use, and so, My Dear Child, I shall bid you Adieu. Beseeching God to bless you and embracing you tenderly I am all yours,

JAMES R.

The Same to the Same

ROME. Sept. 12th, 1746.

If what the Gazettes say, My Dearest Carluccio, of you being again at the head of some of The Highlanders be true, I should hope in that situation you might be for some time at least in a less unsafe way than if you had continued hidding, and that you will be the more easily found out by those who are gone to look out for you, and bring you into France. But with all that all we know of you is so uncertain and the dangers you are exposed to so manifest, that my pain and anxiety for you put me in a condition I cannot well express. While I am all alone here, without satisfaction or comfort of any kind, and without knowing when I can have that of seeing you again, for were you now in France, I cannot go to you, and you could not come here, without abandoning all our affairs. But your Brother is not in the same case, and I even writ him not very long ago upon the subject of his coming to make me a short visit here, after your arrival in France. But with all this, I thank God my health is not worse and has even been rather better than usual this summer. Adieu, My dear Child, for till I know you are in a place of safety I can scarce think or write of anything but what relates to you. God Almighty bless protect and direct you. I tenderly embrace you and am all yours,

JAMES R.

A certain number of letters to the King on the occasion of the Prince's escape from Scotland are now given.

Cardinal de Tencin [1] *to James. His relief at the escape of Prince Charles, for the accomplishment of which he had done so little, rings somewhat false*

FONTAINEBLEAU, *le* 15. 8bre 1746.

SIRE,

Je respire, Le Prince est Sauvé ; il est heureusent arrivé à Rosehof,[2] qui est vieux rade entre Rennes et Morlaix. C'est à Warèn a qui on a eu l'obligation. Je suplie très humblemem Votre Majesté de me permettre de la féliciter de cet heureux Evènement ; Elle ne doute pas qu'en conséquence je ne fasse tout, pour le bien de son service.

Nous avons gagné une Bataille en flandres le II de ce mois,[3] le Marquis d'Armentières en a apporté avant hier la nouvelle au Roy. En même tems, Sa M^{te} a appris que les Anglois qui avoient faite une déscente sur nos Côtes de Bretagne, avoient été obligés de se rembarquer sans rien faire.

Je suis avec un profound respect et l'attachement le plus tendre.

Sire,

De Votre Majesté,

Le très humble et très obeissant Serviteur,

LE CARD. DE TENCIN.

The Duke of York to the King, after the landing of Prince Charles at Roscoff

CLICHY. Oct^{bre} *ye* 14*th*, 1746.

SIR,

Your Majesty may judge how happy I am with the news I send you. I long much to have this Courrier arrive that you

[1] Pierre Guerin de Tencin, Cardinal 1679–1758. Owed his advancement to his sister, the celebrated Madame de Tencin, mistress both of the Regent Orleans and of Bolingbroke. He was minister from 1742 to 1751.

[2] Roscoff.　　　　　　　　[3] Saxe defeated the Allies at Rancoux.

may be well ridd of all the pains and anxietyes you have been under for so long. I am very impatient as you may believe to see my dearest Brother, I am in hopes it will be tomorrow. Sir John is just gon to meet him for the reasons that Obryon mentions. The Duke will make use of all his endeavours to putt in practice the advice Gregory (the King) has been so good as to give him. How is Luke (the Duke) to act if John (the Prince) shou'd not care that he shou'd communicate certain things to Leopold (Mr. Obryen). Your Majesty will see the reason of that question by Humphrey's (the Prince's) letter to Jonathan (the Duke). As I have slept but three houers last night, my head does not permit me to write long. But next post I shall probably make it upp. Most humbly begging your Majesty's blessing I remain with the utmost respect,

your most dutifull Son,

HENRY.

The Same to the Same

FONTAINEBLEAU. *Oct^{bre} ye* 23rd, 1746.

SIR,

Wee are here since Wednesday night and in such a continuall hury and tracas that I wonder how I have gott time at all to write. I think Gregory (*The King*) will have reason altogether to be pleased with the way Cornelius (the *French Court*) has acted, he has certainly been drawn in by degrees, all these are trifles to the mein point, but yet they have allwaise some good in them. It was only the other day I received your Majesty's letter of the 27th last month. My health is not as well as usual, but it will I hope soon turn quite right when I can gett anew some exercise as I know your Majesty will excuse my shortness this post.

Most humbly begging your blessing.

I remain with the utmost respect,

Your most dutifull son,

HENRY.

King James to Prince Charles

ALBANO. *November 3rd*, 1746.

I cannot express to you, My Dearest Carluccio, the joy and comfort I felt in receiving your letter from Morlaix of the 10th Oct^r, after all I have suffered on your account for so many months past. Till I hear from you after your arrival at Paris it is useless to enter into any particular business with you from hence, and specially considering the informations you may have had from the Duke and Obryen, who will show you what I now write to him, for to be communicated to you and to Card^l Tencin, on some particulars, on which I need not therefore enlarge here. I am affrayed you will have little reason to be satisfyed with the Court of France, and that you will not have less need of courage and fortitude in bearing and suffering in that Country, than you had in acting in Brittain, and let me recommend in the most earnest manner to you patience and prudence, for by a contrary conduct you would make things worse, and never better. You have a sure friend in Card^l Tencin and as sure and trusty a servant in Obryen. Nobody can advise you better than they two, and they will I am sure do all they can to serve you.

I need say nothing of the Duke, in whom you will find a great alteration in all respects since you saw him, and you will soon see that he deserves to be your friend, as he is your Brother.

I had promised Mr. Warren that if he brought you back safe from Scotland, I would make him a Knight Baronet,[1] and accordingly you will find here inclosed a Warrant for that effect, which you will give him from me, and I am sure I can never forget the service he has now rendered us. I wish however that he would keep this Warrant secret, because I am absolutely resolved to give no more such, or any Commissions, as long as our affaires remain in the situation they now are.

[1] Warren had hoped to be a Baron, like Walsh.

Sir Thomas is here with me and better in his health than I have seen him these many years.

When I hear further from you, I shall say more on this subject. At present I shall add nothing else but to beseech the Almighty to bless, prosper and direct you, after having deliver'd you from so many dangers, of which I am very impatient to have a distinct detail. I thank God my health has been pretty tollerable all this Summer, and is so yet, tho' we have a mighty bad season of it here. Adieu, my D^{rst} Child. If you knew how much and how truely I love you could have nothing to wish on that article and I think myself as sure of yours for me that it will never alter. God bless you, I tenderly embrace you and am all yours,

JAMES R.

The Prince to the King, showing how childishly he was behaving in Paris

CLICHY, *ye 6th November,* 1746.

I had been a little out of order, it being an Indigestion, but am entirely recovered, as I have had all the Kiks of ye Facalty, except bleeding, that has hindered me from wryting this week as I coud wish. I have had as yet no positive answer from ye F.C.[1] in regarde of our manner of Living here, except a regiro of Mar: Argen^{on} sending his Clark with a verbal message to Obrien, and making a moste scandalous arrangement for us. O. immediately came and asked me what retur to macke to such a message, oppon which after having asked him if Mr. Argen: had writ to him on that subject (to which he said no, shewing me a trifling Letter ye said Minister had just writ to him). I dictated to him immediatly his answer. *Id est* that he had given me an account of what ye said Clark had told him and that I asked if ye M's. had writ anything about that, you said no, that being immediatly said I wou'd not believe a word of any such proposals unles I have it under ye said M's. hand.

[1] French Court.

I find it and am absolutely convinced of it that ye only way of delying with this —— Government is to give as short and smart answer as one can, at ye same time paying them in their own Coin by Loding them with sivilities and compliments, setting apart business, for that Kind of vermin the more you give them the more the'l take, as also the more room you give them the more they have to grapple at, which makes it necessary to be Laconick with them, which is the only way of passifing them, and putting all their sheme upon their backs which they woud fairly strive to shift of by rigiros.   As to Mr. Writ and others I leve spaking of them till a nother time and so I shall end at present moste humbly asking yr Majesty's Blessing. ·

I shew'd this Letter to ye Duke, as I intend also to shew him for ye future, what I write having entier Confidence and trust in his secrecy, but have made him solemly promise to say to no mortal without exception what i trust to him by word of mouth or wryting, for I wou'd be very sory some people should no my heart as I shall more fully explain an other time.

The King's dignified rebuke to the Prince as regards this behaviour has been printed by Browne.   The one printed next, of course, crossed with the above.

King James to Prince Charles (in his own hand)

♦ ROME. *Nov.* 12*th*, 1746.

What a comfort was it to me, my Drst. Carluccio, to find by yours of ye 17 Oct. that you were well and safely arrived at Paris after all the dangers and fatigues you have passed thro. As I never missed a week writeing to you, you will have received a number of my letters together.   Some of them are scarce worth reading now, but others are, particularly those of ye 19 April and 25th July, wherein I opened my heart and my mind to you, for I must allwayes say what I think for your good and service and you must be sensible I can have nothing

187

in view but your advantage. When you write to me on these letters and have been at Fountainebleau, I shall be able to writ more fully and to the purpose. In ye mean time it is useless to fatigue you here with repetitions, or on any other matters besides that I am in a great hurry. I cannot however but add here the comfort I had to find your Brother so pleased with your kind reception and I am sure he will allwayes deserve your love and affection. Tho' you prepare me to be some weeks without receiving long letters from you, I hope and believe you wont be so good as your word. Adieu, Drst. Child, I beseech God to bless you. I tenderly embrace you and am all yours,

JAMES R.

James Edgar, the Secretary (see p. 190) *to*
Sir John Graeme (see p. 198)

ROME, 9*ber* 17*th*, 1746.

I am very glad, my Dear Sir, I can now tell you that alongst with yr Letter of the 17th 8ber, I recd those of the 5th, 10th, 19th and 26th 7ber, so that now there are no more packets due, but the Current one, wch I hope to receive today or tomorrow, since the French Courier now passes through Switzerland. We are happy that our anxietys about the Prince are now over, which for a long time had been a constant article of our Letters. I beg you would do me the honor to lay me, full of zeal and duty at their R.R.H.H.'s feet.

There being now several Gentlemen of the Shyre of Angus now at Paris, with the most of whose fathers I was acquainted, I beg you would let them know that they have one here with a true-honest-Angus-heart, full of concern for the late publick and private misfortunes and ready to serve them upon all occasions, Assuring Lord Ogilvy [1] of my humble respects, and

[1] The territorial magnate of Angus (Forfarshire) now a refugee in France who was shortly after permitted to raise a Regiment of Loyal Scots in French pay, and thus give worthy employment to many fellow countrymen.

188

the other gentlemen of my best and kindest compliments, I am, my dear sir, with all my heart, etc.

Prince Charles to the King

PARIS. 12*th Dec.* 1746.

SIR,

I have received yrs of ye 17th and after it yrs of ye 12 Novem^r, which as its being so long a missing I gave it for lost. I must own my fault but I have not as yet red all yr old Letters that I received in one bundle upon my arrival in this Country, my only excuse is I realy did not immagine their was anything in them that needed be answered immediatly, had I thought otherwise I would have read them, not withstanding my being hurried in a manner every day mostly with trifles, which not withstanding cannot be left neglected. Not being able to find Lord Sempils Cyphers which I must have mislaid or lost since I came hither, this hinders me from reding yrs of ye 19th April and 25 July you point out to me, but shall certainly be able to answer them by next post for I have immediatly sent to Lord Sempil for his Coppy. Wright came to make me a visit t'other day, and by his discourse I find he is entierly of ye same way of thinking as Howel (himself) is in regard of Williams, and by consequence aproved his providings in that respect, at which Howel cou'd not but own to me he was not a little surprised at it. If it was not to much liberty I wou'd make bold to desier yr Majesty to lay me at his Olinesses feet being penetrated with his goodness. I shall leve off, having nothing more to say at present and wanting words to express how much I am sensible at all ye expressions your Majesty is so good as to make me in all yr Letters. I moste humbly ask Blessing and remain

Your moste Dutifull son,

C. P.

The Same to the Same

PARIS, *ye* 10*th Aprill,* 1747.

SIR,

It is a melancholi thing this affair of Murray ye Secretary, of which I send a Coppy of a Letter writ by ye very man that carried a French Commission, he so much pressed for. I have good reason to suspect by putting circumstances together that he (Murray) was in a click with L. George tho he pretended and appeared to be otherwise, this perhaps may be reffining to much, and so shall suspend my judgment upon that till I can make it absolutely clier. I have received a Civill note from Count d'Argenson,[1] in which he desiers I should give him an adress by which he can be always able to communicate to me his master's pleasure without its ever being suspected, which I did, giving him a Cant name, to be sent under cover to Waters jounior, so that now everything is at their door. I am seeking out for a Cuntry house near the town where I shall be able to brese a little fresh air and be aporte for any business that may happen. I have got accounts that B[2] arrived safe, after a very narrow eskape, for he fell into ye sea getting out ye ship in to a littler bote, being pursued by a man of War. I am very impatient to have accounts from himself. I have got a Cold in my head a little troblesom, but of no consequence God willing. I lay myself at yr. Majestys Feet moste humbly asking Blessing.

(*No signature*)

P.S. I have just received by ye Spanish post yrs of ye 27th Janry. and 17th Feby. but have not yet read them.

Of the letters written after the failure of the Rising of 1745 a great number are from and to James Edgar, who was private secretary to King James for forty-eight years, and one of the

---

[1] See p. 158. The Minister for War was the Comte d'Argenson. The Minister for Foreign Affairs was his elder brother, the Marquis René Louis.
[2] Probably Charles Boyd 2nd son of Lord Kilmarnock.

most all-pervading personalities of the vast Stuart correspondence. He wrote a very large number of the letters of the
King who merely signed them. Of such letters as were holograph, Edgar made a copy in his small neat script, if they were
in French, sometimes a translation, and very often the two are
filed together. He was also the recipient of innumerable
letters from Jacobites all over Europe, who relied upon him to
put their cases or their pleas before his master, at a favourable
moment.

He was the son of a small laird in Angus (Forfarshire) and
always had a soft spot for anyone from his own country, as
well as a great though hopeless longing to revisit it.

He had taken an active part in the Rising of the '15. On his
own showing he was present at the raising of the Standard at
Braemar and fought throughout the Campaign. Subsequently
he was lucky enough to escape to France in the clothes of a
friendly farmer (which clothes he scrupulously returned) and
rejoined his master at Avignon, where he appears in the official
list of Scots in that city as "Sous-secretaire." He followed
the King to Urbino, Pesaro and finally Rome, which became
his home until his death in 1764, though he accompanied the
sad little court on its annual visit to Albano. At the very
beginning of the period covered by this volume, viz. in the
spring of 1719, he appears to have (in common with all the
other Jacobites in Rome), resented the arrogance of James
Murray of Stormont, but that is the sole occasion in the whole
mass of correspondence when he was not on friendly terms
with *everybody*. He was one of a large family of brothers,
some of whom wrote him amusing letters, and one of his
nephews, John Edgar, followed in his footsteps and wielded a
sword in the '45, likewise escaping safely to France. He

eventually returned to Scotland, where he became the laird of Keithock. James Edgar died in Rome of a stroke early in 1764. His master was at that time a complete invalid and the days of his correspondence were over, he himself dying two years later.

From the vast mass of letters to and from James Edgar it has been more than usually difficult to make a selection. The first is from the worthy Jacobite of both Risings, Lord Pitsligo, from his own retirement in Edinburgh between the two dates. That, as well as some of the others, indicate the poor Secretary's longing for Scotland and things Scottish, while others show him as the confidant of everyone's interests and troubles, and finally, as straining every nerve to keep up some kind of communication between the wandering Prince Charles, now completely disappeared and his melancholy old Father.

The first few letters are prior to the collapse of the Rising.

Lord Pitsligo, one of the most faithful Jacobites of 1715 and 1745, to James Edgar

EDINBURGH. *Oct.* 8, 1738.

DEAR MR. EDGAR,

I went last year to Bath on account of my Son's health, and I thank God the Journey has not been without success, tho' he is still upon a very low Dyet. Yesterday I saw Mrs. Abercrombie (the honest Doctors widow) who told me you were pleas'd to remember me, as I assure you I ever remember you, with a great deal of Affection, and 'tis a Quality I value my self upon that I can never forget a Friend. But to say no more in my own Praise, I give you hearty thanks for your Friendship to good Mrs. Abercrombie, not doubting your continuance of it for the future. I long much for an Evening's Conversation with you. I believe we could find subject matter for two.

I know not what more I can say. You may suppose me the same man you left me, only about nineteen years older, and I fear with little acquisition of Prudence for so long a time. I have lost a world of Friends, and some of infinite worth, since we parted, but I rejoice when I think of those that remain. This is a poor Letter to be sent so far, but you'll accept of it as it is from a sincere Friend and humble servant.

James Gairdner, a merchant captain, writes from Leghorn to James Edgar

Jan. 11, 1740.

"I am sorry to tell you that I cannot provide you with neither skait nor bannocks, for my ship was never in Scotland, being too large for any business from thence. I carry upon her 24 guns and must battle with ye Spaniards if attackt. Yet I hope one day or other to act in a better cause.

As for news, the most I know of is about yr young people which cannot be any ways entertaining to you. Mr. Carnegie of Brechin and my Grandfather is dead, and Sir David Ogilvie of Enverhartie is married to Finevever's [1] eldest daughter."

John Gairdner writes again to Edgar to inform him that all his friends in the land of cakes are well, but that he (J. G.) has had no occasion to go there, nor to bring the dainties asked for.

The place John Hay occupied in the hearts of his fellow-Jacobites is well shown by the following letter, written at the time of his death to Edgar :

AVIGNON. 26 *Sept.* 1740.

You will be, dear James, equally afflicted and surprised with this letter, which if you happen to open in the King's presence, I wish you took some pretence to retire, in order to deliver the

[1] Finhaven.

enclosed to my Lord Dunbar, that so he may manage a proper time for communicating to his Majesty the death of his faithfull servant, my Lord Inverness.   I am perswaded his Majesty will feel his loss in a most sensible manner, and should therefore be glad he was prepared to receive the account of it.   For that reason I have enclosed to Lord Dunbar my letter to his Majesty on this dismal occasion, which will be one of grief and concern to me as long as I live.   I am dear James,

Yr most affectionate & most humble servant,

JO. GRAEME.[1]

*Robert Edgar, brother of the Chevalier's Secretary, James Edgar,
in Rome, writes from his home in Angus to Rome*

25 May, 1745.

DEAR JACOB (no doubt a joke in connection with the residence of James Edgar in Rome),

As it is dangerous bad time this French war, if it were possible to obtain a French pass for my ship—suppose it were attended with some charge, it would be a great convenience to me.   However, I leave it to yourself and shall be glad to hear your opinion about it.   If it can be done it would come safe to my hand by Mr. Fraser.

My ship is a Brigantine, Pink-sterned—Ninety tunnes burden name of *Success*.   It would be a great advantage in these bad times if I could employ her in a trade clear of contraband.   Your answer will be much wearied for and expected by all friends.   That it may please God to preserve you and in his good time grant us a comfortable meeting is the earnest request of Dear James

Your verie affectionate brother,

RO. EDGAR.

There is no record of whether the honest sea captain obtained his desire or not.

[1] See p. 198.

194

Lady Inverness to James Edgar.

AVIGNON. *Janry.* 1st, 1746.

Many thanks, good Sir, for your kind compliment, receive mine pray upon the same occasion : we have reason to flatter our selves that this year will putt an end to the misfortunes of the Royal family ; I hope in God it will and that I shall soon hear that the King has left Rome to go for England. I wish you with all my heart a good journey and am Sir your most humble servant,

M. INVERNESS.[1]

Rev. Father Flyn to Edgar, hoping that the Court has gone to Scotland following the victorious Prince

ST. GERMAIN. *Jan.* 2nd, 1746.

SIR,

Tho your Silence these two posts past, together with the rumor wee have here of the Kings coming to France, makes me in a manner doubt whether this will find you in Rome, still I shall not discontinue writing Every post untill I have orders to the Contrary, wch I would fain hope to receive soon, for things goe on very well both in England and Scotland. Lord John Drummonds small army is by ye last accts swelled to 8 or nine thousand men, the Prince drives all before him in Lancashire and Chestershire, and the french Embarkment goes on with all diligence possible, tho by the last acctt. from Dunkerque wch was of ye 28th they did not Expect to sett out untill the fourth or fifth of this month. H.R.H. the Duke arrived there that day from Calais. my Lord is honourd wth ye Cordon blue of France I hear.

I enclose Mr. Dillons letter to his Majesty and am with great Esteem

Sir,

your most obedient and most humble servant,

D. FLYN.

[1] See p. 60.

195

As I had finished my short letter arrived a Courier detached by my Lord Marchal from Boulogne, ye 30th at night, wt ye Duke's orders to me to deliver to said Courier two suits of Curaisses, and the arm, without ye helmets.

Anonymous to Edgar—wild rumours from Scotland

Jan. the 10th (1746).

DR. SIR,

By last Genoa letters we had an account in most of the papers, that an officer by name Marquis de la Rochelle was dispatch'd from the Court of Paris to Prince D^n Phillip with the news of a warm action between H.R.H.'s army and that of General Wade with the entire defeat of the latter ; but as noe Courier pass^d by Pisa with such agreeable message, soe noe creditt is given to the same, notwithstanding that both the French and Spanish Consuls maintained the report to be true.

Captn Sprakling, Master of the trading Ship call'd the *Tuskany*, arriv'd here in 26 days from London, which City (he says) is, as if the World was drawing to an End, there's noe Stirring abroad either a horseback, a foot or in Coach, if in the latter you are visited every Corner you pass by to see if you have gott Arms, and even they Search peoples Pocketts to know if they have Pockett-Pistols or letters ; and upon that occasion they robb one another of what money they can lay their hands on ; for noe manner of justice is to be had for such Crimes or misdemeanours ; he tells me, that by fame the Prince is extreamly well lik'd all over London, and that his Vanguards was at Liverpool : the Ladies in the Theatres publickly praise His R.H. and cry out, when shall we have the grace to see, brave King-Charles-of Sweden's brother, what—will he not come from Liverpool to see us : We had an account here that Colonel Drummond's Regiment with the Irish Picketts was then arriv'd from France ; The Captn tells me, whilst he was riding in the Downs at an anchor, that a French Privateer of

20 Gunns was taken with several officers aboard going from Dunkirk to Scotland, and that one of the officers was immediately sent aboard the *Admiral* then cruising in the Channel.

Father Flyn to Edgar, giving the gossip of Paris, while the Prince was in Scotland

ST. GERMAIN. *Jan.* 30*th,* 1746.

SIR,

The Roman post is not as yett come in ; by letters of ye 27th from Boulogne all things there were in ye same state wch I marked ye in my last of 23rd w^t pleases me most is yt H.R.H. the Duke is very hearty and full of good spirits, wch shews ye he has at least good hopes ; its not doubted but ye Embarkment will goe on in proper time, its said they onely stay to be joined by the Brest fleet : wee hear by ye Common report yt some Spanish troops have lately landed in Scotland wth a considerable summe of money. Wee are assur'd yt upon ye Princes retireing from Westmorland his arrier gardes were attacked by Cumberlands advanced gardes, yt the later were repulsed with considerable loss, yt on ye next day the 2nd of this month ye Prince left 400 men and onely 3 pieces of Canon in Carlisle and marched with all the rest of his army he arrived ye 3rd at Dumfries where he found some opposition from ye Inhabitants, for wch Insolence they wer fin'd 2000 pds Sterling, he arrived ye 6th at Glascow without any molestation, for Cumberland did not find proper to pursue or trouble their march, but returned in great hast to London wth part of his army, my Lord John Drummond was at yt time besieging the Castle of Stirling, I hope he is befor now master thereof. Said Lord has just publish'd over all Scotland a manifesto setting forth yr he is sent to yt Country by order of the K. of France to war upon and distress the Enemys of the Royal familly of ye Stuarts, and yt his most Christian Majesty joyntly wth the King of Spain are firmly resolved never to desist acting

197

that way, untill said Royale familly are restored to their own
dominions : this manifesto caused a great Consternation in
London, the Duke of Hanover has sent a Coppy of it to his
beloved friends the States General, after a very mournful tone,
Monsieur D'Argenson minister of war, has lately presented a
memoire to Mr. Van hoy the Holland Ambassador wherein he
complains of the duplicity and knavery of that Republick in
regard of France, and even requires yt a speedy reparation may
be given to his master : the Court of France is still att Marly and
very gay. I finish in conjureing ye to be of good courage, for
I realy hope very firmly yt wee soon will have great and good
news and am with great Esteem, Sir,

   your most obedient & most humble servant,

             D. FLYN.

By the Amsterdam Gazette ye Lord Tyrawly, General
Wade and Admiral Vernon gave up their Employments
and quitted the Court. by a letter arrived this minute from
Boulogne, Bulkeleys Regt. has orders to march towards
Diep in Normandy.

Another man of whom there are a great many letters is
Sir John Graeme, one of the many Scots at the Court in Rome,
who had been with the Prince at one stage of his journey from
Rome to Paris in January 1744. He was afterwards appointed
by King James to accompany the Duke of York to Avignon
and Paris in August 1745, and remained with him there.
Later, he was in the service of Prince Charles, which he left at
his own request and retired, but was in 1759 summoned to his
master's side in Rome by a pathetic letter from King James
which, although given in Browne's *History of the Highlands*, is
too little known and is given on page 247. At that period,
Graeme was created Lord Alford and died on Jan. 3rd, 1773.

The letters here given only begin in 1746—the second

mentions the loss of the good ship *Hazard*—taken at Montrose, renamed the *Prince Charles* and sent to Scotland with money and men under Captain Talbot.

The Prince's estimate of the numbers under his banner is greater than any known computation in the month preceding Culloden, as it seems to refer to those actually with him, disregarding the numbers under Perth and Sullivan in Ross-shire and the Macphersons and Frasers which were no doubt those he expected to join him "in a very little time."

Sir John Graeme to King James, while waiting with the Duke to go to Scotland with the prospective Expedition, or alternatively to join the French Army (the cypher names have, as usual, been translated by the writer or reader)

DUNKIRK. *Apl.* 15, 1746.

SIR,

I had the honour to acquaint your Majesty by last post of the measures the Duke had taken to go and reside in Flanders. In answer to the letter I wrote to Daniel (*The Card*[1]) proposing to him that Ghant, which had been allready granted, might be chang'd to Lille, he takes no notice at all of my proposition, but says H.R.H. may chuse betwixt Arras and St. Omer. Perhaps Charles (*The K. of France*) intends to go straight to Lille, and to remain there some time to concert the operations of the campagne, which may be the reason for not allowing the Duke that place for his Residence and that Daniel (*The Card*[1]) rather than give that reason for it, chus'd to take no notice of the proposition. However H.R.H. in order to leave no time for retracting the permission given to go into Flanders, posted yesterday morning from Boulogne, and will set out from hence on Munday for Arras, which he prefers on many accounts to St. Omer.

Lord Thomond, who commanded there, assures me that Berwick's and Booth's Regiments will be ready to sail in two or three days if the wind serves. One of the two Cutters or advice boats, which the Court has granted for carrying Intelligence betwixt France and Scotland, will be ready about the same time. There will go in those Ships as many of the volonteers as can find room in them, and the rest will go according as occasions shall offer.

There was a report several days ago of a Battle in Scotland where the Prince had obtain'd a great victory over Cumberland's army. This news has not yet been confirm'd, but the publick papers continue to prepare for action, and cannot conceal some little advantages. We are inform'd by Sir James Steuart, whose lady is come lately from Edinburgh,[1] that the rumours there were that the government's army was mightily afraid of the Highlanders, and that numbers of them were sick.

I am always in great hopes of hearing soon good news, and am with the most profound respect, Sir,

> your Majesty's most faithful most dutiful and most
> obedient subject and servant,

Jo. Graeme.

This letter was written on the very day before the fatal battle of Culloden, and the next a fortnight after it, on receipt of the cheering news brought by Richard Warren who skilfully got away from the obscure little port of Findhorn on April 15.

The Same to the Same

Arras. 30 Ap. 1746.

Sir,

Mr. Warren arriv'd here yesterday in ten days from Findorn in Scotland, having left the Prince some days before at Inverness in perfect health, being quite recover'd of a great Cold he had at Elgin. H.R.H.'s affairs go on very well in the Highlands, his partys having had several advantages over those of

---

[1] Lady Fanny Steuart, sister of Lord Elcho.

the Ennemy, and all those that were under Lord Loudon's command being quite dispersed, some of them killed or taken. The joy this good news gave us was much abated by the great misfortune of *Brouns* being taken at Tounge with all the money arms and volunteers, after having surrounded the Orkneys.[1] I realy believe that money, had the Prince receiv'd it in the favorable situation he is in, would have carry'd his affairs a very great length. But if the two Privateers which sail'd from Britany arrive safe, they will, I hope, retrive that loss. The Duke has receiv'd two kind letters from the Prince of the 2nd and 23rd March, O.S. He mentions in the first his having 10,000 men and his expecting some thousands more in a very little time.

JO. GRAEME.

The Same to the Same. (He had now gone with the Duke of York to join the French Army in the Low Countries)

GHENT. 20 *May* 1746.

SIR,

Tho' we have nothing directly from the Prince himself, yet the publick papers are so full of a battle at Colloden near Inverness, where they pretend Cumberland has gain'd a victory, that the Duke—thinking no time was to be lost dispatch'd the day before yesterday an officer with a letter to the King of France to implore his protection for the Prince on this melancholly occassion. He wrote likewise to the Marq[s] d'Argenson, which I accompany'd with a letter of mine proposing to him that the King his Master should immediately intimate to the Elector of Hannover as well as to his Allys, that he never would listen to any proposition of peace till such

---

[1] A long account of the taking of this ship by Captain O'Bryen in the *Sheerness* is to be found in the Archives Nationales in Paris. Another account occurs in an interesting manuscript in the possession of Lord James Stewart Murray, where it is stated that in addition to the large amount of specie to be consigned to the Prince and his commanders there was also a cask of specially blessed rosaries !

time as the Princes person was in safety. I enclos'd the packet to Lord Thomond whom I desir'd in the Duke's name to deliver it out of his own hand to the Minister, and to insist upon the contents of it by all the reasons his zeal and attachment to the Royal family could suggest to him. Tho' I flatter myself things are not so bad as they are given out, yet we thought it would be extreamly imprudent to allow ourselves to be lull'd asleep with vain hopes after seeing the Elector address'd by the House of Lords for a victory, whilst H.R.H. might be in danger of falling into the hands of his Ennemys. I receive this moment by an Express a letter from the Minister acquainting me that the King allows the Duke to go immediately to Antwerp to the siege of the Citadelle of that Town commanded by the Comte de Clermont Prince of the blood, as his aide de Camp.

The Same to the Same

ANTWERP. *May 27,* 1746.

SIR,

On Wednesday at six in the Evening the Duke got on horseback with his small retenue and went with the Count de Clermont to view the Camp. From that we went to see the Parc of Artillery, and from thence to the Depot. At half an hour after nine we came to the place mark'd for the opening of the Trenches before the Citadel, where having stay'd a little to see the *Travailleurs* file off with great order and silence, we retir'd a little towards one of the gates of the Town, and there remain'd about an hour when the Ingeneers came to inform the General that they were almost cover'd ; and he finding there was no more occasion for his presence, we went home to our Quarters in Town. During the opening of the Trenches the enemy did not fire above four or five Canon shot, and that at random, whence it is probable they did not know what we were about, tho' it was moon light, and at a small distance from the Citadel. Yesterday betwixt five and six in the after-

202

noon we went with the General to the Trenches from one end
of the Parallele to t'other, and I need not tell your Majesty that
the Duke kept the best Countenance in the world, and walk'd
as upright and steady as he would have done at ten miles
distance from Canon shot. Now it is the Ennemys turn to
burn powder, but we shall soon have ours. This afternoon
our mortars will begin to play, and tomorrow or Sunday at
furthest our Canon.

The Count de Clermont takes great care to instruct H.R.H.,
and your Majesty may be assur'd he never will allow him to
risk his person but in his presence, and *a propos* I don't doubt
but you will think fit to write him an obliging letter.

Clement (Marqs. D'Argenson) told us that he had accounts
at last of the Swedes being sail'd. I pray God they may arrive
in time. I enclose a *Placet* in favour of a person who was very
much recommended to the Duke by Sir Charles Wogan
whilst we were at Arras.

I am with the most profound respect,

Sir,

Your Majesty's most faithfull most dutiful and most
obedient Subject and Servant,

JO. GRAEME.

The Same to the Same

NAVARRE. *July* 31, 1746.

The Duke receiv'd yesterday morning your Majesty's letter
of the 4th with one enclose'd for the Duc de Bouillon which I
have forwarded, and a Copy of your letter to Cardinal Tencin.
Since my last nothing new is happen'd except poor Mr.
Murray's [1] misfortune whom the gazettes mention to have
been taken in the Low-lands near his own house, and on whom
I am affraid the government will have no pity. They are
going on very fast in their proceedings against the prisoners

[1] John Murray of Broughton, who turned "King's Evidence" against
Lord Lovat and others.

they have in their hands, and they are bringing a new bill of Attender against forty-four persons of which number I am sorry to find in an English Paper Sir James Steuart and Mr. Carnegy. I wish with all my heart Clements' (Marquis d'Argenson) letter to the miner 628 (Dutch Ambassador) had been more nervous. Remonstrances of that kind ought to be short and strong. I propos'd to him at Antwerp to intimate to the English Secretary of State by that minister's channel, that the King his master would take so much to heart any vigour that might be us'd against the Prince or his friends, that tho' he had actually no British prisoners at his disposal, he was resolv'd to make reprisals on those who should fall into his hands during the course of the war. A Remonstrance of this nature might have had some effect ; but he excus'd himself by saying such Reprisals would be of a very dangerous precedent and introduce a great deal of blood-shed over and above what must be necessarily spilt in the war. Never was such a step made as the excepting a ransom for those who were taken at Fontenoy, and at so critical time. Were they now prisoners in France, I am persuaded that even without having recourse to threats, they would have sav'd the lives of many honest men.

As to what your Majesty writes of the motives of the Prince's Expedition which might be learnt from Sir Thomas, I don't believe the Duke [1] talk'd to him much while he was here upon that Topick, all his thoughts being employ'd about his Brother's safety ; and I doubt even if he can tell us much more upon the subject than what we imagin'd from the beginning which is—That H.R.H. being quite tyr'd of the manner wherewith he was us'd in *Durham* (France) and of the delays of *Cornelius* (The French Court) resolv'd at last to try what he could do of himself, in hopes that his appearing at the head of a body of men would encourage them to send him succours for their own sakes, once the danse was begun ; to which I believe we may safely add the common exagerations of well

[1] Of York.

meaning men with regard to the numbers of those he might expect to joyn him. And I make no doubt but H.R.H. has been told that he had but to set his foot on British ground and he would carry all before him, which is a language I have hear'd on more occasions than one. All these are strong motives to engage a brave and generous Prince in an undertaking, where so much glory and reputation was to be gain'd besides the restoring of his Family to a Crown which is their undisputable right. He has acquired the first, and if it shall please God to bring him safe to this side I hope still to live to see the accomplishment of the last.

I have always observ'd in the Duke so much tender love respect and deference for the Prince his brother that I am persuaded nothing will be ever captable to alter their Union, and should any Impression have been given at any time to the Prince, which I flatter myself is not the case, I am confident their first meeting will set all right.

They write from Paris that the four Irish officers [1] who are to go on board the fregates are to part for Bretany on Munday or Tuesday at furthest. As the late gazettes make no mention of the Prince, it is to be hop'd he is either come away, or that his Enemys are quite ignorant of the place where he is.

The Duke took physick two or three days ago, but I cannot say he has yet recover'd his appetit. H.R.H. has writ to the new King of Spain upon his accession to the Crown. He has likewise writ to the Marquis d'Argenson charging him with his Compliments to the King of France on the death of his Uncle and Daughter in law.

I am with the most profound respect
Sir,
Your Majesty's most faithful most dutiful and most obedient Subject and Servant,

Jo. Graeme,

[1] O'Sullivan and his friends.

The Same to the Same

CLICHY. *October* 14, 1746.

SIR,

This being the happiest day of my life [1] I beg leave to rejoice with your Majesty on the Prince's safe arrival in france. As I am about seting out to meet His Royal Highness I have not time to make this longer which I leave with the Duke to be forwarded by a Courier he intends to dispatch tonight.

I am ever with the most hearty zeal and profound respect,

Sir,

your Majesty's most faithfull most dutifull
and most obedient Subject and Servant,

Jo. GRAEME.

The Same to the Same

CLICHY. *October* 17, 1746.

SIR,

Your Majesty will be glad to know that the Prince is arriv'd at Paris in perfect health and in high spirits. Tho' the fatigue, the want of all necessarys, and the dangers he has undergone are beyond imagination, yet he looks as well as when I had the honour to see him more than two years ago. Nothing was ever so tender as his first Interview with the Duke, which I am sorry I was not witness to, having met him on the road in the night time, and found them together on my return next morning. It is an unspeakable pleasure to me to see how much they love one another, and I hope in God it will always continue so. Col¹ Obryen is gone to Fontainebleau to concert his Interview with the King of France. We wait his return with impatience to know the manner of it, tho' by some letters already writ from thence we have reason to fear that the Court will insist upon its being done privately, which will not be at all to the Prince's taste, and it is no wonder.

---

[1] This phrase was also used by Richard Warren, who actually brought the Prince from Scotland.

Besides Messrs. Warren, Sheridan, Obrine and Lynch that went to look for H.R.H. there are come over with him Lochiel, his brother Doctor Cameron, Lochguery and Roy Steuart. He also brought over one Macdonald of Barestal [1] against whom there were proofs that his intentions were treacherous, and has recommended him to the care of the Intendant of Britany. H.R.H. has been very private at Paris since his arrival, and will be so for some days longer. The Duke din'd with him on Saturday and yesterday, and after dinner they came out together to this place, where the Prince stay'd about an hour and return'd again to town.

There being no letters from your Majesty by last post I shall only add the profound respect with which I am

Sir,

your Majesty's most faithfull most dutifull and most obedient Subject and Servant,

JO. GRAEME.

It is said that the English who landed near L'Orient are reimbarked. [2] There has been an affair in flanders where the french have had a considerable advantage, but the particulars are not yet come our length.

After the return of the Prince
James Edgar to Prince Charles

ALBANO. *Nov.* 3, 1746.

SIR,

My heart is so full of joy on Your Royall Highness safe landing in France, that I most humbly beg leave you would permit me to lay myself at your feet on that happy occasion, full of thankfulness to God for your miraculous preservation, and of most fervent wishes that Your Royal Highness may not be long without having another opportunity to exert your

[1] Barrisdale, a traitor to both sides.   [2] See p. 183.

valour and heroick virtues in relief of your distressed Country, and attended with all the success you so highly deserve. I shall think myself happy in the meantime if I can contribute in any thing to Your Royall Highnesses satisfaction by obeying any commands you shall please to lay on me.

JAMES EDGAR.

Extract—Sir John Graeme to the King
(The Prince had left Paris)

PARIS. Feb. 27, 1747.

SIR,

There are several letters at Paris which bear Humphry's (The Prince's) departure from Avignon, but neither Jonathan (The Duke) nor I have heard from thence since the letter which Luke (O'Bryen) sent you by last post. We have here a very troublesome task by the impossibility of contenting so many people as we have to do with. Every body imagines to himself he has as much merit as another and deserves from the Court as considerable a gratification. Others are quite out of humour that some few have had the Cross of St. Louis or a Commission of Colonel, and thinking they have as good or a better pretention to such favours are dunning us continually.

Lord Ogilvy is at Versailles these eight days past waiting for a final decision concerning his Regiment. This will be an occasion of placing several of our unfortunate Country-men. There is lately a private letter from London which gives some hopes that there will be soon an Act of Indemnity,[1] in which case I suppose many of those who are not attented and have any thing to return to will go home. I am with the most profound respect,

Sir, Your Majesty's most faithfull, most dutiful and most obedient Subject and Servant,

JO. GRAEME.

[1] The Act of Indemnity was passed that summer, but eighty-three prominent Scotsmen were excepted from its provisions.

Extract—Prince Charles to the King

PASSY, *ye* 18 *June* 1747.

. . . I have been made a Curious present, be ye Sossety of Jesuits here, it being the Cross that Queen Mary of Scotland wore when she was beheded. I proffite of this sure occasion of sending it to yr. Majesty, as I flatter myself it will be acceptable. Moste humbly asking Blessing—I remain . . .

The Same to the Same, on hearing of his brother's intention of taking Holy Orders

ST. OUEN, *ye* 10*th July* 1747.

SIR,

I have received yrs of ye 13th and 20th June had I got a Dager throw my heart it would not have been mor sensible to me than at ye Contents of yr first.

My Love for my Brother and concern for yr Case being the occasion of it. I hope your Majesty will forgive me not entering any further on so disagreeable a subject the shock of which I am scarce out of so shall take ye liberty of referring to next Post anything in yours to be answered. I lay my self full of Respect and Duty at your Majesty's feet moste humbly asking Blessing

your most Dutifull son,

CHARLES P.

The Duke of York had left Paris secretly to rejoin his father in Rome, with the design of entering the Church, which design had been accomplished before the Prince heard of it. It was without doubt a great blow to the Cause.

Henry Duke of York to Prince Charles, while still under his brother's displeasure for having become an ecclesiastic

ALBANO. *June ye 20th,* 1747.

DEAR BROTHER,

Tho I have still the mortification to be without hearing from you I think it my duty to continue to write to you and to assure you of my most respectfull and tender love and affection, until you lett me know more plainly than by the silence of a few weeks that my letters will not be acceptable but I trust in God that will never happen and that you will never do me, and give me leave to say, yourself the wrong of breaking with a Brother who you will be sensible at last is not unworthy of your kindness. I remain, dear Brother, with the utmost respect,

your most loving Brother,

HENRY.

Extract—Father Myles McDonnell to King James, voicing the opinion of many Scots on this step

PARIS. *July* 14, 1747.

MOST GRACIOUS SOVEREIGN.

The complyance I owe to your Majesty's dread commands and the bent of my own natural inclination will not permit me to be silent upon his R.H. the Duke of York's late change of condition. The general distraction is only equal to the confusion your Majesty's subjects here are in agreeing in nothing so unanimously as in thinking it a mortal deadly stroke to the Cause ; especially at this present juncture, when the War is at the Height and prosperous and the Usurpers General Pardon just published at home. Many and various are the conjectures as well as the resolutions taken upon this occasion, and I am heartily grieved (tis unthinkable submission to say it) that not one of them is favourable to your Majesty's person or cause. The People at home were never so ripe, so well disposed, nor in greater hopes of another successful attempt, being determin'd

210

to second it with all their power to make amends for their late supiness. This I know from Gentlemen of distinction and quality lately come from England and just returned thither. I endeavour'd to persuade them that when your Majesty's reasons for consenting to the late event were known they wod certainly justify the Proceedings. This is all I co'd say, but alas, that will be of little force at home, where all the old bugbears of Popery, bigotry etc. will be renewed with (I am afraid) too much success. Wherefore I humbly apprehend and with the utmost submission remonstrate, that it will be proper to dispatch some discreet persons to England speedily, furnish'd with all the arguments and reasons imaginable to justify that step, and ward off if possible the dreadful storm the cause is threaten'd with. For my part I am determin'd to go at all hazards to throw in my little mite of assistance if I can scrape up enough to carry me, but I shall wait for the return of the Post to know yr. Majestie's pleasure.

His R.H. the Prince (I am told, for I don't go near him) has shutt himself up for several hours alone upon his hearing that news, the Duke's health is no more drank nor his name mentioned at his table. He is teazed about his safety and made to believe that his life will be in danger, being now alone and unmarry'd, and this upon a report that the Duke is to go into Holy Orders immediatly.

I have been searching my poor imagination for reasons to account for this sudden resolution of his R.H. and can find no other except that he was Peaked, and full of resentment for the most audacious base and perfidious attempts of some people to insult and vex him, at leastt to ridicule and make him unpopular. Your Majesty was as little spared which I hinted in my lastt. I cannot say whether or no this highly crimenal behaviour of those wretches arriv'd to the Duke's knowledge, but I don't think it co'd presently escape him.

I call Heaven to witness my terrours and dread for the Prince of Wales's safety, which I can't cease thinking not only

Precarious but in iminent danger whilst he is in the power of both the Kelly's. I co'd demonstrate that they are both of 'em, false, Perfidious, ambitious and sordidly avaricious, at leastt in private life and indeed it ever was the inherent characteristick of their respective familys. Thus far I make free with my kindred from a motive not inseparable from my Dutty. And therefore I do most solemnly give your Majesty warning of it in discharge of said Duty . . .

Your Majesty's most duttifull and ever loyal subject,

MYLES MACDONNELL.

Extract—Father Myles Macdonnell to Edgar

PARIS. *July ye* 15th, 1747.

DEAR SIR,

My heart, mind and soul are so possessed with the fears and terrours of the frightful consequences that a late very singular event is naturally productive of, that tho I am in no worse plight than my fellow subjects here, I am still unfitt to entertain yo with any thing better than that I am determin'd (when I have recd. proper instructions from thence) to seek England at all hazards in order to employ my poor influence to prevent the dreadful effects of an inconsiderate and fatal step out of all reason. If I can be useful to you or yours in that country I flatter myself that I need not urge or enforce any new arguments to convince you of my hearty and cheerful dispositions to acknowledge your many and singular favours.

Lord George Murray has been here some days. I am told that the Prince of Wales has sent him a message not to appear in his presence, and to withdraw forthwith from Paris. If that great man be innocent, Heaven comfort him and confound his enemys.

.   .   .   .

Pray forgive the liberty I take to convince myself that you

are my friend, and do me the justice to believe that I am no less unworthy of it, than I am most respectfully Dear Sir

your affec. humble servt.

MYLES BONEY.

The King to Prince Charles

ALBANO. Novemr. 7th, 1747.

I have received My Dearest Carluccio's of the 16th Octr, and am very glad Lockyel has at last got a Regiment ; I remark and take well of you that you do not directly ask of me to declare Lockyel's Tittle, for after what I had already writ to you on such matters, you could not but be sensible that those were things I could not do at this time ; were I not to declare all the latent Patents (which are in great number) and which it would be highly improper to do, I should please but one, and disgust a great many other deserving people, and in Lockyels case, I should particularly disoblige the other Clanns, who have all Warrants as well as he. Neither is Lord Lismore's [1] case a precident for others, since his Tittle had not been declared without he had come here to be about me in the way he is in. Lockyel's intrest and reputation in France will make him more considered there than any empty Tittle I could give him, and as he knows the justice both you and I do to his merit and services, I am sure he is too reasonable to take amiss my not doing now what would be of no use to him, and would be very improper and inconvenient for us.

I was the more concern'd for poor John Stewart's death,[2] that I easily foresaw the miserable condition his Wife and Daughter would be in. You know my Situation as to money matters, which grows worse and worse, so that I can promise nothing to any body, but as far as I am able, I shall be always ready to assist her, as I have hithertoo done to many others.

[1] Daniel O'Bryen recently created Lord Lismore on becoming Secretary of State.

[2] John Roy Stuart, whom Ruvigny states to have lived until 1784 !

Poor David Fotheringham [1] is very ill in Rome, I am affrayed it is the *Mal d'aria*, he having slept in the *Campagna* as he came from Civita Vecchia.

We have had a mighty fine season of it here this year, but it cannot last always, and I reckon to return to Town the beginning of next week.

Adieu, My Drst. Carluccio. I pray God bless and direct you and am all yours,

JAMES R.

The majority of the letters of the Prince in 1748 are just like this :

PARIS, 8 *July* 1748. SIR, I receive yr of the 18 June. The Weather here is at present as hot as I ever felt it in Italy, which is surprising enuff. I lay myself at your Majesty's feet most humbly asking Blessing. Your moste dutifull son,

CHARLES P.

The King of F. hunts today, so that there will be a great destruction of game. . . .

A better one is the following of 7 weeks later :

PARIS, *ye 25 Aug.* 1748.

I enclose here the usual letter. It is useless and grievous for me to mention ye melancholy situation poor Glenbucket [2] is in. I cannot but say by his mismanagement. However as long as I have bred, I shall share it with so honest and Worthie an old subject—still regretting I cannot hitherto do everything of that kind to my wishes. Adieu.

(Not signed but written in Charles's hand on the back of a letter from Edgar to him.)

---

[1] A merchant of Dundee, made Jacobite Governor of the town.

[2] The famous John Gordon of Glenbucket. Like Alex. Robertson of Struan he took part in three Jacobite risings, both being boys at the date of Killiecrankie.

(Endorsed "Nov. 1748." Copy of a note from the King of France notifying to Charles Edward the Treaty signed at Aix-la-Chapelle in October 1748 and expressive of the King's wish that he should retire from France.)

Mes Ministres plenipotentiares aiant signé à Aix-la-Chapelle le 18 du mois dernier le traitte deffinitif de la paix générale, par le quel toutes les puissances de l'Europe ont renouvellé les engagements qu'elles avoient déjà contractées en différentes occasions, pas raport à la succession au throne de la Grande Bretagne, mon intention est d'executer ce qui a été stipulé à cet egard. J'attends du Prince Charles Edouard qu'il m'en facili tera les moiens en se retirant incessament des états de ma domination. J'ay trop bonne opinion de sa sagesse, et sa prudence pour adjouter foy aux bruits qu'on a affectés de répandre sur la resolution dont on lui attribue le projet. Mon Cousin le Duc de Gesvres lui expliquera plus en détail quels sont mes sentiments. Je souhaite que la response du Prince Charles Edouard justiffie de plus en plus l'affection que j'ay pour lui, et la disposition je suis de lui faire eprover les effets. A Fontainbleau le 4 9bre 1748.

LOUIS.

Unfortunately the Prince was so foolish and obstinate as to disregard the plain wishes of his kind host ; and the even more positive commands which followed both from King Louis and his father. He presumed too far on what he believed to be his own popularity in Paris, and forced the French government to have him ignominiously arrested, confined for the night in the Château of Vincennes and next day conducted over the French frontier towards Avignon.

James Edgar to Mr. Waters

ROME. 31st *Dec.* 1748.

SIR,

I begin to write this before the Post comes in, and in finishing it I hope to be able to tell you that it is arrived.   A Courier arrived here Thursday night from Paris, and brought me accts of the Prince's being forced to leave France.   This is so moving a subject and swells my heart to such a degree that I cannot express what I feel upon it.   I earnestly pray God to preserve and support H.R.H. in all the tryals and hardships he is put to, and I beg when you hear any thing particular about him personally you would let me know it, for you perhaps may hear some things wch I may not know otherways than by you.

You will find Inclosed an order of the King's for paying 200^d to the order of Mrs. Stewart the Colonels [1] widow.

James Edgar to (Sir) John O'Sullivan

ROME. 21st *Jan.* 1749.

SIR,

I have received yours of the 15 Xber, and wont delay to let you know that I have had the honor to lay it before the King, and that H.M., doing justice to your merit and attatchment to him and his family, was pleased to take the contents of it very well of you.   You may be sure I shared with you in your uneasyness occasion'd by what happen'd lately to the Prince. But understanding last week that he was at Avignon and in good health I am now much easyer on that article, and pray God he may be allowed to stay there undisturbed as long as he finds it convenient for him.   The Duke took very kindly of you the assurance of yr duty wch you made him, and commands me in return to make you many thanks and Compliments in his name.   I beg of you that you would be well

---

[1] John Roy Stuart.

216

assured that my best wishes will ever attend you, and that I shall be always glad of occasion where I can show you how truely and sincerely I am, etc.

The King to Prince Charles

ROME. *Dec.* 30*th*, 1750.

Tomorrow you end your 30th year. May you see many more than double that number, and happyer ones than those you have already past. The hardships you have gone through and do perhaps still undergo are not so small, and it is to be hoped they will contribute at last to what they are chiefly directed. But in the darkness you keep me as to all that relates to you, I can pray and wish, but I can neither judge nor advise, except on one single article, which is so obvious and so important, that I should think everybody who really wishes you well should be of the same opinion in that respect, and that is your securing the succession of Our Family by marrying. I cannot think you so selfish as to have yourself only in view in all you do and suffer. The happiness of our Country must undoubtedly be your motive, and by consequence you would never surely restrict that happiness to your own life only, but endeavour to perpetuate it by a succession of Lawful Kings, who may have no other intrest but those of Our Country. Your giving lawful heirs to The Crown will not only be a constant security to your own person, but it will make you more considered and respected abroad, and will undoubtedly give new life and vigour to The Cause and your friends, whose zeal can never be so warm when all their hopes are centred in you alone. Had you enter'd into the view I formerly gave you, you had been probably at this time the Father of a Family, with a Wife whom it would not have been beneath you to have marryed, had you been in England. But it is useless to look backward, and what gives me the greatest concern in all this is, that you have put yourself in a situation and way of living,

217

which renders your marrying anybody absolutely impracticable. This as long as it lasts, must appear extraordinary and singular to persons of reflexion and sense, because the motives and object of your marrying are obvious to all, and that those of your pursuing your present conduct and scheme, whatever they may be, can be only known to such as are the authors and promoters of them. For my part, I can have no other view but your real good and advantage, and I am so much convinced of the necessity of your marrying, that I could almost say that I would rather see you marryed to a private Gentlewoman, than that you should not be it at all. And therefore I cannot but recommend earnestly to you to think seriously on the matter, and as you cannot now hope to make a marriage suteable to yourself, to endeavour to make one that may be at least as little unequal as possible, for I can only on this occasion exhort you in general, since I cannot think of any particular person to propose to you, who might be anyways proper, and at the same time willing to marry you. If this letter has the same fate with many others I have writ to you, I might have saved myself the trouble of writing it, but whatever reception it may meet with, or impression it may make, I shall still have the comfort of having acquitted myself of the duty of a Father, in telling you what I really think for your good, and of showing you at the same time that no behaviour of yours can alter the warm concern I shall ever take in all that relates to you, whom I beseech God to bless protect, prosper and direct upon all occasions.

JAMES R.

Prince Charles to the King

VENISE. *ye* 17*th May.*

SIR,

I writ last to Edgar ye 26 Aprill, but by an unforceen accident it was not forwarded in time, so that perhaps this will arrive before it. My health is perfect and hope soone to give your Majesty notice of my being well received and protected here. In ye mean time I keep myself absolutely in private for iff their was the least sent of it many oppositions wou'd be made to hinder me from remaining in a Place that next to France is the best for my Interest, and the only one in Italy. I lay myself at yr Majesty's feet moste humbly asking Blessing,

your moste

Dutifull Son,

CHARLES P.

Lord Dunbar to James Edgar on his joining the Roman Catholic Church

AUTUN. *Sep.* 23, 1751.

I have to impart to you dear Sir, a thing relating to myself which may perhaps surprise you, which is that God of His Mercy has given me the Grace to be reconciled last Sunday to the Catholick church. If you are anxious to know the reasons which determined me you will find them *first* in Mons de Meaux's exposition of the doctrine of the Catholique Church and 2^d in his history of the variation of the Protestant churches in 4 vols in 8vo and lastly in the Perpetuité de la foy etc. by Mr. Arnaud, in 4 vol in 4to. You may get these books from Card. Monti and if you read them, with a sincere desire to see the truth, I am persuaded you will find things that will astonish you. It is certaine that we whome providence has conducted into Catholique countrys and obliged to live and probably to dy in them are of all men the most unexcusable if we neglect to examine seriously the grounds of the separation of our ancestors from the Universal church, and a serious examen can never divert you from the truth if you are in the right way, because, as you well know besides the force of truth itself education, habit and in spite of all resolutions to the contrary a strong prevention on their side. But this is more than

219

enough on this subject. I believe I shall set out on my way home next week and therefore my next will be from Belvedere. I am Dear sir ever yr . . .

He wrote on the same day to the King, hoping that the news "would give his Majesty some pleasure, on account of the goodness yr Majesty was pleased to show me during the course of the many years which I had the honour to pass in your service."

The following delightful bits of gossip are culled from the later letters of Lord Dunbar to his old friend. The former's nephew had in fact married Henrietta Frederica, daughter of Count Bunau. This nephew became Viscount Stormont in 1748, Earl of Dunbar in 1770 and finally Earl of Mansfield in 1793, in succession to his distinguished Uncle.

Lord Dunbar, Avignon, May 3rd, 1759, to James Edgar

"I cannot but give you a piece of news which regards our family which cannot surprise you more than it did me. Lord Stormont, who has been English Minister at the King of Poland's Court for four years past, has marryed a Saxon lady of great quallity in that country, a young widow of twenty years of age and they say she has admirable qualities of body and mind, yet you will easily feel that a foreign alliance cannot be agreeable to any of his relations.

I believe My lord Marischal is somewhat embarrassed as to his journey to England, and has a mind to see whether these flat-bottomed boats are in gest or earnest before he goes over."

This was on the occasion of the Earl Marischal's pardon from George II. The flat-bottomed boats were dispersed for ever by Admiral Hawke 20th November in this year.

Dunbar from Belvidere, Oct. 12, 1759, to Edgar

"I am much obliged to you, dear Sir, for the account you send of my Saxon niece."

When his younger brother, William,[1] had been made Lord Chief Justice of England, he told Edgar he had heard the rumour of it, but as he had not had a letter from home for 30 years, did not know if it were true or not.

James Edgar to Lord Dunbar

ROME. *May 4th,* 1751.

MY LORD,

The post not being yet come in, I have little to say to your Lop at present. I am more curious now than usual about the news from England, because tho' the Duke of Hanover be in an ill state of health, some of the English Gentlemen here have letters from London giving an account that he had got a new Mistress, one Miss Gunning, an Irish Girl, and one of the handsomest that can be seen, and we may also see in a short time what consequences his eldest Son's death may produce. The royal family here is very well, and design next week to go to Albano for the Villagiatura. There is nothing new here that I know of worth mentioning. I offer my most humble service to my Lady[2] and am with great respect, My Lord, etc.

James Edgar to his nephew, John, who had been a Jacobite of 1745 (see p. 191).

ALBANO. *Oct.* 10, 1752.

I wish your sisters either by themselves or their directions would make or get made as much strong linen for me as will be a dozen and a half of shirts, the thread of the linen big and even but not coarse, wrought close, but so as not to be ready

---

[1] Lord Mansfield.　　　　[2] Lady Inverness.

to cut and that it be well bleached. Let the shirts be made, but without ruffles and after that once washed. Your uncle Robert can send them to London to be put there aboard of the first ship going to London and underneath for M. Marsi. A bill of lading for this bundle, may be sent to Mr. Scroop by the post. This is all I have to say on this particular, but that I shall take care that my friends shall be no losers on account of this Commission. You see I desire the shirts to be made and I think you have the measure of my neck and wrists.

I wish your uncle Robert would send me with a ship coming to Leghorn with fish—

A dozen of dryed skait.

Half a dozen of Ling and a few Rattray Codlings.

2 or 3 dozen of Cosyed haddocks or Creil capons.

2 dozen of Bervy haddocks (no matter though they be a little spoiled by the carriage).

10 or 12 dozen of the little dryd Montrose whittings.

3 or 4 mutton hams and a dozen of Montrose oat bannocks —double baked.

You will copy this in your own hand and send it home with your conveniency.

endorsed "To Capt. Edgar."

Six days later John Edgar writes to his uncle, James Edgar, from Paris: "Two days ago I took my dogs out of the College, and gave them to Forbes, who has taken them with him to Boulogne from whence I hope they will be sent safe to Scotland."

The Same to the Same

Undated (1753).

DEAR SIR,

You'll have heard before now of poor Archy Cameron being made prisoner in Scotland. By what I can learn he and several others have certainly been sent by the P's orders. I know nothing of the affairs they are gone about, neither is it my business to enquire. Ld. Thomond and Ld. Ogilvy have got the minister to promise that he will write to the Duke de Mirepoix concerning Mr. Cameron that he may make proper applications for the saving of his life. This day Mr. Murray Ld. Elibank's brother, told me in confidence that he had been with a person lately come from the P—e who says that H.R.H. is exceeding anxious about Cameron's life. Mr. Murray desired me to acquaint you of this, that you may communicate it to the King and its to be hoped that H.M. will prevail on the French Court to interest themselves heartily for Cameron or any others that shall have the misfortune to be taken.

I had lately a letter from one of my sisters—all your friends in Scotland are well and have a most kind remembrance of you. Your shirts are to be gone about with all diligence. My Commission will be out in 3 or 4 weeks. I propose to join the Regiment in eight days.

Your most affectionate Nephew and most
obliged humble servant,

JOHN EDGAR.

David Areskene to Edgar, in reference to a peculiar cure for rheumatism

TERAMO. *August* 18, 1757.

"I am sorry we are at so great a distance, as not to be able to show you the esteem I have for barley broth, 'tis true I would not have dishonoured and spoiled their good taste with the burnt head of a tup [1] and as for your haggis, I always knew it to be a bad french hachis boiled in a stinking sheep's bag, that always tastes of the wool and often of something that is yet worse. Having still a coldness in my legs ever since my great sickness in Orbitello, I intended last Summer to take the hot

---

[1] Sheep.

sands at Ischia but my affairs at Naples would not permit it so I am resolved the beginning of next month to bathe up to my knees in a tub of the ripest grapes I can find in this cold climate, and be so good as to give my kind service to Doctor Irving and tell him that I intend to do so, but that I am not in the least like the Laird of Lundie's fowler, he will explain to you what that means."

Later. "I am now taking my baths every evening in a tub of grapes well braized and fermenting, but I cant say I perceive any great good."

John Carmichael to Edgar, who had to act as the channel between his master and the innumerable claimants for the latter's bounty

FOUNTAINE GAILLARDE PRE SENS.
20 *Dec.* 1757.

SIR,

It is with the outmost reluctancy I am obliged to have recourse to his Majesty's bounty. Were it possible for me to subsist otherways I assure you I would be the last person that would presume to trouble my Royal Sovereign. If nothing better should come to pass I hope I shall soon be in a condition to subsist my family as I have now taken a house and a small farm in Bourgogne where the ground is not very dear, but what I have not got and still must have to furnish it is mostly on Credit and without I can get that paid I must infallibly faill in the undertaking wheras the sum of 6 or 700 livres would put me in a way of supporting myself . . . It is no want of inclination to industry that has rendered me so necessitous but the affliction of a distrest spouse who this three years has not been able to put on her own cloaths, a numerous family and destitute of the means to procure them assistance.

Jn. Waters to Edgar (the last, 1758)

I received in the usual way the packet and your letter to me of the 6th Inst. The one you then sent to me for Mr. Douglas [1] was immidiately forwarded and I enclose to you one from that Gentleman. I left the King's letter for the Bishop of Soissons with the Fitzjames family's Swiss, for his Lordship was somewhere in the country near to Paris and expected in a day or two so I may well suppose the Bishop got that letter before now. I am very glad the King enjoys good health and H.R.H. the Duke also. It gives me great pleasure to find from several here what an influence he has in the Conclave. God send he may succeed in getting elected a Pope that may prove a steady friend to the Royal Family. (*This was Clement XIII.*)

I am yr most humble and obed. Servt.

Jn. Waters.

Dr. Flyn to Edgar, from St. Germains, 15 Oct. 1758

"I must now, to my great concern trouble you on ye subject of Col. Cameron this honest worthy gentleman whose loyalty was well known upon all occasions is of a long time very heavie and helpless. he pensions at a french house here at ye rate of 700 livres a year for his table and lodging, his yearly income is a thousand livres on the Court of france, soe yt after paying his 700 L. he had onely 300 L. a year to furnish cloaths, washing, fire, candles, tobacco, etc. however he went through very decently until it pleased God to afflict him some time agoe with a violent fit of apoplexy and palsie and remained in danger of death 10 or 12 dayes, during which time there was 3 or 4 people constantly about him whose wages and diet together with the expenses of physitians etc. brought him indebted considerably for one of his circumstances who had not a penny before him . . . His case is soe desperate that I am obliged (after begging humble pardon)

[1] The Prince.

225

to pray you may lay before his Majesty how much he is in want of some present relief to pay his debts. In all appearance he cannot live long."

Robert Fotheringham to Edgar

ST. GERMAINS. *Dec.* 22, 1759.

"I heartily pray Almighty God to send his Majesty all the Blessings and Felicitaties that a new year can possibly bring along with it, and that the year sixty may prove as propitious to our unhappy countrys as it did last Century by restoring to them the inestimable blessing of the Royal Family, and as I cannot figure to myself any earthly happiness superior to the seeing of it, I heartily wish you may not only live to see it, but in great good health happily to enjoy it for many years to come."

James Edgar died in 1764, in Rome, after nearly fifty years' faithful service to his Royal Master. After Edgar's death his work was taken on by Andrew Lumsden, who had previously been his assistant.

Andrew Lumisden as he himself usually spelt it, was one of the family settled as merchant burgesses in Edinburgh for four generations. They came originally from Berwick and the spelling in the thirteenth century, when they were first heard of, was "Lummisdayne," while the branch settled in Aberdeenshire, at Cushnie and Clova, which provided stalwart Jacobites both in 1715, and 1745, and still flourishes, have always spelt it Lumsden. Andrew's grandfather and great-grandfather were Episcopal parsons at Duddingston, near Edinburgh, and the latter was "ejected" or "extruded" in 1688 and became a Non-Juring Bishop. Two of his sons, John and William, were Jacobites, William being the father of Andrew above. William's wife was Mary Bruce of Kennet

226

and the only children were Andrew and Isabella who became the wife of Robert Strange, the artist and engraver, and was a much more ardent partisan of the Stuarts than was her brother in his youth. Andrew had been "bred as a writer," and when Prince Charles and his Court came to Holyrood and John Murray of Broughton, the secretary, found the need of professional assistance, young Lumisden was recommended by his relative, Dr. Alexander Cunninghame. He was employed throughout the campaign in "keeping the books," and after the disaster of Culloden, Cluny MacPherson was specially desired by a message from the Prince to "take care in particular of Lumisden and Sheridan, as they carry with them the sinews of war." Lumisden seems to have remained for some months hidden in the Highlands and then reached Edinburgh disguised as a groom, where he lay concealed in his father's house. He next, in October 1746, proceeded to London disguised as a poor teacher, and eventually got safely to Rouen. His was the last name but one on the list of exceptions to the Act of Indemnity of 1747, and he is there called "Andrew Lumsdale, otherwise Lumsden, son to William Lumsden, writer, Edinburgh."

A good many letters of his to his father have been preserved in the family. At first they only deal with the novelties of life in France ; his observations on the first time he heard an Italian Opera are of charming naïveté.

"There appears to me some thing so very ridiculous in the composition of an opera, that I confess I have no taste for it. Can anything be more unnatural than for a king to sing three or four minutes to his valet to give him his gloves, and the valet to quaver out as many minutes in saying he will bring them?"

He seems to have been a very serious-minded young man and begs his sister to send him from Edinburgh a great many books, that he may continue his studies. Also some necessary articles of apparel. He mentions that with him in Rouen were Mr. Hamilton of Bangour and Sir Stewart Thriepland, and concludes by begging, as so many exiles had to do, for a little money to be sent him, to keep him from starving, "till I can put myself in the way of bread." £40 a year was at last grudgingly promised by his father. Andrew's letters at this period show a good deal of criticism of the two young Princes still in France, though Henry was very shortly to return to Italy and don the mantle of a Cardinal. Lumisden says, "Everything seems to conspire to their ruin. I am sorry to say they will owe it chiefly to themselves, since from their conduct of late in many things, one is almost led to think they had given up all thoughts of further attempting to sit upon the British throne." Andrew Lumisden was still in Rouen when Prince Charles was expelled from Paris in December 1748 and in the list of Gratifications given by the French Court to needy Jacobites in June 1749, he appears as receiving a much-needed 600 francs, and before the end of that year he had reached Rome, travelling in company with Edward Daniel, brother of Captain John Daniel. Lumisden was shortly after his arrival appointed Assistant Secretary to James Edgar at a small salary, and continued there after Edgar's death until that of the King—January 1766. A few years later, he was allowed to return to England and received a pardon in 1778. He died 1801.

Andrew Lumsden to James Edgar on his first arrival in Rome

ROME. 13*th* Dec. 1749.

SIR,

As I know your inclination and zeal to serve every one in distress, I presume to trouble you with this letter, in order to have your friendly advice how to lay my situation before his Majesty in the most respectful manner.

Tho' I have the honour to be descended from two families equally remarkable for their loyalty and antiquity, Lumisden of Cushnie and Bruce of Clackmannan, yet I shall not waste your time by going further back than my grandfather the deceast Sir Andrew Lumisden, Bishop of Edinburgh, who, for his steady attachment to his late Majesty, was at the Revolution deprived of his living, and from that period till his death, about the year 1723, warmly preach'd up principles of loyalty, and supported himself on his paternal estate, wch was greatly diminished by educating a numerous family.

My father, treading the footsteps of so virtuous a guide, was one of the gentlemen who attempted to surprise the castle of Edinburgh in the year 1715 ; and, after joining his Majesty's army at Perth, was appointed governor of the town of Burntisland, and upon the separation of the army was oblig'd to abandon his country for some time. And tho' he has had many advantageous offers made him, provided he would have taken the state oaths to the Elector of Hanover, yet he always rejected such offers with disdain, having preferr'd his honour to his interest. Such principles however have made him an object of the Usurper's resentment, which he has felt on several occasions, and particularly on his royal highness's late expedition when he was made prisoner and confined in the Castle of Edinburgh, where his health was so impair'd that they at last allowed him to find bail.

Animated with these examples, upon his royal highness's landing in Scotland, I early offer'd him my service, and he

229

was graciously pleas'd to appoint me his principal under-secretary, and at the same time entrusted me with the keeping of his seals : And such was the confidence he was pleas'd to repose in me that I was likewise entrusted with the receiving and giving out of all his money. How far I answer'd expectation or acted with exactness and fidelity in these stations would be unbecoming in me to say : but his royal highness has been pleas'd to express himself on all occasions well satisfied with every part of my conduct ; and I flatter myself that all my countrymen will also bear me the same honourable testimony. The acting in these offices necessarily made me very remarkable, and the usurpation has accordingly done me the honour to attaint me, and thereby am excluded from ever returning to my country but with the royal family.

From this short narrative it plainly appears how much we have suffer'd by a firm attachment to his Majesty : my grandfather robbed of his benefice ; my father by his unshaken principles unable to enjoy any employment in the government, and by a late Act of Parliament absolutely disqualified from being employ'd in any branch whatever of the Law to wch he was bred ; and myself in this early time of my life banish'd my country and cut off from all rights of succession, and already in effect depriv'd of a very considerable one, viz. 2000 £ ster, by a person's altering his destination on my having join'd his royal highness, besides several yearly settlements given me by my friends for managing their private business. We never receiv'd any of his Majesty's money. We all along serv'd on our own charges, which has been very great both in the year 1715 and in the late attempt, from my father's imprisonment and the expences I was put to in the army and since, wch has so far diminish'd his fortune as to make him unable to support me abroad. And tho' I have receiv'd a gratification of 600 livres from the Court of France, I am uncertain if that sum will be continued annually, and supposing it should 'tis obviously insufficient to support me in the character of a gentleman as the prices of things are so greatly encreas'd every-where. I do not indeed desire, nor is it to be expected that I should live in the same easy manner as when at home ; at the same time I flatter myself that his Majesty, whose royal breast is fill'd with such extensive clemency, will not allow one born a gentleman, and whose family as well as himself have been so remarkably attacht to him, to want the necessaries of live or to be oblig'd entirely to give up that character. 'Tis therefore indispensably necessary for me to throw myself at his Majesty's feet and to implore his generosity and goodness in such manner as he shall judge proper, that I may be enabled to dedicate the remainder of my life in acquiring such knowledge as may render me more capable to serve the royal family.

That his Majesty may live to accomplish his restoration, and to make his subjects a free and happy people by the continuance of his wise government, is the ardent and daily prayer of him who is with the greatest esteem and respect,

Sir,

your most obedient and very humble servant,

ANDREW LUMISDEN.

Nine years after this, when Lumsden had become the Under Secretary, King James, in order to try and re-establish some kind of communication with what Edgar calls "the dear wild man," decided to send Lumsden to Paris, and issued the following instructions (in Lumsden's own hand !) :

"You will set out for Paris with all convenient speed, and after you have seen and conversed with the Prince you will regularly write here, giving an account of what passes betwixt you. When you have anything of a certain consequence to say you may write directly to myself and by every post to Edgar and when you have with the Prince's conveniency finished all with him in consequence of my instructions and of what I have charged you by word of mouth, you will return hither with all convenient diligence.

You will let the Prince know that I could say a great deal here on his politic affairs and present situation, but my health does not allow me to do it, neither is it indeed necessary. The Prince has been sufficiently informed of my sentiments and reflexions by the great number of letters I have writ to him these years past and you have yourself seen many of them and have been informed from my own mouth of my way of thinking which you will represent to the Prince in the strongest and fullest light. In two words, the Prince must be convinced by his own experience, how little he has to expect from the English alone and that he has as little to hope for in, any respect, from any foreign power except France, so that if he does not seriously endeavour to gain and cultivate the friendship of that Crown, it is in some manner next to renouncing all human hopes and means of a restoration and putting himself in the necessity of leading for the rest of his days the same ignominious, indecent life which he has led for so many years past and which will put the seal to his own and our family's destruction.

You will also inform the Prince of the situation of my health, which renders me incapable of much application or of any fatigue, so that whatever may happen I can never hope to go out of Italy and indeed not far out of Rome. The Prince will be sensible that in the situation I am more desirous than ever to abdicate to him but he will easily feel, also, that the circumstances of the times render it not advisable to take such a step at present. It might make me less useful to him abroad, it would be in reality yielding to him what I have not as yet and giving him an empty title which would be a load and of no service to him. Were he once in England, that alters the case entirely ; and in general I cannot think of taking such a step but in concert with France.

232

You will also explain to the Prince the comfort and satisfaction it has been to me to hope from some accounts I have
received that Mrs. Walkinshaw is, or will be, soon separated
from him. This is an article on which I had thought myself
obliged to have writ to the Prince long since had I thought
my writing would have had any effect, but that particular
for some time past was become so public and was of so much
prejudice to his honour and interest as well as to his conscience,
that it cannot but be of extreme satisfaction to me on all accounts
to have reason to hope that he may have at last taken, on that
head, a resolution becoming himself.

Given at Rome this 7th day of October 1758.

(signed JAMES R.) "

The above is a good and somewhat touching example of
what Andrew Lang has called King James's "sad lucidity."
He really saw, fairly clearly, that the cause was lost, also that
his own opinions and advice had little or no weight with his
son.

Some of Andrew Lumsden's letters to Edgar, written on
his journey north, show that, unlike so many of his refugee
countrymen, he seems to have taken a deep and intelligent
interest in the artistic and antiquarian treasures of the towns
he passed through. He writes from Florence, Oct. 13, 1758,
to Edgar :

DEAR SIR,

"You see I am so far advanced in my journey. I shall
use all diligence to accomplish the whole and may it turn
out according to our wish. Last night I arrived here and
having rested today, I set out tomorrow for Bologna . . .
At Viterbo I examined Salvi's church. I think it is an elegant
performance. It was no doubt a great restraint on the archi-
tect to be confined to build on the foundations of the old

233

church. Such a genius however, could get the better of every difficulty. He intended certainly to cause a picture to be put over the high altar, which would prevent seeing the choir and thereby the present disproportionate length of the church would be removed.

I found M. Brompton in the Tribune here, finishing a very fine copy of Titian's Venus. He was so kind as to be my antiquary, no small compliment from one so diligent as he is, and notwithstanding a very rainy day, I have seen as much of the beauties of Florence as my short stay would permit."

From Bologna on Oct. 17 he writes :

"The rivers are so swelled with rain, that unless it soon cease, my vetturino says it will be impossible to set out to-morrow for Modena . . . I have spent a melancholy day here. I went to the palace of Tampieri, but it was so obscure with the rainy day that I could not see distinctly that choice collection of pictures. In such weather it was idle to go to any other palace and the same with the churches,—I amused myself with looking at the oddities in the Institute. I am ignorant of what is now doing in the world. I have not seen a newspaper since I left Rome. From Turin I shall write you again."

TURIN. *Oct.* 28, 1758.

DEAR SIR,

Notwithstanding of great and constant rains since I wrote to you from Bologna on the 17th, Yesterday I arrived here. To shorten my journey at Piacenza I intended to have gone by Pavia, Tortona, etc. but being informed that the road was impracticable after such rain I went by Milan where I remained only half a day. At Bologna I contracted a severe cold by the sudden change of the weather, but I think I have now almost got the better of it by fasting. I took this morning

234

a dose of salts wh I reckon will complete my cure. In such a situation you will easily suppose how many disagreeable hours I have spent since we parted. I grudge however neither fatigue of body or mind when I am doing what is my duty to do. I have bargained for a chaise to carry me to Lyons ; we set out tomorrow morning, and in seven days I hope to inform you of my arrival there. In the meantime, I beg you will do me the honour to lay me at the King's feet. Assure him of my constant fidelity and zeal, and that I shall lose as little time as possible to execute his royal commands. May I have the happiness to find on my arrival at Paris that H.M. is again able to go abroad and take his usual exercise.

The bad weather has greatly disappointed me in satisfying my curiosity. It was so dark that I could make nothing out of Corregio's great works in the cupola at Parma. I saw, however, two pictures of his, one at the Dominicans and the other in the new accademy, which fully answered my expectation. They might indeed make him say, after he saw the works of Raphael "ed io anche son pittore."

At Milan I had only time to see the Cathedral and the Ambrosian Library. I regretted that I had so little time to examine the latter. It contains many valuable pictures and drawings by the greatest painters as well as a vast number of curious MSS. I looked over the book of drawings by Leonardo da Vinci and the other celebrated Masters for which King James the 6th offered 3000 *doppie* but the gentleman to whom it belonged, Sig^r Galazzo Arconate of Milan, would not deprive his country of such a treasure and therefore refused H.M.'s offer and generously bequeathed them to the Library and for which they have erected his bust in marble.[1]

Here are preserved all the letters wrote to St. Charles Bor-

[1] It is curious to think that but for the public spirit of this gentleman, all these drawings might now be at Windsor, as presumably King James would have brought them with him from Scotland.

235

romeo with copies of his answers. As he was consulted in most of the ecclesiastical transactions of his time, this collection will be of great use to one who writes the ecclesiastic history of the period.

Adieu my dear sir. It seems already an age since I left you for night and day you occupy the grateful thoughts of Your most affectionate and most obedient humble servt.

ANDREW LUMISDEN.

From Lyons, on November 6, he writes again :

"Yesterday at noon I arrived here and immediately went to the bureau of the Diligence, but unfortunately all the places were taken up for this day—there remained only the last place in the Diligence that sets out on Wednesday morning which I have taken, so I lose two days here. I can assure you, however, that although I was for some days in a condition more proper to have remained in bed than to have travelled—I lost no time on that account. I am now, thank God pretty well, and hope to continue so that I may the sooner have the pleasure of seeing you again."

On reaching Paris, he writes again :

PARIS. *November.* 14, 1758.
"I arrived here late last night and I flattered myself that I had at last got to the end of My journey, but Mr. Waters' directions to me are that I must go by the stage coach to Sedan and there wait for further instructions. I have taken a seat for tomorrow morning. We shall be six days on the road, being a journey of 160 miles. I have a few zeckins still remaining which I shall preserve for my return to Italy and have therefore taken 600 livres per Mr. Waters."

From Bouillon, Lumisden wrote to the Prince, since he had been told to put what he had to say in *writing.* Nov.

236

21. 1758. The letter is chiefly concerned with the great necessity that exists for the Prince to be on friendly terms with France. He writes again to Edgar on Nov. 30 : "I offer my compliments to all our friends. I know you would have them with you this night, celebrating the feast of our good saint,[1] as I have the honour to do with Mr. Arthur, who has particularly drunk your health."

Dec. 9 Lumisden again wrote the Prince, as ordered, setting forth in fuller language, the King's views as to his own abdication. Obviously as yet Charles had refused to see Lumisden, making the mission of his father's faithful Under-Secretary as difficult as possible ! Charles had lost a good deal of the spontaneous courtesy and charm which had so endeared him to all hearts when in Scotland. Hope deferred and the atmosphere of intrigue in which he lived had not brought out the best which was in him.

Letters of Prince Charles during his years of wandering about Europe and of some of his faithful followers to him

George Kelly to Prince Charles

AVIGNON. 31st *May*, 1752.

SIR,

I hope you will not disapprove of my going to Paris, since a stronger reason has happen'd for it, than what I had the honour of mentioning to your Royal Highness, for the Scotch, who remain there, make a strange racket, and are much offended at my being in your family. They have, no doubt, a desire to come into it, and makes the World believe, they can do great matters for you. As I have, Sir, nothing so much at heart as your Interest, I should never forgive myself in such a case, to be any obstacle to it, or even thought an

[1] St. Andrew.

237

author of the least prejudice to your affairs. For as I have had the honour to inform Y.R.H. already ; if I cannot serve, I never will be instrumental in disserving you.

I hope, Sir, you are fully persuaded of my zeal and that no people's ill-grounded Envy nor any other reason will ever prevent my obeying your Commands whenever you have the least occasion for me. I have the honour to be with the greatest respect and Submission—Sir

your Royal Highness's

most faithfull and most devoted humble servant,

GEORGE KELLY.

Kelly was one of the seven men who had landed in Moidart with the Prince in 1745. He had previously been mixed up in the Atterbury plot and been imprisoned in the Tower from which he escaped and became secretary to the Duke of Ormonde at Avignon, until the latter sent him to join the Prince. He latterly quarrelled with the Prince and at his own death in 1762 had not seen his master for many years.

Undated. On the back of someone else's letter, in Prince Charles's hand—addressee unknown

(The Prince did not assume the name of John Douglas till after 1750.)

You know I do not think it proper to aply directly untill things be in a different situation—However as I do not neglect for that to assist my friends as much as possible, I desier you when next at Paris to represent the hardship of Mr Gordon and John Hay's case to yr Majestys and instead of retrenching the former gratifications to augment both by cutting off Eneas Macdonald, whom I know myself to be unworthy and one Steward who was taxed by his own countrymen of being guilty of several bad things. I find Sir J. Steward has been true also, and as no people can have more merit than these

238

three, it will give me great concern to see them so ill-rewarded for their sufferings. The receiving some small support from their own country can be no reason for this treatment for they are still at the mercy of the E. Government and may be entierly deprived of it at their pleasure. I therefore desier you to Inform me what effect the representation has had, and to give in a memorial pursuant to it setting forth the hardships of their case in the strongest terms. I remain your sincere friend J. D. (John Douglas).

Send yr answer to this as soon as you can to J. Waters who will forward it to me.

Stafford [1] *and Sheridan* [2] *to Prince Charles, circa 1752*

(FROM AVIGNON)

Yesterday we received a letter without a name desiring us to send Daniel to Paris. We followed your instructions. We should have informed you sooner had we known your address—that we changed lodgings, sold the coach and eight horses—the coach for 1976£ seven horses at 600f a horse and the eighth for 16 Louis d'or—one dyed of the staggers. Another we still have on our hand. Shall sell him to the first that bids money for him ? The letter desires us to give the keys to John Stuart. You know that you ordered us to put all your effects into the Vice Legates custody which we did, accordingly ; except the papers in Mr. Sheridan's keeping.

When you think proper to give us your address, shall lett you know what passes here. Sir James has wrote for his books.

Your most obedient servants

H. STAFFORD

M. SHERIDAN.

[1] Henry Stafford of the Prince's household.
[2] Michael Sheridan, nephew of Sir Thomas. These two remained for years in Avignon, looking after the possessions of Prince Charles, who

Prince Charles to Stafford and Sheridan

ye 10*th April* 1753.

MR. STAFFORD AND SHERIDAN,

My last was of ye 18th Jan^ry. This is to Let you know that as I am extremely necessitous for want of Money it Engages me out of Economi to send for Daniell Obrions [1] Close which you are to Pack up in his own trunc and to send it adressed to Mr. Woulfe at Paris, but Let there be in ye Trunc none of Daniels Paipers or any thing else except his Close. I expect daily Accounts from yr Parts. in ye mean time I remain yr. sincere friend

JOHN DOUGLAS.

Prince Charles to Edgar

ye 31 *July* 1754.

I received yrs. of ye 1st May, 11th June and lastly ye 16th July. My situation is terrible, the more that in reality I cannot see any method or appearance of its Bettering. Shall give an Account to my Master [2] of all my proceedings as soon as in my power, for the present it is not possible to put severall things in writing ; you cannot immagin how many Crosses I meet with, but never any shall hinder me from doing what I think to be for ye Best. Be pleased to assure my Master of my moste humble duty, and believe me for ever yr sincere Friend

J. DOUGLAS.

My Health is good, and am overjoyed to here that my Best friend [2] is quite out of Dangire and in a way of Recovering Perfectly.

seems to have had masses of clothes (some of which unfortunately became moth-eaten) and many other objects which he expected his servants to be able to sell. They themselves were often short of money.

[1] His valet. [2] His father.

240

King James to "Mr. John Douglas" (Prince Charles)

Dec. 31st, 1754.

Tho' it is always a comfort to me to receve My Dear friends letters, yet I own that yours of the 24th Nov. was at the same time of great concern and affliction to me. What you had writ some months ago made me hope you were beginning to open your eyes as to your present situation, but from what you now say you appear to be more fixed than ever in your former scheme. I cannot it is true absolutely form a judgement of matters of which I am entirely ignorant, but what can I think, and what may I not fear from a scheme, which, whatever it may be, has drove you into the situation you now are, and which it would appear from what you say will keep you in it till some change or new event happens. I have been myself expecting such things all my life, and they have never happened with success. Who can assure you it may not be the same with you, and in that case you will pass your life in obscurity, you will let our Family end for want of providing for its succession, and all the labour and pains you will have taken will be lost. It is very commendable in you to be resolved to pursue your point to the last, but is the way to succeed to think you want no advice, and to exclude me from all your Secrets and Councils, while you do me the justice to believe that you have not a better friend, and to content yourself with calling me Master, as I really am, without giving me the least mark of that confidence and deference you owe me. All this cannot be your own thoughts or work, but those of others. It is remarkable that the first steps you took in entering into your present scheme seemed to be calculated to seperate you entirely from all that could be useful, or ought to be dear to you, and after so many years it is not seen what new friends you have got, or what advantage you have reaped from such measures, which have forced you to deliver yourself up entirely to those who now direct you. You look upon them to be sure to be your friends, and I cannot say they are otherwise, because I know them not. But I can see, and so may all the world, that if they were your greatest enemies, they could not have taken more effective measures to ruin both your intrest and reputation, and to put you under a sort of necessity of never getting out of their hands. They have drove you into a labyrinth, out of which it will be hard for you to extricate yourself, without you exert vigorously that Spirit and Courage which God has given you, and prefer a due submission to a loving Father to the slavery of those who are now in reality your Masters. In the dispositions you seem now to be, and at the age I am of, I can scarce hope yo see so happy a change, and must prepare to pass the rest of my days in grief and anxiety for you, and all that is left for me to do is to submit to the dispositions of Providence, and to beseech The Almighty continually to bless you, to enlighten you and to restore you to me, and indeed to yourself, which would be also the most effectual means of restoring you to what will one day belong to you.

May you see many of these days and not another in the situation you now are but in all circumstances the blessing and prayers of a loving father will allways attend you.

Stafford to the Prince—re selling his wine stored at Avignon

1757.

"The wine can't be sold, as the good can't be distinguished from the bad, nobody will buy all together. I believe it will be best to keep them until you drink them yourself."

The Same to the Same

AVIGNON. *Oct.* 31, 1757.

SIR,

I received the honour of yours of the 21st inst. and shan't miss the first opportunity of selling the Chair, it may lye on my hands for many months without I sell it at a under price. I have a gold watch and some other moveables which I'll sell or pledge, as for credit I have none. If you could employ the footman elsewhere, it would lessen the expence, he is quite useless to me. I have only bought wood enough to boil my pot, and shall endeavour to pass the winter without fire. I am with due respect

Sir yr most obed. hum. servant,

H. STAFFORD.

If I am hear the 1st of Feb. must pay 6 months rent for my lodgings.

Answer from the Prince

11 *Nov.* 1757.

MR. STAFFORD. Sir, I receive yours of the 31 Octobre and ye contents give me concern. You should apply to Lady Inverness to lend you one hundred Louidors. Shure Shee won't refuse you when I answer to guet it be remitted to her in six months—the servant may still be kept in this manner and yr self to as usuall. Do not delay answering.

Yr sincere friend,

J. DOUGLAS.

A letter of Stafford's of November 23rd (while in doubt) is as follows :

"Sir,

I yesterday received the honour of yours. Lady Inverness is at present in the Country. Shall take a horse and ask her in your name for the money. Shall let you know her answer. In case she refuses shall either pledge or sell everything I have even to the last shirt, for yr service."

(Noted on the Prince's letter : In consequence of this letter I received a hundred louis d'ors from Lady Inverness. Avignon. Dec. 3, 1757. H. S.) Sheridan had left.

BELVEDERE. *Nov.* 4, 1757.

(Lord Dunbar sending some scurvy grass water, which had cured Lord Lismore of a soreness in the gums, proceeding from scurvy,[1] which Dunbar thinks might also be of use to the Duke of York who in his youth suffered from scorbutic affections.)

"That H.R.H. may receive some scurvy grass water without loss of time I have written to Mons. Gastaldi (who is an excellent Physitian,) giving him the commission to send it by the first pedon, and as several persons use continually that remedy I hope he will be able to procure of the best sort. I have also desired that he would write at the same time to you a letter containing directions for the use of this water if any be necessary. All I know is, that one must begin by cleaning the teeth, because otherways the nastyness touching the gums would if not prevent, at least diminish the good effect. It makes the gumms smart and it is by that it operates the cure."

Prince Charles to his Father

26 *May* 1758.

Mr. Orry [2] Sir, I doe not find to have anything to add on certain subjects to my last of 19 currt expressing my thoughts about them. I have a very good opinion of Lumisden and in case ever you had occasion to speak such matters as could not be well expressed in writing you cannot pitch on a more proper person than the said Lumisden. Allow me sir to remain with profoundest respect, your obedient humble servant, J. D.

[1] This disease seems to have been common among the Jacobite exiles— perhaps due to lack of exercise and the keen air to which they were accustomed at home.

[2] A cypher name of that particular date.

The King to Prince Charles

Sept. 18, 1758.

"What would I not give to have some few hours conversation with you. I am persuaded it would be of advantage to our affairs, as it would be of a singular comfort to me especially in the situation of health I now am. Could you not contrive even this winter to find some idle weeks in which you may have neither important business nor immediate expectations, to come and pass a few days with your old father who has nothing in view but your good, who tenderly loves you and beseeches God Almighty day and night to bless you and direct all your counsels."

Alexander Murray of Elibank trying to give the Prince good advice :

"Campbell" to the Prince

29 *Sept.* 1758.

". . . that infamous creature Lady Primrose has propagated over the whole kingdom that you are a drunkard. the only and most effectual way to convince your friends of the falsity and malice of her villainous lyes is to drink very little while these gentlemen are with you, in case any of them should propose drinking for God's sake evite it yourself because your character and success depends upon the report of these gentlemen at their return."

A letter from a deputation came to the Prince from England giving no names except—

". . . you can't shew too much civility to Sir Rowland Hill's son who is one of them that will have the honour and pleasure of seeing you . . . If the Court of France enter vigorously into your affair it will be absolutely necessary that you endeavour to get Marshal Keith to command the troops.

245

Your worthy friend who will deliver you this is charged by your friends on the other side of the water to mention this to you. I am persuaded the Court of France would be very glad to make him quite the King of P. and that things might be so contrived as to bring it about. You see that I was not mistaken in the character of your noble friend, who is more if possible attached to you than myself. God preserve you." Aix. la Chapelle.

Another letter, King James to Prince Charles, Oct. 7, 1758 :

"By means of Lumsden's mission we shall I suppose understand one another better than I think we do, but I hope that will not hinder you from coming here yourself as soon as you can. Do not deny me my dear Child the comfort of embracing you once more before I dy."

Lumisden's journey was to take a month. Elaborate instructions were given him. The King hopes "Mrs. Walkingshaw is, or will soon be, seperate from him (the Prince)."

As might be expected, numbers of letters exist among the later Stuart papers referring to Prince Charles Edward and Clementina Walkinshaw.

Before those dealing with the period when Clementina had felt herself obliged to retire with her child from the Prince's neighbourhood, there is one among the undated which obviously refers to the time when the little Charlotte was the darling of both parents who, however, seem to have left her temporarily in the care of the faithful Thibault (Intendant of the Duc de Bouillon), while she seems to have been suffering from whooping cough. The anxiety about the partridge-pie has a pleasant domestic ring.

Thibault—apparently in charge of the little Charlotte (of Albany)—
to Prince Charles

No date, but circa 1757 or 8.

Monsieur j'attend avec la dernier impatience que vous aye la bonte de me faire mander votre arrivée à bon port. Mlle. Pouponne se port bien. Elle a cependant de temps en temps des quintes de toux, mais cela ne prend pas sur sa sante. Elle se tranquilise dans l'espérance de revoir bien tôt son cher papa et sa cher maman dont elle demand des nouvelles tous les jours. Madame peut être sure qu'on a pour la petite, toutes les attentions inaginables.

Nous sommes dans un grand embarras par rapport au pâte de perdreaux rouges de Perigueu qui est arrivé ici mardy. Nous craignons qu'il ne deperisse avant votre retour. 'attende les ordres la dessus.

Votre très humble et très obeissant serviteur.

THIBAULT.

King James to Sir John Graeme, six years before his death

ROME. 9ber 20th, 1759.

SIR,

You will, I am sure, be concerned for poor Lord Lismore's death. I am myself very much, and with reason ; for I have lost in him a true friend, and an old and most faithful servant ; but at our age it is a wonder when we live and none when we die ; so that we are yet more obliged than younger people to be always prepared for that great and last hour ; but still, as long as we are in this world, it is our duty to acquit ourselves of the obligations of the station in which Providence has placed us. While the ill state of my health at present makes me unfit for almost any application,—so that, after serious reflexions, I have determined to call for you here for to replace Lord Lismore, and assist me, as he did, in quality of minister, but without the title of Secretary of State. You will see by this resolution the place you always retain in my esteem and good opinion, and I do not foresee your having any difficulty in complying with my desire to have you about my person. This climate is favourable for old people, and I am persuaded you will be able to live very comfortably in this place. I shall continue to you the same pension you have so long enjoyed. You will have an apartment in the house with a scrivener and two horses at your disposal; and tho' I am now no more able to eat but alone, you shall have your table, in one shape or another, and after that I shall endeavour to secure a small portion to you after my death. It is also my intention to give you, when here, the title of a Scotch Earl, and I even wish you could now send me the Titles you desire to have that I may give you the warrant at your arrival here, and that you may take upon you that title at the same time. I would have you inform Lady Lismore of your coming here, and it will be necessary that you settle a correspondence with her, tho' it need not be constant nor regular, for what may occur for my service, and you will find here inclosed a letter of mine to give her, with another to introduce you to the Duke of Choiseul, with whom I am glad to find you are acquainted and protected by him. However, if Cardinal de Luynes be at Paris, it will be fit that he should carry you to the minister, and therefore you will find a letter from me for him also, which you may destroy should he be at Sens or at a distance from Court, since he could not then carry you there, and that I write another letter to him secretly by this post. You know, I believe, enough of my present situation to foresee you will have little fatigue or business here; but that little is more than I can always do myself. I think that I have now sufficiently explained all I intended to say in this letter. As for the time of your setting out, in general, the sooner the better; but with all proper regards for the season and your health. And you will find here inclosed an order of 2000 livres upon Waters for the expenses of your journey. I

248

heartily wish it may be favourable and of no detriment to your health. Assuring you of my constant friendship and kindness, of which you can have no doubt.

J. R.

Sir John Graeme to Prince Charles when he had actually joined the King and changed his name

ROME. *20th Feb.* 1760.

SIR,

It is my duty to acquaint your Royal Highness of my arrival here and of the honour the King has been graciously pleas'd to confer upon me by creating me a Peer of Scotland by the Title of the Earl of Alford. The kindness your Royal Highness has been so good as to shew me on many occasions makes me confident this will be agreable to you, and I am perswaded you don't doubt of the satisfaction it will be to me to have occasions of rendring you all the service which may depend on me who, I am confident, you know never had any other view than the wellfair and interest of the Royal Family ; and may all that is good and great ever attend you is my dayly prayer and the constant and sincere wishes

I am with profound respect

Sir,

Your Royal Highness's most dutiful most obedient

and most humble Servant,

ALFORD.

The three letters which follow are, strictly speaking, outside the limits assigned to this book, which should terminate with the death knell of all Jacobite hopes at Quiberon Bay, Nov. 22, 1759, but one is included as showing Prince Charles on an unchronicled visit to England, and the next as almost the final appeal of the old Chevalier to his wayward son to visit him ; he had nearly six years more to live, but from this time onward failed visibly and at last became bed-ridden and almost speechless. He gave up the burden of his long and sad life on the 1st of January 1766.

The letter of Sir Richard Warren gives the contemporary view of the Battle of Quiberon Bay.

(*Endorsed the Prince—to Mr. John Dixon—in the Prince's handwriting.*)

SIMONS INN COFFY HOUSE, LONDON, CHANCERY LANE.

2 *Feb.* 1760.

SIR,

Since a great while our Correspondance has failed neither by your fault or mine, in fine let us not look Backwards, and it is time now to spake plane. Iff any of P. fords Relations will come from their Letargy, no time is to be Lost and some trusty person shou'd be sent to him, not only to inform that young Lad of ye situation, Life or death of his Cuntrymen, the being now so many years absent and in so distant a Country, as also to remit him sum funds which have been due to him since he saw a near Relation of his ye year 1753 in Flanders ; you know how P. Ford quitted London ye year 1750 and my concern for him is great when breding together in Oxford : Do not delay answering me this, that I may once for all Let my friend know what he has to depend upon and in case you can immediatly forward him sum supply of money, in ye mean time that is to say, untill he can regulat his affairs entirely, you have only to advise me ye sum and in what manner it is send. My adress is——

as I sign, your most sincere friend

JOHN DRUMLAG.

P.S. You will plese to put a Cover over my Letter—addressed to Mr. Thompson who lives in ye houses ye wido of Mr. Dormels at Anvers in Flanders.

ye second Feb. 1760.

M^dme LA VEUVE D. DE BEAU LIEU À ANVERS.

250

The King to Prince Charles

ROME. *3rd March* 1760.

If I have not writ you for some time, my dear Son, you would wrong me much if you attributed to want of sincere concern and tenderness for you. They encrease with my age and make me more desirous than ever to see and embrace you once more befor I dye. My health is much in the same state in which it has been for a long while, and I do not even hope it can ever grow much better, and I have now, besides the accidentail ail of my convulsive cough, which generally lasts me a long while, tho' it is not as yet so severe a fit as the last I had was, so that if ever you desire to see me again you would do well not to delay your visit too long. And the present situation of affairs seems favorable for it, for whatever the public may say or the French Court give out I cannot conceive that the last can be able to act for our cause for a long while, and I reckon that a couple of months may be sufficient to you to make me the kind visit I so much desire, and which you seemed formerly to wish as much as I. I think I formerly writ to you, the road will be very safe and secure for you as long as the war lasts. You may be here as privately as you please, and tho' it should be suspected in the present juncture that can be of no consequence. And when you are here you shall be entire master of seeing none but those you think fit. In fine, my dear Son, all circumstances concur to facilitate and encourage you not to delay the giving me the greatest satisfaction I can have in this world. I am continually thinking of you and have nothing so much at heart as your welfare and happiness. God Almighty preserve you, my dear Son, and pour down upon you all those blessings which your own and my heart can wish for you, and then I am sure you will have nothing left to desire. I embrace you tenderly and am all yours.

P.S. Not knowing how you may stand at present in relation to money matters, and that nothing may retard your journey here I send you enclosed an order for Waters to keep at your disposition 12000^{ls}. So that whenever you think fit to call for that sum he will, by virtue of that order, send it to you either altogether or in parcels as you shall direct.

J. R.

(*Copy of the order to Waters*)

You will give the sum of 12000^{ls} to the Prince whenever he sends you this order either in whole or in part as he shall desire and state the same to my account which you keep with Marsi.

Charles Edward did not come ; he survived his father for twenty-two years, dying on January 31st, 1788, and some months afterwards one member of the present editor's family wrote to another (the letter still exists) saying, "The King is dead."

Poor Carolus III, whom even the Pope would never recognize.

Sir Richard Warren to King James

VANNES. *6th May* 1760.

SIR,

I received with the deepest sentiments of respect and gratitude the Commission of Major General your Majesty has been pleased to send me, and begg you may excuse the wants of words to express them.

Positive orders from the Court have kept me on these coasts, and hindered me from marching with your Majesty's Loyal Brigade, Happy if where I remaine I may be, at least indirectly, more usefull to the Royal Cause, tho' the projected

Prince Charles Edward as King Charles III

From an autotype of the original drawing in the collection of Archibald Hamilton Dunbar

Expedition seems dropped for some time by the unexpected event of the last sea fight.[1]

I am with the most profound Respect

Sir,

Your Majesty's

most humble, most obedient, most devoted Servant, and most dutyfull Subject,

RICHRD WARREN.[2]

---

[1] Quiberon Bay, November 20th, 1759, which practically put an end to all idea of a Stuart restoration with French help.

This memorable battle has been mentioned more than once. In its consequences it really extinguished all the hopes of those whose dreams and plans we have been following in the Stuart papers. In another letter Warren seems to think that the British victory was due to mistaken tactics on the part of the French Admirals. The result was really due to the marvellous seamanship of Admiral Hawke, who fought the action on a rocky coast in a gale. It is recorded that he replied to the pilot's warnings : "You have done your duty in showing me the danger, now you will obey orders and lay me aside the *Soleil Royal*," the French flagship. Two French ships struck their colours in the action, four were sunk and the rest ran for shelter. With the loss of sixty-four ships during that autumn the French Navy became for the time almost negligible.

[2] Sir Richard Warren died at Belle Isle in 1775.

Appendix

PETITIONS to the King in Rome occur in great numbers, and many are amusing. The two following are in themselves interesting though it has been impossible to discover the identity of the writers.

Madame Gausé, née Everhardt, reveals a quite unknown episode in the life of King James and there seems no real reason to doubt her veracity. The incident, if it occurred at all, must have taken place in February 1716 during the passage of the Old Chevalier and the Duke of Mar from Montrose to Gravelines. It is not at all intrinsically impossible that they should have set foot in Holland en route. The voyage lasted a week, but it was entirely foreign to the character of James Stuart to forget any obligation.

The other petitions are merely specimens of numbers received.

Something seemed to have been given to every petitioner.

Madame Everhardt

DRESDE. *Aug.* 21, 1747.

SIRE,

Le destin m'aiant favorisé et rendu assez heureuse de pouvoir être utile à Votre Majesté lorsqu'à son retour d'Ecosse. Elle arriva en Zélande, ou Elle étoit mise a prise, je me prosterne très humblement à ses pieds pour la supplier de se souvenir que je suis la femme qui l'a reçu chez elle avec my Lord Maarr et vous mit a couvert dans sa maison, en attendant qu'elle vous procurait un batelier qui vous fit passer l'eau. Vous disant, quoique déguisée elle avait l'honneur de vous connaître. Votre Majesté fit alors un mouvement pour lui donner quelque chose, mais la crainte qu'elle eut que le moindre delai n'apporta du préjudice au départ de votre Majesté, l'obligea de luy dire précipitament de partir, et de persuader le batelier de les passer comme gens de sa connaissance. Votre Majesté, ensuitte, écrivit quelque chose sur ses tablettes et en la remerciant lui promis sa recompense si jamais l'occasion s'en présentoit. C'est dans cette confiance que j'ose avec la plus respectueuse soumission, représenter à Votre Majesté que la vississitude des tems et le changement de ma famille qui à embrassé la Religion catholique Romaine, nous ont transporté à Dresde ou nous implorons la secours du ciel et ou nous osons espérer aussi que Votre Majesté daignera nous accorder le sien. Nous obligeans d'aller à Rome nous jetter a ses pieds, si elle vouloit nous l'ordonner, nous ne cesserons cependant de prier continuellement le Seigneur pour la conversation to votre Majesté et pour celle de toute la famille Roiale.

ANNE MARIA DE GAUSÉ
NÉE DE EVERHARDT.

Enclosed in Dr. Flyn's letter. It has not unfortunately been found possible to identify the Sieur Fox who with his father, uncle and six brothers claimed to have fought at the battle of the Boyne and subsequently in Scotland.

Aug. 20, 1747.

A Sa Magesté-Bretany. Qui à Rome.

SIRE,

Le sieur fox represente très humblement à votre Majesté que son père, son oncle et lui, six jeunes frères, son venue d'Irlande avec Jacque seconde votre père d'heureuse Memoire, où ils son continu dans le service de france ou ils son tous sacrifié, et votre

Majesté m'a ordonné d'aller en Ecosse, étain votre sujet j'ai obey tout asitos avec beaucoup de zèle, Comme toute ma famille aves pour la famille royale.

Je beaucoup souffert en Ecosse par le frois et la dissette, je fus pris à la bataille de Collodon de là on nous a mené par Merre à Londres ou il m'on chargé de soixante livres de fer sur mes deux jambes. Qui mon rongé jusqu'ausau, tombé malade par cinq fois et abandonné des Medicins et actuallement toujours malade. Et per dussus tout, mes manbres ataqué d'un rumatise unyversel, et une fièvre lente donc je ne peut pas bougé de mon lits qu'à force de bra, et Banny des trois royaumes parce que luis qui est en possession de notre bien en Irlande. Comme j'ay un fils qui est tou ce qui reste de notre famill qui est étudiant et que je n'aurai à lui lessé je supplié très humblement votre Majesté de vouloire bien optenire un Benefice pour vivre j'offriré toute ma vie des vœux au siel pour la Resteration de votre famile royale.

Thomas Gardener to James

1747.

To his sacred Majesty James *King of Great Britain.*

SIR,

Please your Majesty Thomas Gardener, Irish Sealor, lately deserted from an English man of War which happened to touch at Leghorn and being in a Miserable Condition in my Travel from Leghorn to Rome that I was forced to sell my Rags of Cloes. Now having nothing to support me, please your Majesty for a little Charity which wou'd be a great service to me in the Distress I am in please your Majesty. I being prested this three year and two months never had the oppertunity of getting away until now lately in Leghorn— No more to your Sacred Majesty—

Your well wisher

THOMAS GARDENER, Irish Sealor.

*To his most sacred Majesty James the 3rd King of Great Brittaine,
France and Ireland*

1747.

SACRED MAJESTY.

Your humble and most faithfull subject *Anthony Smith* who
has been often relived ftom his great misery haveing the misfortune being sick these nyne months past and those torments
dayly increasing as Dr. Wright can aver he was so good as to
come and see him, what little incom we have between us is not
half sufficient for the dayly expense of her ailments begging the
grace of Your Majesty be gratiously pleased to order some
small relief and as in duty bound shall always pray as always
does for the preservation of Yr Majesty's health and all the
Royal family.

Noted on back of letter (*Tre Zecchini*)

Michele Vezzosi to James Edgar

S'OUEN. 27 *Aug.* 1747.

SIR,

His Royal Highness has been so very good to recommend
two of my sons to his Majesty to do them the charity to provide them of some kind of benefice not for any other end but
to get them a suit of Cloaths this year, for realy where they are
they do not get enough to keep themselves decently cload,
that I am obligst to do for them. Sir you know that I am ould,
and still with two distempers on me which keeps me always
low and if I should day they would be left miserable it would
give me very great consolation if I could see them in any
way provided . . . Hopping in his Majesty's charitable disposition to raccommend them either to the Pope or the
Cardinal Davario. I say so for I know no better. Sir I hope
you will now and then speak to his Majesty in their favour.
I am persuaded of your goodness and protection. I never fail

258

nor my sons to offer our prayers to Almighty God for the preservation of the Royal family, and this is what sticks in my heart and I hope that God Almighty will protect em and give them joy and health in this world and a happiness in the next. This is all my wishes and remaining

Yr very very hum. and obedient servant,

MICHEL VEZZOSI.

Michele Vezzosi was originally a servant to the Venetian Ambassador to London ; he helped Lord Nithsdale to escape, went with him to Rome and was thirty years in the employ of King James. He then accompanied Prince Charles on his expedition to Scotland, was made prisoner, released as a foreigner and sent back to France where he died in 1764.

George Flint to James Edgar

PARIS. *March* 4, 1748.

SIR,

In mine of the 11 Dec. last I gave you a short account of the many tryals that my wife and I went through in the last 4 months of the last year—Which having reduced us to distress we most humbly begd. that the Royal Bounty might come to relieve us this year as soon as the King thought fit. But haveing had no answer at all, we in the depths of consternation do in this most humbly repeat the same supplication. This we do by force and with the utmost reluctance. I was 17 months in Newgate and 20 months in the prison of Callis, still accompany'd in both by my faithful generous wife. But that was thirty years ago in the prime of our age, and when the good cause for which we suffered gilded the gloom of the Prisons. ، We suffered for God, King and Country. But now in our old age, to be thrust into prison for debt which tho' contracted by force is still scandalous, this I dread much more than death.

259

. . . Two such conspicuous old stagers as my wife and I both are will I hope meet with mercy from God and from the King. . . . Yr most devoted and most obedient Humble Ser.

GEORGE FLINT.

Mrs. Flint

Monday, May 7, 1753.

MAY IT PLEASE YOUR MAJESTY—

With most profound humility and even with fear, I presume to let your Majesty know my situation. Since the death of my dear husband, which is 2 years, I have lived in the hospital general near Paris, for I have done with the world intirely after forty years mariage with one of the best of men. I pay here 12 livres a month not to be mix'd among all sorts of people— we are poorly maintained but what is much worse, there are great mortifications almost continually which I cannot sure always to bear as I ought to do. By the advice of my confessor, I would put myself into a community hard by which is much more honourable where I may be for 200 livres a year and better maintained much than here.

If Your Majesty would be pleased to allow me some small matter a year to help me with the 100 livres I have upon the Eaeconomats I could live for which I can't trouble your Majesty for long, being now 70 years of age.

With all humility I beg yr Majesty's pardon for this letter Yr M. most dutiful subject and servant,

MARY SPENCER FLINT.

Two Other Sailors

May it please yr Majesty Yr humble petitioner John Wright of London which left the *Ambscade*, Man of War in Lighorn and about a fortnight ago received your Royal bounty, which he laid out in a shirt and Breches and other necessarys being almost nacked and being now to pursue his journey to Napales humbly begs for your Majesty's charity to help him on his jorney. Oct. 1757.

Noted on back (Mezzo Zecchino)

J. R.

Please your goodness my greate King etc.

Plese my King to look upon me, being come from a man of war from Naples, they pressed me in Margate when I went over to make the harvest. I come heare to you to gett some money to by Cloths and victuals and cary me to Leghorn and Depend I will love you for ever while my name is Patrick Sarsfield.

Gold bless King James. My grandfather fought for your father in Ireland against King William.

Answer on back, for Patrick Sarsfield uno zecchino (worth about ten shillings).

The following shows some of the peculiar cases with which King James had to deal :

"Letters of an excentric Jacobite Peer, The Earl of Dumbarton." (He himself, invariably spelled it with the N)

George Douglas, second Earl of Dumbarton and Lord Douglas of Ettrick, was born 1687,[1] and died circa 1750.

His father was Lord George Douglas, fifth son of the 1st Marquis of Douglas and Lady Mary Gordon, and was for long in the French army ; Charles II created him an Earl in 1675. Ten years later he commanded the army which defeated the rising under Argyll in Scotland—(an operation not demanding any great military skill !) and was nominated by King James II as one of the eight original members of the revived Order of the Thistle.

[1] As announced by his uncle the Marquis of Douglas, who, in a letter of 2nd May, 1687, excuses Lord Dunbarton for not writing, saying " For it is a great business for him to have a son and air, his title will be Lord Ettrick."

He was also one of the four Lords who went with the King when he fled to Rochester (Arran being another), and both he and his wife died at St. Germains, three years later. The son, George, seems to have been somewhat eccentric from his youth. At 17 he wished to become a monk but was dissuaded, did a little soldiering and was at one time sent to Russia. In later life he would seem to have spent his time going from one monastery to another and apparently more than once entering a religious order and then leaving it. His letters reveal a curious personality.

He was always in want of money and appears to have borrowed it indiscriminately from any fellow Scot, including Lady Traquair and many others.

He frequently took it upon himself to write or send messages to the Pope with regard to Ecclesiastical preferments, transfers, and the charges made for Papal bulls. It is to be gathered that at length no one took him quite seriously. Edgar writes towards the end that he *hopes* Dumbarton will now remain where he is (i.e. Douai) for the rest of his life.   .

Lord Dumbarton—probably to J. Southcott in Paris (he was then aged 40 and was in his first religious retreat)

St. Riquier. Oct. 2, 1727.

Dear Sir,

Give me leave to return you my most sincere thanks for all your favours and for the tender concern you expressed in everything that relates to me. I am very well satisfied that the step I have lately made in abandoning my country and its service will meet with approbation from some people, as it will also be blamed by others, but I bless God I am thoroughly easy in every respect, and am convinced that I not only acted in it like a Christian, but like a man of honour ; in a word, after the life I had had for twenty years I thought it proper to

262

putt a space betwixt life and death ; thanks to the Almighty for the favorable opportunity his mercy gives me so plentifully to repair my youthfull frailties by a retired solitary life. I must beg the favour of you, dear Sir, to assure his Majesty of my duty. I ever loved and honoured him and no one thing in life but my unhappy situation heretofore could ever have separated me from his person or his service. I had the honour to be brought up with his Majesty and to receive severall marks of his Royal favours in my younger dayes, so that nature and inclination concurred with my duty towards him. After what has passed of my life, I dare not write to the King till I have his leave. I must own I should be glad before my death, to kiss his Majesty's hand and once more pay my duty to him and endeavour to make some atonement for my past behaviour. Heaven bless him and protect him. I desire to hear from you on this subject. With my hearty service to my Lord of Rochester and to our good friend Mr. Inese—I have writ by last post to Lord Stafford. Adieu dear sir—be assured that I am, in all *intimo cordis.*

Your faithfull humble servant,

DUNBARTON.

He then apparently joined the Capuchin Order, and had begged that "Brother George de l'Angleterre" [1] should be allowed by the Pope to come and visit him. This was granted. He seems next to have been a member of an Order called the "Recollets" (Reformed Franciscans).

Four years later, when he desired to leave that order Father Lewis Innes writes to the King :

17th May, 1731.

"I have the honour of your Majesty's last, of 28th April and with it that of Lord Dumbarton, whose demand I think most

---

[1] Brother George has not been identified.

unreasonable, that poor Lord forgetts, quite, that he is a *fryar*, and will be one as long as he lives, however little he complies with the duties he is bound to by his three solemn vows. It would I fear make your Majestie's credit very cheap if your name were made use of in asking what not only would be certainly refused, but would reflect on your Majesty in giveing in so easily into asking a thing so unusuall and unreasonable in itself."

Innes however, apparently did what the King wished and writes 20 May, 1731 :

I am press'd by Lord Dunbarton to give your Majesty some account of what your Majesties recommendation produced in his favour. Card. de Bissy told that Lord that, on his return from Rome, he had pass'd by the Grand Chartreuse and had gott the Generall's promise to receive him into their order upon tyrall, which was what Dunbarton desir'd. But after putting him off for 2 or 3 months, the Generall at last positively refused receiving him on any account. I believe the reason of this refusal was that the Generall had been inform'd that this Lord had allready changed 3 or 4 religious houses without fixing any wher, which is but too true. He is at last, with much ado, admitted amongst the Benedictins of S. Maur, in a Convent of theirs near Autun, where he promises to end his dayes, without changeing any more. I wish he may keep this promise better than he has done many others.

The King to Dumbarton (two months later)

ROME. *July* 10, 1731.
"I have received yours of the 5th of June and would very willingly contribute to what might be for your satisfaction and advantage, but am persuaded that my writing about you to the General of the Carthusians would signify nothing since what

has been represented to him on your behalf has hitherto been without effect. You are best judge whether you have any new motives to offer to him, but if you have not, I cannot but strongly recommend you to come to some resolution as to your state of life with the advice and assistance of an able director and when you have once taken a good and solid resolution, to stick to it for that will I am confident be conducive to your present ease and quiet."

Dumbarton then writes three years later from the Abbé dé la Charité by Besançon, to the King, with a new demand :

This 11 *Dec.* 1734.

SIR,

May not I take the liberty to assure your Majesty that your poor and faithfull Dunbarton loves and honours you beyond imagination. Yes, soe I doe, and my constant and daily prayers to the Almighty God are that he bless you in all manners—in this life and if he pleases restore you in your kingdoms. God of heaven send it, I shall ever wish it with all my soul. I must take the Liberty to beg of your Majesty to be so kind as to interest yourself for me and to endeavour to gett me a pension of two thousand livers a year which will make me easy. You see Sir that my demand is not exorbitant ; if your Majesty will be pleased to cause writ to the chief minister of France and desire him in your name to be so kind as to give me a pension of 2000 liv. upon some Abbaye or Bishoprick it will be done, and you see, Sir, that the scheme for it is personal, and easy on every side ; I abandonne it to your Majesty's goodness. As for myself, be assured, Sir, that whenever you are please to call me, that moment I fly towards your royal service with all despatch—and perhaps the time approaches that God Almighty will be pleased to restore you for the good and benefit of every honest English man. God send it soon, I humbly beg it of him and shall continue daily in my poor

265

prayers to the great God of Heaven to recommend Your Majesty in that manner. May I not hope that you, great Sir, will be pleased sometimes to think of your poor faithfull Dunbarton, who honours and loves you beyond imagination. I am and ever shall be with the most profound respect etc.

P.S. I take the liberty to tell your Majesty that the Bishop of Verdun who is here, told me that is the way, for me to gett a pension upon an Abbaye.

A little over a year later, he writes again to the King with another specious plea for pecuniary assistance—He was actually still in the same religious house, at Besançon.

LA CHARITÉ, *ce* 27 *Mar.* 1735.

SIR,

Its a trespass upon your Majesty's goodness, to trouble you with such an idle correspondence as mine,—I beg leave to assure you that its not possible to love and respect your Majestie as I doe and shall continue to do for as long as I breath. I received the honour of your letter and thank you for all the good and charitable advice you give in it—but I must take the liberty to insinuate to your Majesty that the only reason of my asking a pension was not to help myself but to endeavour to doe something for the poor for I take charity to be an excellent virtue. I submit it entirely to your Majesty as I doe myself and shall continue my poor but daily prayers to Almighty God—that he may be pleased to bless you and restore you in your kingdomes and grant you hereafter his eternal rest and am and ever shall be etc.

Two years later the King writes to Dumbarton on February 4, 1737, hoping he is busy and contented and continues :

"I should always be glad to contribute to make you so, but, after God, that depends on yourself alone and with a true spirit

266

of retreat and of pennance, you cannot fail of being happy both in this world and the next which I sincerely wish, having always for you a particular regard and kindness."

Another two years elapses and Dunbarton writes to Edgar wishing to become a Jesuit :

DOUAY, *the 8th of Marche* 1739.

DEAREST SIR,

I write to you these linnes to beg of you the favour of your friendship and to beg of you to assure his Majesty of my most humble and sincere respects, and that as I have been very ill, I pray his Majesty to be so kind as to speake to Mr. Wayes who I am told is at Rome with his Majestie, to entreat him to write to English Colledge at Douay, to desire the vice-president who is a friend of mine to take me in the colledge, where I hope with the grace of Almighty God to live and dye amongst my countrymen. This is the great favour which I beg of you and to be assured that I am unalterably your friend and Humble servant

DUNBARTON.

At Douai he appears to have spent a great part of the rest of his life, though two years later he is found appealing for help to the ever-generous Lady Traquair—on what grounds does not appear.

George, Earl of Dumbarton, to Mary, Countess of Traquair

RUISSEAUVILLE, *the 14th June* N.S. 1741.

MADAM,—It's a trespass upon your Ladyship's goodness to trouble you with a letter from your poor cozen Dunbarton, and I flatter myself that you will be pleased to excuse it, and impute it to the iust concern I haue for you will be yours, and which shall euer and euer be the same, be assured of it.

I know the concern you was pleased to express for me, and I thank God Almighty euery day of my poor life fir the fauours you are pleased to honour me with, and of which I beg the continuation. God of heaven return you His blessings. Excuse me if I trouble you at present, but realy the terrible necessity I am reduced to is the only occasion of't. If your Ladyship would be so kind to your poor cozen as to send him fourty pounds sterling, it would be the greatest charity in the world, for I am reduced so low, that I am oblige(d) to be in want of seuerall that are necessary in human life. May not I hope for success in your Ladyship's goodnesse, in yoir charity, and in the honour I haue of been your near relation ? If you will be so kind as to send it to me, you may cause writ to Mr. Charles Smith, who liues at Boulogne, who will forward it to me ; and I pray the good God of heaven to bless you and yours in this transitory life, and then take you to His divine presence. How does my good Lord Traquair ? My hearty and sincere wishes attends him ; and if I may be so bold, I pray your Ladyship to assure him of my most humble respects, not forgetting my dearest Lord Linton, and his dearest brother. I flatter myself that your Ladyship is assured that I am, and shall euer be, with the greatest respect and sincerity, madam,

Your Ladyship's most humble, most obedient servant,

and most affectionat cozen,

DUNBARTON.

He then apparently returned to Douai.

Dunbarton to Edgar

DOUAI, 18*th of March*, 1748.

DEAR SIR,

I received yours of the 6th February for which be assured of a most hearty and sincere thanks and be persuaded that in all occasions whatever you and yours shall ever find in me a true and sincere friend. I beg you'll be so kind as to present to his Majesty my most sincere profound and humble respects and to tell his Majesty that after looking over and over all my papers I can not find the Dispense I got from the court of Rome. I think it is one and twenty years since it was obtained under the name of Mr. Douglas to hide my name and quality, I then been in England. The contents say nothing as I can remember. Only that I shall live in a regular community— that is all as near as I can remember of the dispense. I pray you be so kind as tell his Majesty that as I am growing very infirm and that as I have a mind to live and dye among the good *Recollets* of the province of St. Andrew, beg his Majesty to be so kind as to procure me a bref from his Holiness the Pope by which I may be in the said province and as the Recollets have no property shall give them in alms (viz. to their mother Syndique) the pension for me and my servant as she and I will agree upon.

I beg you'll represent to his Sacred Majesty that this is my last and final request [1] to him and that every day of my life I think it is an indispensable duty to pray the good God of heaven for the Prince of Wales and the Cardinal Duke of York. I am and ever shall be, etc. I beg your answer as soon as you can. Adieu, dearest Sir. Look upon this as my last affair in the world and may the Heavens ever reward you.

Three weeks later, to the same correspondent

DOUAI. *April* 5, 1748.

SIR,

I trouble you with a Line, and beg you'll be so kind as to present my most humble duty to His Majestie and give him the inclosed letter, and when there is an answer, pray send it to me, and be assured Sir that I am sincerely your friend and humble servant.

[1] Of course it was *not* !

269

The enclosure

Sir,

I take the Liberty to writ to your Majesty to assure you that I daily think of you and recommend you to Almighty good God and to Heaven. I beg the favour of yr Majesty to be so kind as not to forget me and to be so gracious as to speak to the father general of the Jesuites who's at Rome that I may be admitted amongst our fathers who are my countrymen, and to engage the general of the Jesuites to writ to father Rector here Father Crookshank to be admitted to board right here and in so doing yr Majesty will eternally oblige me and be assured dearest Sir of the great respect and sincere truth with which I am and shall ever and ever be

Yr Majesties Most faithfull and ever devoted subject,

DUNBARTON.

In a letter from this nobleman to Lady Jane Douglas, dated Douay, January 7, 1749, he says, "As for me, I live quietly here with a gentleman that boards me and my servant, and I try to make a shift with my poor fortune" (*Defender's Proof in Douglas Cause*).

In the following year there is another letter :

Lord Dunbarton to the King

FROM THE SCOTCH COLLEGE AT DOUAY.

Octobre the 20th 1750.

MAY IT PLEASE YOUR MAJESTY.

I take the Liberty to writ these linnes to yr Majesty to tell you know that I am excessively well pleased in our dear Scotch Colledge at Douay, that I receive infinit favours from our good father Crookshanks who is rector and whom I hope your Majesty will be pleased to honour with your protection and speak to the Father general of the Jesuites and recommend him

270

to his favour in order for his continuing rector which would
be to me the greatest blessing that's possible and the only thing
I desire being with all my heart and my soul Your Majestie's
most dutyfull and ever Loyal Subject and servant,

DUNBARTON.

The reply—Edgar writes

"I had the honour to deliver to the King Yr Lop's letter.
H.M. desires me to acknowledge receipt of it and to make you
his compliment. He is glad to find you have so good an
opinion of your Rector Father Cruikshanks of whom H.M.
has also heard much good. He will therefore recommend him
to his General as you desire for being continued as Rector at
Douay, but will delay doing it until he knows that the father
himself wishes it."

The *Complete Peerage* states that Dumbarton died in 1749,
but in view of the above letters it appears his decease must have
taken place a little later.

*Letters of Lord Wintoun (as he himself spelt it), another
example of an almost crazy refugee, like Lord Dumbarton*

George, 10th Lord Seton and 5th Earl of Winton, was born in
1678 out of wedlock, but was afterwards "legitimated." His
father died in 1704, but George was not served heir until
July 4th, 1710, as he was abroad at his father's death, and the
family did not know his whereabouts. He was actually
working as a journeyman blacksmith in France, "having
always had a taste that way." He was considered to be very
eccentric and by some people as quite mentally unbalanced.
Although a Protestant, he was suspected by the Government
of Jacobite leanings, and was among those Peers and Lairds
who were summoned to appear at Edinburgh on the outbreak

of the Rising. He did not, of course, obey the summons and was said to have ordered his vassals to join Mar's army in September and even collected them. He himself joined the force under Kenmure at Moffat on October 11th and commanded a troop of his servants and friends ; this command was due to his rank and not to any military experience. When the disputes began between Kenmure, Mackintosh and Foster as to whether the joint forces should proceed alternatively to England, or to the West of Scotland, or endeavour to take Argyll in the rear (which latter would have been much the wisest course), Winton was strongly averse to going into England and even threatened to go home sooner than cross the border, in which proposal he had the support of a large number of his fellow-Scots (and about 400 actually did so). He was, however, eventually won over to the idea of proceeding south, and persuaded the majority of his own men to follow him to the disaster of Preston, where he was among the Scots Lords taken, carried to London and committed to the Tower. His trial took place March 15th, 1716, when he pleaded not guilty, but was convicted of high treason, attainted and condemned to death ; after several reprieves he succeeded in making his escape from the Tower, either by his own efforts or the connivance of his jailers. It is said that he induced a laundress to bring him a file concealed in his linen, and with his blacksmith's knowledge succeeded in picking the locks or breaking the bars, and eventually got to France and so to Rome, where he remained, drawing a monthly pension, for thirty-three years, and died on December 19th, 1749. His eccentricities seem to have increased with his age, and with his ideas of his own importance. He never married, but claims were afterwards made on behalf of a man who said he was his great-grandson through a secret marriage in 1710 to Margaret Maclean, daughter of an Edinburgh doctor ; the claim was not established.

Mackay in his *Secret Memoirs*, describes Winton as "mighty subject to a particular caprice, natural to his family," a polite manner of alluding to his mental aberrations. Winton is said, before he joined Kenmure, to have buried a quantity of treasures, plate and jewels, etc., somewhere near Seton and to have returned from the Continent to look for these in company with the blacksmith who helped him to bury them, but failed to find the spot, while the family of the blacksmith was observed to become, later, unusually well-to-do !

His pension was drawn with great regularity from succeeding paymasters of King James's household in Rome. Of no one are there so many signatures among the Stuart papers, but he seems to have been perennially dissatisfied with what was allowed him and to have asked for (and sometimes obtained) additional benefits.

The first letter alludes to one somewhat unusual device for augmenting his resources ; he seems to have forgotten that such things were no longer in King James's gift.

James Murray to John Hay (who was in Paris)

ROME. *Dec.* 3, 1720.

"Since my last to you, the most remarkable thing which has happened at this place was a request my Lord Winton made to the King in an audience he desired of purpose, in which he is not likely to have many rivals. It was to be made Governor of the Bass ; and he told his Majesty that the appointments as he understood were formerly £25 a year but that Doctor Magie had told him that one might make £100 a year besides, by selling of the geese. I believe you'll agree that the Govern-

273

ment would be well bestowed, providing he was obliged to *reside in it.*" [1]

The next letter is of seventeen years later and voices the first of many complaints :

Lord Wintoun to the King

ROME.

Jan. 14, 1737.

SIR,

Were I treated as a gentleman, I would not have the occasion to inform your Majesty how little respect is given to those of your following in this place (wich in consequence falls upon your Majesty) by the message sent me from Mr. Steuart by Mr. Slezer on the 7th instant, threatening me with murder without any reason and which is not to be neglected either in jest or earnest, since all wise men agree that Courage, Honour and Honesty can never agree with buffoonery. If those about your Majesty would have ventured to inform your Majesty of this, I would not have troubled your Majesty with it, and wish that their refusal upon this and several other occasions do not give occasion (*turn over* !) the Enemys of your Majesty's Person and Family to say it proceeds from your being surrounded with favourites, flattering and ignorant, who always

[1] The forfeited estate of Lord Wintoun was the largest of those confiscated by the Government in 1716 ; while those of the Earl Marischal and the Earl of Mar, (both of far more importance politically) were respectively computed at £1669 sterling and £1884 sterling, per annum ; Wintoun's, which lay in the lowlands, amounted to £3393 10s. 5d. The items are curious—

	£	s.	d.
Money rents only accounted for	266	7	9
Wheat, Barley, Oats and Straw	2073	12	8
The poultry given up by tenants	53	10	0
And a round £1000 for the Salt and Coal . . .	1000	0	0
	£3393	10	5

has been and will be the ruine of Kings and Princes and of all other persons whatsoever that trust in them. I hope your Majesty will take this in your serious consideration and give satisfaction to me and all honest men and oblige Sir

    Yr Majesty's most humble, obedient and faithfull
       servant and subject,

WINTOUN.

The reply in Edgar's hand

"The King having read your letter, Commands me to tell you in answer to it that he thinks you ought to take it well of Mr. Stewart his informing you of what he heard. That he is sorry you are uneasy. That he cannot but recommend it to you to live quietly and peaceably with your neighbours as all the other Lords and gentlemen of H.M.'s following have done and H.M. says he expects this of you, which is the only way he thinks will bring you out of your present embarras."

Ten years later

Lord Wintoun to the King

ROME. 12, 13, 14 April 1747.

"Preliminaries for an Audience."

      (Wintoun had 40 scudi every month.)

SIR,

I want an audience of your Majesty, to lett you know that at present I have neither money nor credit and therefore one of the greatest objects of charity that depends upon your Majesty.

And that I do not, nor ever did rely upon Pensions and upon what your Majesty has been pleased to give me from time to time.

And to lett you, Sir, understand that when your Majesty is pleased to do me Justice, I'll know better how to manage my own affairs than any of the Politicians that are or that I ever did see about your Majesty.

275

The Same to the Same, eighteen months later

ROME. *27th October,* 1748.

SIR,

Your Majesty having ordered those of your retinue to put on mourning for the Duchess of Parma, Grand Aunt to the Prince and Duke, and I not having money to doe it, I want to know by your Majesty's orders to Mr. Marsi how far your Majesty will be pleased to assist me.

I am Sir, Your Majesty's most humble and faithfull subject, and servant,

WINTOUN.

Lord Wintoun to the King

ROME. *5th December* 1749.

SIR,

I told your Majesty some time ago of my want of mony and I have neither money nor health, so I hope to hear from your Majesty how far your Majesty will be pleased to assist me in my present circumstances. The bearer can inform your Majesty of the State of my affairs.

These letters to the King are comically abrupt in tone, and at the foot of the page as already seen he writes curtly, *turnover.* Wintoun's counsel at the trial which had resulted in the verdict of High Treason in 1716 had concluded the case as follows (and the words aptly describe his condition in his old age in Rome) : "My Lords, I have nothing else to say on behalf of this unhappy Lord, unhappy as being in that doubtful state of memory, not insane enough to be within the protection of the law, nor at the same time sane enough to do himself in the least respect any service whatever."

George, Fifth Earl of Winton, 1749

Wintoun's death occurred in Rome December 19th, 1749,[1] but it is not known where he was buried, as the records for the Protestant cemetery near the Porta del Popolo only begin from the year 1775.

His portrait shows him in the uniform of an official of the Vatican.

[1] His forfeited honours remained dormant until 1840 when Archibald William, 13th Earl of Eglinton, was served heir male—general to George Seton, 4th Earl of Winton, father of the Jacobite, and granted the title of Earl of Winton in the Peerage of the United Kingdom. How this came about was that the 4th Earl had been granted, in 1686, a Novodamus of his titles, with remainder to heirs male of his body, of which at that time he had *none*, whom failing, to *anyone* whom he should name, and the Eglinton family was descended from the brother of his first wife, daughter of Hugh, 7th Earl of Eglinton.

Alexander Seton, 6th Earl of Eglinton, who took the title on the death (in 1612) without heirs of the 5th Earl, was brother to George, 3rd Earl of Winton. He had to pay £8,000 to the crown, to be allowed to succeed to his cousin, in 1612.

Index

Barry, Dr., 122.
Bartram, Consul, 13, 14, 19.
Bass Rock, 273.
Battoni, Pompeo, 32.
Bell, R. Fitzroy, 37.
Belle isle, 129, 133, 253.
Bellew, Lady, 83.
Bellisk, Monsieur, 70
Bellona, frigate, 145, 173.
Belloni, 126.
Benedict XIII, Pope, 63, 86.
Benedict XIV, Pope, 32, 164, 169, 189.
Benedictine Order, 9, 264.
Bervie, 222.
Berwick, 1st Duke of, 8.
Berwick, 2nd Duke of, 89, 90.
Berwick, Regiment of, 199.
Besançon, 265.
Bissy, Cardinal, 92, 264.
Blaikie, Dr. Walter, 6.
Blair's College (Aberdeen), 30.
Blau, John, 123.
Boisdale, Macdonald of, 137.
Bolingbroke, Lord, 8, 45, 183.
Bologna, 54, 68, 80, 233.
Bonelli, Angiolo, 14, 15, 21.
Booth's Regiment, 199.
Boradale, 161.
Borromeo, St. Charles, 235.
Bouillon, town of, 236.
Bouillon, Duke of, 154, 203, 246.
Boulogne, 49, 102, 141, 160, 166, 196, 222.
Bourbon, 56.
Bourbon, Duchesse, 65.
Bourgogne, 224.
Boyd, Charles, 190.
Boyer, Alex., see D'Eguilles.
Boyne, Battle of the, 113.
Braemar, 44, 49, 191.
Braye, Baroness, 23, 30
Braye, Lord, 34.

Brechin, 193.
Brest, town of, 137, 144.
— fleet, 144, 172, 197.
Brett, Capt., 136.
Bristol, 80.
Brittany, 136, 169, 183, 201, 205, 207.
British Museum, 23, 29, 34, 35, 60.
Britt, cypher name for Scotland, 180.
Brompton, Mr., 234.
Brougham, Lord, 27, 31.
Broughton, see Murray.
Brown, Capt. N., 151, 201.
Browne, Dr., 2, 37, 187, 198.
Bruce, Mary of Kennet, 226.
Bruges, 18.
Buchanan, Duncan, 131.
Buckingham House, 4.
Bulkeley's Regiment, 198.
Bunau, Count, 220.
Buonioni, Monsieur, 93.
Burnet, Mr., cypher name for Prince, 123.
Burntisland, 229.
Bury, Monsieur de, 96.
Bury, Rev. Edward, 31.
Buti, Monsignor, 30.
Butler, Abbé, 131, 151, 161.

Calais, 51, 195, 259.
Callaghan, 6.
Cameron, Archibald, 151, 207, 222.
Cameron, Colonel, 225.
Cameron, Donald of Lochiel, 105, 132, 151, 207, 213.
Cameron, Donald, a boatman, 132.
Camillo, Messenger, 90.
Campana di Cavelli, Contessa, 5, 37.
Campbell, cypher name for Murray of Elibank, 245.
Campbell of Auchinbreck, 105.
Campbell of Glendaruel, 57.
Campo-Florido, Prince, 93.
Cancelleria, Palazzo della, 9.

Dennis, Consul, 28, 31.
D'Este, Cesare, 7.
Dettingen, 123.
Devonshire, Duchess of, 26.
Dicconson, Mr., 107.
Dickson, Dr. W. K., 5, 37.
Dictionary of National Biography, 66.
Dillon, Arthur, 62, 73, 80.
Dillon, Mrs. 195.
Dixon, Mr. John, 250.
Douai, 262, 270.
Douglas, cypher name for Prince, 225, 238.
Douglas, Marquis of, 261.
Douglas, Lady Jane, 270.
Dover, 50.
Dresden, 255.
Drumlag, cypher name for Prince, 250.
Drummond, see Perth.
Drummond, Lord John, 173, 195, 196, 197.
Dubois, Cardinal, 70.
Duddingston, 226.
Dumbarton, Lord, 261.
Dumfries, 197.
Dunbar, Lord, see Murray.
Dundas, Henry (Lord Melville), 13.
Dundee, 214.
Dunkirk, 134, 199.
Durham, cypher name for France, 204.
Du Teillay, the Prince's vessel, 134.

Eardley-Simpson, Major, 6, 37.
Edgar, James, 8, 45, 68, 190, 226.
— — Letters to, 102, 130, 135, 140, 156, 192, 196, 197, 223 passim, 233, 268.
— — Letters from, 140, 156, 188, 216, 221.
Edgar, John, 191, 221.
Edgar, Robert, 194.

Edinburgh, 138, 149, 226, 271.
— Castle, 15, 229.
Eglinton, Earl of, 277.
Eigg, I. of, 138.
Elcho, Lord, 173, 200.
Elgin, 22, 200.
Elibank, Alex. Murray of, 245.
Elliot, H., brother of Lord Minto, 10.
Ellis, H. J., Diary of, 29.
Erskine, David (Areskine), 223.
Erskine, Frances, 50, 53, 76.
Erskine, Thomas, Lord, 45, 74, 76.
Erskine, Will, of Pittodrie, 76.
Ettrick, Lord, 261.
Everhardt, Madame, 255.
Ewald's, Life of Prince Charles, 5.

Falkirk, Battle of, 142, 165.
Fantucci, Senator, 80.
Fénélon, 25.
Fenzi, Procurator, 160.
Findhorn, 200
Finhaven, Carnegie of, 193, 204.
Fish, Scotch, sent to Rome, 222.
Fitzgerald, Mrs., 103.
Fitzjames, Abbé, 103.
— Country seat, 124.
— Regiment, 144.
Flanders, coast of, 167.
Fleury, Cardinal, 105, 118, 123.
Flint, George, 259.
Flint, Mary, 260
Florence, Letters in, 9.
— Procurator of, 160.
Flyn, Father, 195, 197.
Foligno, 109.
Fontainebleau, 29, 183, 206.
Fontaine Gaillarde, 224.
Fontenoy, 123, 129, 204.
Forbes, Charles, of Brux, 50, 69, 222.
Ford, cypher name for Prince, 250.
Fornacette, 160.

286

287

289

Lightning Source UK Ltd.
Milton Keynes UK
UKHW022120170822
407469UK00010B/97